BERTRAND RUSSELL
on
God and Religion

D1558870

I believe that when I die I shall rot, and nothing of my ego will survive. I am not young, and I love life. But I should scorn to shiver with terror at the thought of annihilation. Happiness is nonetheless true happiness because it must come to an end, nor do thought and love lose their value because they are not everlasting.

—Bertrand Russell
Why I Am Not A Christian

BERTRAND RUSSELL
on
God and Religion

edited by

Al Seckel

Prometheus Books

59 John Glenn Drive
Amherst, New York 14228-2197

Dedicated to Laura, Pearce, and John

Cover design by Scott White

Cover drawing courtesy *Punch Magazine,* London, England

Published 1986 by Prometheus Books

Copyright © 1986 by Al Seckel
All Rights Reserved

No part of this publication may be reproduced, stored in a retrieval system, or trans-
mitted in any form or by any means, electronic, mechanical, photocopying, record-
ing, or otherwise, without prior written permission of the publisher, except in the
case of brief quotations embodied in critical articles and reviews. Inquiries should
be addressed to Prometheus Books, 59 John Glenn Drive, Amherst, New York
14228–2197. 716–691–0133. FAX: 716–691–0137.

Library of Congress Catalog Card Number: 85–63409
ISBN 0–87975–323–4

Printed in the United States of America on acid-free paper

Acknowledgments

No one person could bring together such a collection of essays without assistance. First and foremost, I owe a debt of gratitude to Laura Seckel and to Steven L. Mitchell, college division director of Prometheus Books, for their advice and opinions. Both spent many hours reading through pages of proofs, correcting numerous errors, and making helpful suggestions. My appreciation extends as well to Paul Kurtz, president of Prometheus Books, for the encouragement he gave and for his willingness to undertake this project. I also want to thank my close friends John Edwards and Robert Davis (former president of the Bertrand Russell Society) with whom I spent countless hours discussing Bertrand Russell's ideas in general and his views on religion in particular.

I would like to express my appreciation to the Bertrand Russell Archives in Toronto, Ontario, for providing copies of several of Russell's more obscure essays, ones that I did not have in my own collection.

Most of all I want to thank Drs. L. Pearce Williams of Cornell University and Richard Feynman of California Institute of Technology. As both mentors and friends, they spent much of their valuable time encouraging me to think and to question, for which I shall always be grateful.

Finally, thank you Bertrand Russell, wherever you are not, for having so many fascinating things to say on such an important subject.

Contents

PART FOUR

PART FIVE

Preface

"I think all the great religions of the world—Buddhism, Hinduism, Christianity, Islam, and Communism—both untrue and harmful. It is evident as a matter of logic that, since they disagree, not more than one of them can be true. With very few exceptions, the religion which a man accepts is that of the community in which he lives, which makes it obvious that the influence of environment is what has led him to accept the religion in question."[1]

It has been almost thirty years since Bertrand Russell penned these words to the preface of philosopher Paul Edwards's edited collection, *Why I Am Not A Christian and Other Essays on Religion and Related Subjects*. Although this is a wonderful compilation of some of Russell's more popular essays on religion, many of his essays on the subject still remain buried as obscure pamphlets, as chapters in books, and as articles contributed to various periodicals not readily available. The purpose of this collection is to bring together in one handy volume some of Russell's most delightful and thought-provoking essays on religion, which he defined in 1920 as "a set of beliefs held as dogmas, dominating the conduct of life, going beyond or contrary to evidence, and inculcated by methods which are emotional or authoritarian, not intellectual."[2] Recently, in the United States and around the world, there has been a tremendous resurgence of religious fundamentalism, whose effect is being felt in both the political and the social spheres. It brings back the old dogmas and intolerances against birth control, sex education, equal rights for women, homosexuality, and evolution. The list could go on and on. It is therefore important to reexamine religion critically, and Bertrand Russell was certainly one of the most eloquent and creative thinkers to expound a critical viewpoint.

Russell has two primary objections to belief in the existence of God, religion, and the dogma that belief in them engenders: the first being intellectual while the second is moral. The intellectual objection is directed at various specious arguments that attempt to prove such propositions as the existence of God. "As for God—well, there are a great many arguments that have been advanced in favor of the existence of God, and I thought, and I still think, that one and all they're invalid, and that nobody would have accepted such arguments if they hadn't wanted to believe in the conclusions."[3] As a matter of fact, Russell states, "I've observed that the belief in the goodness of God is inversely proportional to the evidence. When there's no evidence for it at all, people believe it, and when things are going well and you might believe it, they don't."[4] He does not find the proposition that such a being exists unintelligible, or logically impossible; Russell maintains that after carefully examining the evidence, there is not the slightest reason to think it true. It is not up to the skeptic to disprove the proposition; rather, it is up to the person making the claim to offer evidence in favor of the proposition.

The general intellectual position Russell adopts is that of "rational skepticism," i.e., of withholding judgment where the evidence is not sufficient, or, even more so, when there is contrary evidence. As for faith, Russell writes: "We may define 'faith' as the firm belief in something for which there is no evidence. When there is evidence, no one speaks of 'faith.' We do not speak of faith that two and two are four or that the earth is round. We only speak of faith when we wish to substitute emotion for evidence. The substitution of emotion for evidence is apt to lead to strife, since different groups substitute different emotions."[5]

Russell's moral objections to religion are numerous. "I am as firmly convinced that religions do harm as I am that they are untrue."[6] This approach is to insist that dogmatic claims inhibit social changes essential for the happiness of mankind. "The Catholic condemnation of birth control, if it could prevail, would make the mitigation of poverty and the abolition of war impossible. The Hindu beliefs that the cow is a sacred animal and that it is wicked for widows to remarry cause quite needless suffering."[7]

The second moral argument against religion concerns the ever present danger of the enforcement of official creeds, with the discouragement of inquiry and other attendant evils: "It is thought virtuous to have Faith—that is to say, have a conviction which cannot be shaken by contrary evidence. Or, if contrary evidence might induce doubt, it is held that contrary evidence must be suppressed. ... The above evils are independent of the particular creed in question and exist equally in all creeds which are held dogmatically."[8]

Russell's writings show that the history of religion and Christianity in particular left much to be desired. He has also raised the question of the degree of blame that can be assigned to various religions with respect to the subjection of women, and he has attacked the idea of the supposed moral and social desirability of a doctrine of sin and damnation. "There is one very serious defect in my mind in Christ's moral character," said Russell, "and that is that He believed in hell. I do not myself feel that any person who is really profoundly humane can believe in everlasting punishment."[9] In the end, Russell believes that the dogmatic inflexibility of religion has been its undoing. "The fact is that religion is no longer sufficiently vital to take hold of anything new, it was formed long ago to suit certain needs, and has subsisted by the force of tradition, but is no longer able to assimilate anything that cannot be viewed traditionally."[10] Russell believes that only the opposite attitude of rational skepticism will result in the emergence of a happier society: "The world that I should wish to see would be one freed from the virulence of group hostilities and capable of realizing that happiness for all is to be derived rather from cooperation than from strife. I should wish to see a world in which education aimed at mental freedom rather than at imprisoning the minds of the young in a rigid armor of dogma calculated to protect them through life against the shafts of impartial evidence. The world needs open hearts and open minds, and it is not through rigid systems, whether old or new, that these can be derived."[11]

In conclusion, there is a marvelous anecdote from the occasion of Russell's ninetieth birthday celebration that best serves to summarize his attitude toward God and religion. A London lady sat next to him at this party, and over the soup she suggested to him that he was not only the world's most famous atheist but, by this time, very probably the world's oldest atheist. "What will you do, Bertie, if it turns out you were wrong?" she asked. "I mean, what if—uh—when the time comes, you should meet Him? What will you say?" Russell was delighted with the question. His bright, birdlike eyes grew even brighter as he contemplated this possible future dialogue, and then he pointed a finger upward and cried, "Why, I should say, 'God, you gave us insufficient evidence.'"[12]

NOTES

1. Bertrand Russell, *Why I Am Not A Christian and Other Essays on Religion and Related Subjects* (New York: Simon and Schuster, 1957), p. v.

2. Bertrand Russell, *The Practice and Theory of Bolshevism,* second edition. (London: George and Allen Unwin, 1949), p. 74.

3. Bertrand Russell, *Bertrand Russell Speaks His Mind* (Cleveland: World Publishing Co., 1960), p. 24.

4. Ibid., p. 31.

5. Bertrand Russell, *Human Society in Ethics and Politics* (New York: Simon and Schuster, 1955), p. 203.

6. *Why I Am Not A Christian,* p. vi.

7. Ibid., pp. vi-vii.

8. Ibid.

9. Ibid., p. 17.

10. Bertrand Russell, *Prospects of Industrial Civilization* (London: George and Allen Unwin, 1923), p. 48.

11. *Why I Am Not A Christian,* p. vii.

12. [Anon.], "The Talk of the Town," in *The New Yorker* (21 February 1970), p. 29.

The Life and Wisdom of Bertrand Russell

"Three passions, simple but overwhelmingly strong, have governed my life: the longing for love, the search for knowledge, and unbearable pity for the suffering of mankind. These passions, like great winds, have blown me hither and thither, in a wayward course, over a deep ocean of anguish, reaching to the very verge of despair.

I have sought love, first, because it brings ecstasy—ecstasy so great that I would often have sacrificed all the rest of life for a few hours of this joy. I have sought it, next, because it relieves loneliness—that terrible loneliness in which one shivering consciousness looks over the rim of the world into the cold unfathomable lifeless abyss. I have sought it, finally, because in the union of love I have seen, in a mystic miniature, the prefiguring vision of the heaven that saints and poets have imagined. This is what I sought, and though it might seem too good for human life, this is what—at last—I have found.

With equal passion I have sought knowledge. I have wished to understand the hearts of men. I have wished to know why the stars shine. And I have tried to apprehend the Pythagorean power by which number holds sway above the flux. A little of this, but not much, I have achieved.

Love and knowledge, so far as they were possible, led upward toward the heavens. But always pity brought me back to earth. Echoes of cries of pain reverberate in my heart. Children in famine, victims tortured by oppressors, helpless old people a hated burden to their sons, and the whole world of loneliness, poverty, and pain make a mockery of what human life should be. I long to alleviate the evil, but I cannot, and I too suffer.

This has been my life. I have found it worth living, and would gladly live it again if the chance were offered me."[1]

—Bertrand Russell

Bertrand Russell (1872-1970) was without question one of the most productive and brilliant thinkers of the twentieth century. The American philosopher W. V. Quine summed up Russell's career with these words: "Russell's life coincides with an era in the history of philosophy that can be defined in any of three almost equivalent ways: philosophy since John Stuart Mill, or the past hundred years in philosophy; or, most significantly, The Age of Russell. . . . His life was as broad as it was long. Off at one edge of Russell's broad spectrum, he was a logic-chopping technician, a mathematician's philosopher and a philosopher's mathematician. At the other edge of his spectrum he was a social reformer, advocating revision of the family and of sexual mores and was even communicating with the world's political leaders, doing what he could to decide the fate of the empire."[2]

Bertrand Russell gained worldwide recognition as a bold man and a wise thinker even among those who were not competent to assess his mathematical and philosophical works. In 1962, Secretary General U Thant of the United Nations had this to say about Russell: "To my knowledge there is no other person who feels so concerned about the future of humanity and who is prepared to risk anything for the cause of humanity. He certainly deserves the highest recognition that human society and all organizations can accord."[3]

Russell, a great master of English prose, wrote and published over seventy-five books as well as countless articles, essays, and pamphlets, many of which have undergone frequent reprintings and have been the impetus for a vast secondary literature concerning his life and his views. In addition, Russell had numerous honors conferred upon him during his lifetime: the Order of Merit (1949), the most exclusive honor given in England; a Nobel Prize for Literature (1950); the UNESCO Kalinga Prize (1957); and the Danish Sonning Prize for contributions to World Culture (1960). This recognition confirms Russell as a powerful thinker of perennial importance for our time.

Bertrand Russell believed in reason, and he demanded that every proposed rule of conduct pass the test of reason. The most intense human suffering, he thought, is due to mankind's failures to adhere to rational principles. Russell argued logically against such illogical attitudes as fear of an angry God or feelings of guilt about harmless sexual pleasures. In fact, he urged that no good reason exists for believing in God at all or for waging war in an age of nuclear weapons; but above all, Russell rallied for thought: "Men fear thought as they fear nothing else on earth—more than ruin, more even than death. Thought is subversive and revolutionary, destructive and terrible; thought is merciless to privilege, established institutions, and comfortable habits; thought is anarchic and lawless, indifferent to authority, careless of the well-tried wisdom of the ages. Thought looks into the pit of hell and is not afraid. . . . Thought is great and swift and free, the light of the world, and the chief glory of man. But if thought is to become the possession of many, not the privilege of the few, we must have done with fear. It is fear that holds men back—fear lest their cherished beliefs should prove delusions, fear lest the institutions by which they live should prove harmful, fear lest they themselves should prove less worthy of respect than they have supposed themselves to be."[4]

Russell's parents married in 1864, when they were each twenty-two. His older brother Frank used to boast that he was born nine months and five days after the wedding. Russell's father, Viscount John Amberley, was a gentle, but austere freethinker, who had run for Parliament in the general election of 1868. Unfortunately, his political ambitions were wrecked by his unpopular support of birth control and the introduction of a bill into Parliament that would have legalized the holding of secular debates as well as the giving of lectures on Sunday. Disillusioned, he retired to the country, where he wrote one of the great classics of freethought, posthumously published as *An Analysis of Religious Belief,* which was to have a profound effect on young Bertrand.

Bertrand Russell was born on May 18, 1872, apparently the result, as he later learned, of a failure in that unmentionable practice of birth control, which had already led his father into political isolation. Russell was first described by his mother, Viscountess Kate Amberley, when he was just three days old: "The baby weighed eight and three-quarter pounds is twenty-one inches long and very fat and very ugly like Frank. . . . I have lots of milk now, but if he does not get it at once or has wind of anything he gets into such a rage and screams and kicks and trembles till he is soothed off. . . . He lifts his head up and looks about in a very energetic way."[5]

In June of 1874, Russell's mother fell ill with diphtheria and died. Russell's father, a man of delicate health who had depended on his wife's vitality, rapidly became more invalid and in January of 1876, he, too, died. "Good-bye my dears forever"[6] were his last words to his children. He had appointed two atheists as guardians for the boys, but this was too much for Russell's grandparents, who succeeded in having the will set aside. Bertrand and his brother Frank were put in the custody of their eminent grandparents at Pembroke Lodge. Russell's grandfather, Lord John Russell, had been one of the most important prime ministers of the Victorian period, whose career included the introduction of the Reform Bill of 1832 that launched England on the road to democracy.

Young Bertrand's childhood at Pembroke Lodge was a regimented existence of puritan piety, austerity, and loneliness; hardly an atmosphere conducive to free thought. He found the loneliness unbearable, and he later recalled that at the age of five he reflected that if he would live to be seventy, he had thus far endured only a fourteenth part of his life, and he felt that the years of boredom ahead of him would be unendurable. "There were family prayers at eight o'clock every morning. Although there were eight servants, food was always of Spartan simplicity, and even what there was, if it was at all nice, was considered too good for children. For instance, if there was apple tart and rice pudding, I was only allowed the rice pudding. Cold baths all the year round were insisted upon. . . . My grandmother never allowed herself to sit in an armchair until the evening. Alcohol and tobacco were viewed with disfavor although stern convention compelled them to serve a little wine to guests. Only virtue was prized, virtue at the expense of intellect, health, happiness, and every mundane good."[7]

Russell's grandfather died in 1878, so it was his grandmother, Lady Frances Russell, who decided the manner of his education. Although a Scottish Presbyterian, her religious proclivities were moving toward Unitarianism, so Russell found himself taken on alternate Sundays to the Parish Church and to the Presbyterian Church, while at home he was taught the tenets of Unitarianism. He was not taught the doctrines of eternal punishment or the literal truth of the Bible. Beyond a suggestion to avoid playing cards on Sundays for fear of shocking the servants, there was no Sabbatarianism practiced at home.

On his twelfth birthday, Russell received a Bible, with his grandmother's favorite texts inscribed on the flyleaf: "Thou shalt not follow a multitude to do evil," and "Be strong, and of good courage, be not afraid, neither be thou dismayed; for the Lord thy God is whithersoever thou goest." These texts profoundly influenced Russell's life and retained some meaning for him even after he ceased to believe in God. Later he was to write: "I remember when I was about four or five years old lying awake thinking how dreadful it would be when my grandmother was dead. When she did in fact die, which was after I was married, I did not mind at all. But in retrospect, as I have grown older, I have realized more and more the importance she had in molding my outlook on life. Her fearlessness, her public spirit, her contempt for convention, and her indifference to the opinion of the majority have always seemed good to me and have impressed themselves upon me as worthy of imitation."[8]

Lady Russell dreaded the influence of public schools, so young Bertrand was not sent to school. Instead he was taught by tutors, including his older brother Frank, who introduced him to the study of Euclid. "Before I began the study of geometry somebody had told me that it proved things and this caused me to feel delight when my brother said that he would teach it to me. My brother began at the beginning with the definitions. These I accepted readily enough. But he came next to the axioms. 'These,' he said, 'can't be proved, but they have to be assumed before the rest can be proved.' At these words my hopes crumbled. I thought it would be wonderful to find something that one could PROVE, and then it turned out that this could only be done by means of assumptions of which there was no proof."[9] Throughout Russell's philosophical career he had only one constant preoccupation: to discover how much can be known and with what degree of certainty. "From the outset I wished to persuade myself that something could be known, in pure mathematics if not elsewhere."[10]

During Russell's early years he had no opportunity for contact with other children; consequently, he had abundant time for reflection, and at the age of fourteen his thoughts turned to religion. For four years, he thought about and successively rejected free will, immortality of the soul, and belief in God. He kept his thoughts private because he feared the ridicule of his elders. Russell had an agnostic tutor, a stout defender of reason, with whom he discussed his evaporating faith in immortality and God. When these secret discussions were overheard, the tutor was fired.

Most of Russell's time during his mid-teens was taken up by the study of mathematics, but the emotional drive that ignited his thought was the doubt he experienced regarding the fundamental dogmas of religion. The resulting loss of his faith left Russell miserable for a time. He wrote down his thoughts in a secret diary, using Greek letters and phonetic spelling for concealment. "My loss of faith has taken away cheerfulness and made it much harder to make bosom friends and, worst of all, it has disbarred me from free intercourse with my people, and thus made them strangers to some of my deepest thoughts."[11] Two days after his sixteenth birthday Russell confided to his diary, "I should like to believe my people's religion, which was just what I could wish, but alas, it is impossible. I have really no religion, for my God, being a spirit shown merely by reason to exist, his properties utterly unknown, is no help to my life. I have not the parson's comfortable doctrine, that every good action has its reward, and every sin is forgiven. My religion is this: to do every duty, and expect no reward for it either here or hereafter."[12]

At the age of eighteen Russell left Pembroke Lodge and entered Cambridge University to study mathematics. A whole new world opened up to him; for the first time he could engage in lively discourse without fear of ridicule or punishment. This was a source of great comfort that helped him overcome his earlier misery. "Cambridge was important in my life," Russell recalls, "through the fact that it gave me friends, and experience of intellectual discussion, but it was not important through actual academic instruction. . . . Most of what I learned in philosophy has come to seem to me erroneous, and I spent many subsequent years in gradually unlearning the habits of thought which I had there acquired. The one habit of thought of real value that I acquired there was intellectual honesty. This virtue certainly existed not only among my friends, but among my teachers. . . . It was a blow to me during the [First World] War to find that, even at Cambridge, intellectual honesty had its limitations. Until then, wherever I lived, I felt that Cambridge was the only place on earth that I could regard as home."[13]

Although Russell's shyness gradually began to dissipate amid intellectual matters, it remained a crippling obstacle where young women were concerned. In 1892, at the tender age of seventeen, having had little or no association with young women, he fell in love at first sight with Alys Pearsall Smith, the daughter of an American Quaker family. He proved a rather taciturn and embarrassed suitor, though a most determined one. After almost four years of courtship Russell announced his plans to marry her.

The reaction from Russell's family to his emancipated fiancée was not pleasant. He was warned that "she was no lady, a baby-snatcher, a low-class adventuress, a designing female taking advantage of his inexperience, a person incapable of all the finer feelings,"[14] and a woman whose vulgarity would perpetually put him to shame.

There was, indeed, some reason for caution. Russell was told by a family doctor some hard facts, a few of which he had already suspected. Uncle Willy was mad, Aunt Agatha had broken off her engagement following insane delusions, and the family appeared to have been perpetually tottering along a narrow path above a mental precipice. Other skeletons may well have been brought out of the closet to support concern for the mental health of any children that might result from this union. However, more than this was needed to stop a Russell at the mercy of first love. He and Alys responded with the decision to have no children.

Alys was a believing Quaker when Bertrand married her in 1894, and he used to boast that after six months she dropped her religion. Alys was relieved to hear that Bertrand had no objections to a Quaker ceremony. "Don't imagine that I really seriously mind a religious ceremony," he wrote. "Any ceremony is disgusting and the mere fact of having to advertise the most intimate thing a little more or less doesn't make much odds. . . . I shall be glad to get the damned thing over and done with."[15]

The young couple's plans for the future were earnest but modest. Russell had inherited a large legacy from his father so he did not need to earn a living. (He later gave this fortune away to various causes, including his friend the young struggling poet T. S. Eliot.) Time therefore could be devoted to a leisurely pursuit of satisfying intellectual work. Alys had her good causes: the emancipation of women, teetotalism, and the advocacy of free love (a practice that she favored until, some years later, Russell began to use her theory for his practice). Bertrand was, for the most part, drawn to economics.

Bertrand and Alys decided in 1895 to investigate the German Social Democratic Party, to interview its members at all levels, and to probe beneath the skin in order to understand the status and prospects of the party. Published in 1896, Russell's first book, *German Social Democracy,* predicted with uncanny foresight, Germany's future of dictatorship and war.

The next few years were devoted to writing a book on Leibniz and a work on the philosophy of mathematics. Russell made every effort to incorporate as few assumptions as possible into his mathematical philosophy. Using Occam's razor, he cut out all unnecessary elements in his statement of a philosophical idea. "What is the smallest number of simple undefined things at the start and the smallest number of undemonstrated premises of which you can define the things that need to be defined, and prove the things that need to be proved?"[16]

Part of the answer to Russell's problem in mathematical philosophy was provided by the mathematician Giuseppe Peano, who had set out pure mathematics as a system that could be deduced from five axioms containing only three undefined terms: "0," "number," and "successor." Russell's aim was to deduce the axioms themselves from logical laws and to define the three words in purely logical terms. Russell's most famous analysis of mathematics into logic, his definition of number, is filled with the highly technical language of the philosophy of mathematics "Number is a way of bringing together certain collections, namely those that hae a given number of terms . . . it is simpler logically to find out whether two collections have the same number of terms than it is to define what that number is. Two classes are said to be 'similar' when there is a one-to-one relation which correlates the terms of one class each with one term of the other class in the same manner in which the relation of marriage correlates husbands with wives."[17] All collections with the same number of members have in common a number. The number two is the characteristic of all pairs. The number three is the common characteristic of all triplets. Twins and triplets may have almost nothing in common with other twins and triplets but they do share the distinguishing numbers two and three. "Accordingly, the number of a class is the class of all those classes which are similar to it."[18]

Peano had shown that all pure mathematics was about numbers; Russell showed that numbers were classes of a certain kind. He argued that "class" is a logical notion. This work ultimately resulted in the *Principia Mathematica,* his magnum opus, in which Russell argued that arithmetic, and pure mathematics generally, is nothing but a prolongation of mathematical logic. This concentrated mathematical work, Russell's greatest intellectual achievement, was carried out against a background of emotional chaos, and it would be unrealistic to believe that the latter did not influence the former.

It was during the writing of the *Principles of Mathematics,* the precursor of the *Principia,* that Russell had an experience not unlike what the religious call conversion. For years Russell had been an imperialist, a political position that had led him to support the Boer

War in South Africa. But early in 1901, "In the course of a few minutes I changed my mind about the Boer War, about harshness in education and in the criminal law, and about combativeness in private relations."[19] Russell's "conversion" was the result of his recent vivid awareness of the state of utter loneliness in which most people lived, and a passionate desire to find ways of diminishing this tragic isolation. This agonizing experience was to produce what is arguably his most famous essay, *A Free Man's Worship*.

In 1907 he decided to stand for election on a platform advocating women's suffrage. He had been a keen supporter of women's rights even before coming under the influence of his wife Alys. Later Russell said of the election: "In 1907 I even stood for Parliament at a by-election, on behalf of votes for women. . . . When, in later years, I campaigned against the First World War, the popular opposition that I encountered there was not comparable to that which the suffragists met in 1907. The whole subject was treated, by a great majority of the population, as one for mere hilarity. The crowd would shout derisive remarks: to women, 'Go home and mind the baby'; to men, 'Does your mother know you're out?' . . . Rotten eggs were aimed at me and hit my wife. At my first meeting rats were let loose to frighten the ladies, and ladies who were in the plot screamed in pretended terror with a view to disgracing their sex."[20] Against Henry Chaplin's 10,263 votes, Russell could muster only 3,299, some 4,000 less than the Liberals in the previous year's election.

Although Russell was still actively preoccupied with his work in mathematical logic and the theory of knowledge, with the advent of the First World War he became passionately concerned with social issues. It is probable that Russell would have remained mainly academic and abstract but for the war. It "shook him" out of many prejudices and made him reexamine a number of fundamental questions, and it became emotionally difficult for Russell to remain attached to a "world of abstraction" in the midst of the slaughter of the Great War. "All the high-flown thoughts that I had had about the abstract world of ideas," he wrote later, "seemed to me thin and rather trivial in view of the vast suffering that surrounded me."[21] The attitude of ordinary men and women during the first few months of the First World War amazed him, particularly the fact that they found a kind of pleasure in the excitement, at least until the casualties were brought home. Russell was struck by the connection of politics and psychology and he began to realize that the action of the masses are dictated by the results of shared passions.

This caused him to disagree with the pacifists that wars were the result of devious tyrants who forced them on reluctant populations. According to Russell, the majority of human beings in our culture were filled with destructive and perverse impulses, and no scheme for reform would achieve a beneficial improvement in human affairs until the psychological structure of the average person was suitably transformed through an education that stressed rational thought, a skeptical attitude, cooperation rather than competition, and kind feelings instead of strife and prejudice.

Russell never believed that much tangible good would come from opposition to the war, but he felt that "for the honor of human nature those who were not swept off their feet should show that they stood firm."[22] Russell's pacifism was not unshakable. He never had the view that the use of force is always wrong or that war cannot possibly be justified. It was simply that this war in these circumstances was not worth all the pain and lying of all the parties. As a matter of fact, Russell favored the Allies during the Second World War on the ground that Hitler was absolutely intolerable and if the Nazis had conquered the world, as they obviously intended to do, the world would become an absolute hell. The Kaiser's Germany, by contrast, was "only swashbuckling and a little absurd,"[23] allowing for a good deal of freedom and democracy.

Prior to World War I there had been strong pacifist sentiment in all the major Western countries, especially among the intellectuals and the powerful socialist and liberal parties. When war came, only a tiny minority of these pacifists remained true to their convictions. Overwhelmed by their need to conform and in many cases by what Russell had regarded as their primitive impulses, many of them became the most violent jingoists. Russell was bitterly attacked for his pacifist activities, not only by conservatives and professional patriots, as one might have expected, but also by many of his closest friends. H. G. Wells, for example, publicly heaped abuse on Russell knowing full well that his victim was already in trouble with the authorities. Russell's political philosophy, according to Wells, amounted to a "tepid voluntarism," and he (unlike Wells) had no right to speak for British socialism. Wells even went so far as to abuse Russell as a mathematical philosopher. "Russell," he wrote, "is that awe-inspiring man who objected to Euclid upon grounds no one could possibly understand, in books no one could possibly read."[24]

Public sentiment started to turn against Russell. For example, at Cambridge University, his former teacher and friend John McTaggart lead a move that resulted in Russell's dismissal; public meetings addressed by Russell were broken up by violent mobs without any police interference. Then, in 1916, Russell gave a series of anti-war lectures that increasingly gained adherents. Published as *Principles of Social Reconstruction* (in America under the title *Why Men Fight*), they made considerable impact in the United States, and led to the proposal that Russell should lecture on the same subject at Harvard University. Lytton Strachey said of the lectures, "Governments, religions, laws, property, even Good form itself, down they go like ninepins, it is a charming sight."[25]

Russell was unable to accept Harvard University's invitation and was effectively stopped from giving these lectures abroad when the British Government revoked his passport. He was also banned from lecturing in the coastal towns of Britain (they feared that he might signal to German submarines!), an admission that Russell had reached an almost unique position in the official demonology.

If Russell's ability to draw intellectual rings around officialdom frequently gave a boost to men and women in the No-Conscription movement, there was another way in which he helped the pacifist cause. Few members of the movement had lines open to those who made decisions. Russell, on the other hand, through his family and social contacts with what would today be called the Establishment, moved in circles where the prime minister could drop by without causing surprise. The government knew this and from an early date regarded Russell as an enemy to be handled with great care.

In the spring of 1916, Russell wrote a leaflet dealing with the imprisonment of a young conscientious objector, Ernest Everett. After six men had been sent to prison for distributing the leaflet, he wrote a letter published by the *London Times* that ended, ". . . if anyone is to be prosecuted, I am the person responsible."[26] Russell was fined £100.

Two years later, in 1918, Russell was sentenced to six months imprisonment for an article he wrote in the *Tribunal,* a pacifist weekly, in which he said, "unless peace comes soon . . . the American garrison which will by that time be occupying England and France . . . will no doubt be capable of intimidating strikers, an occupation to which the American army is accustomed when at home."[27]

In a fierce denunciation accompanying his sentence, the magistrate, Sir John Dickinson, referred to Russell's offense as a "very despicable one," and added that he "seems to have lost all sense of decency."[28] It should be added that only as the result of the intervention of the then British Foreign Secretary Arthur Balfour was Russell treated with any consideration while in prison.

On his arrival at the prison gate, Russell was much cheered by the warder who had to take particulars about him. He asked Russell to state his religion, whereupon Russell replied that he was an "agnostic." The warder asked how to spell it, and then remarked with a sigh, "Well religions are many, but I guess they all believe in the same God."[29] This remark kept Russell cheered for about a week. His time in prison was productively spent finishing work on two books, *An Introduction to Mathematical Philosophy* and *An Analysis of Mind.*

When the Armistice was announced, Russell felt strangely solitary amid all the rejoicings. He recalled, "True, I rejoiced also, but I could find nothing in common between my rejoicing and that of the crowd. Throughout my life I have longed to feel that oneness with large bodies of human beings that is experienced by the members of enthusiastic crowds. The longing has often been strong enough to lead me into self-deception. I have imagined myself in turn a Liberal, a Socialist, or a Pacifist, but I have never been any of these things in any profound sense. Always the skeptical intellect, when I have most wished it silent, has whispered doubts to me, has cut me of from the facile enthusiasms of others, and has transported me into a desolate solitude."[30]

The war of 1914 changed everything for Russell. He ceased to be academic and took to writing a new kind of book. He changed his whole conception of human nature, and became for the first time deeply convinced that puritanism does not make for human happiness. Through the spectacle of death, Russell acquired a new love for what was living. During this period of redirection, he grew increasingly discontented with his wife Alys, and drifted in and out of a series of affairs. Russell remarked to one of his female companions, "Chastity, I gave it a good try once, but never again."[31] In 1919, he met Dora Black, who was to become his second wife, on account of her desire to have children.

In 1920 he was invited to join a Labor delegation to the Soviet Union. Russell seized the opportunity to see what was happening in the wake of the revolution he had so ardently welcomed. He was able to meet and talk with Lenin, Trotsky, and Gorky. "He preferred to go about himself," Emma Goldman, then in Russia, commented of Russell. "He also showed no elation over the honor of being quartered in a palace and fed on special morsels."[32] The Bolsheviks were heard to whisper, "Suspicious person, that Russell."[33]

Russell returned to England a few months later in a state of total disillusionment. Though the British socialists thought it wrong at the time to criticize the Bolsheviks openly, Russell saw fit to publish his verdict. Although admitting to a sympathy with the aims of Bolshevism, he could accept neither their methods nor the final submission to the state. Some of Russell's friends argued that any criticism of the revolution would play into the hands of the reactionaries who wanted to reestablish the old order. After some hestitation, Russell decided to publish the truth as he saw it. "Russia," he wrote, "seemed to me one vast prison in which the jailors were cruel bigots. When I found my friends applauding these men as liberators and regarding the regime that they were creating as a paradise, I wondered in a bewildered manner whether it was my friends or I that were mad."[34]

Russell's *Theory and Practice of Bolshevism* is remarkable for, among other things, its prescience. Long before most Westerners had heard of Joseph Stalin, Russell predicted, point by point, the reactionary features that came to characterize his Soviet regime: its militarism and nationalism, the hostility to free art and science, its puritanism, and the gradual ascendancy of bureaucrats and sycophants over the early idealists. Russell was able to reprint the book in 1947 without a single alteration.

His isolation after returning from Russia was even greater than during the First World War. The patriots had not yet forgiven him for his opposition to the war, while the majority of his former political friends denounced him for his opposition to the Soviet regime. But Russell had never been known to play to the galleries. As on many previous occasions he acted in accordance with his favorite biblical text, "Thou shalt not follow a multitude to do evil." Russell was indeed more impressed by prerevolutionary China, where he spent a year teaching at the University of Peking in 1921.

In 1927, owing to the birth of his two children, Russell became increasingly interested in education and sexual morality. His controversial views were closely linked with his observation of the joy people took in fighting and killing during the war. He believed that these characteristics were largely the outcome of experiences and teachings people were exposed to at an early age. A peaceful and happy world could not be achieved without drastic changes in education. In sexual matters, although not only in these, irrational prohibitions and dishonesty were exceedingly harmful. "I believe," he wrote in *Marriage and Morals*, "that nine out of ten of those who have had a conventional upbringing in their early years have become in some degree incapable of a decent and sane attitude toward marriage and sex generally."[35] Conventional education was judged to be at fault, through its general tendency to cramp creative impulses and to discourage a spirit of free inquiry.

Although puritanical moralists professed to be violently shocked by Russell's views on sex and education, it is worth emphasizing that his recommendations are not extreme and his writings on sex form only a small segment of his published works. As Russell later stated in an interview, "only about one percent of my writings are concerned with sex, but the conventional public is so obsessed with sex that it hasn't noticed the other ninety-nine percent of my writings, and I think one percent is a reasonable proportion of human interest to assign to that subject. I should deal with sexual morality exactly as I would with everything else. I should say that if what you are doing does no harm to anybody there's no reason to condemn it. And you shouldn't condemn it merely because some ancient taboo has said that this is wrong. You should look into whether it does any harm or not, and that's the basis of sexual morality as of all others."[36] It would be overly simplistic to regard Russell as an "advocate of wild living." On the contrary, he had no such intentions. In *Marriage and Morals* he wrote: "The morality which I should advocate does not consist simply of saying to grown-up people or to adolescents: 'Follow your impulses and do as you like.' There has to be consistency in life; there has to be continuous effort directed to ends that are not immediately beneficial and not at every moment attractive; there has to be consideration for others; and there should be certain standards of rectitude. . . . But this does not mean that we should be dominated by fears which modern discoveries have made irrational."[37] Russell could see nothing wrong in sexual relations before marriage, and he advocated temporary childless marriages for most university students. It is wrong to regard Russell as an enemy of the institution of marriage, though he did object to continuing a marital relationship when no love was left. What shocked people a great deal was his remark that a permanent marriage need not exclude a few temporary extramarital affairs.

Russell's views on education were so revolutionary in the twenties that he and wife Dora decided to open their own private school.

"We wanted," Russell wrote, "an unusual combination: on the one hand, we disliked prudery and religious instruction and a great many restraints on freedom which were taken for granted in conventional schools; on the other hand, we could not agree with most 'modern' educationalists in thinking scholastic education unimportant, or in advocating a complete absence of discipline."[38] Needless to say, Russell's school aroused controversy. Typical of the levity with which it was viewed is the following verse:

> His formal education done
> He scorned the lesser types of fun
> And started a Progressive School
> Untrammelled by Pendantic Rule
> Combining Roses round the Trellis
> With interludes from Havelock Ellis.[39]

The most widely publicized example, however, is that of the little girl and the rector. As the tale goes, the local rector upon ringing the doorbell at Telegraph House was greeted by a little girl who was quite naked. "Good God!" he exclaimed. "There is no God!" the child replied while slamming the door. Yet in common with other such apocryphal tales, this one has as little claim to reality as the doorbell which Telegraph House did not have.

The school was not a success; it claimed a large amount of time and financial resources. Indeed, many of Russell's writings at that time, and American lecture tours, were undertaken to provide the necessary money. In addition, the school attracted a fair number of problem children, and Russell had great difficulty in effecting his idea of the right balance between freedom and discipline. Though Russell left the school in 1932, it continued in Dora's hands into the 1940s, even after their marriage had ended. In 1938, Russell married his third wife, Patricia Spence, who had been a teacher at the school.

Meanwhile, Russell's older brother Frank had died in 1931, making Bertrand an Earl. "I inherit from him a title, but not a penny of money, as he was bankrupt. A title is a great nuisance to me, and I am at a loss of what to do. . . . There is, so far as I know, only one method of getting rid of it, which is to be attainted of high treason, and this would involve my head being cut off on Tower Hill. This method seems to me perhaps somewhat extreme."[40]

Russell's views on sexual morality and religion featured prominently in the 1940 case involving the City College of New York

(CCNY). When Russell was teaching at the University of California in Los Angeles, he was unanimously invited by the board of higher education in New York to join the staff of the City College of New York to teach a graduate course in logic and mathematics. This appointment was intended to give the school great prestige, for by this time, Russell had achieved an outstanding international reputation as a brilliant scholar and lecturer in these esoteric fields. Accepting this position, Russell resigned his professorship in Los Angeles. A protest against his City College appointment was soon started in the New York papers by Bishop Manning of the Anglican Church. He declared that Russell's position should be revoked on the grounds that "Russell was a recognized propagandist against both religion and morality and who specifically defends adultery."[41] The next step was to pressure the local board members to reverse their decision. A taxpayer's suit to annul the appointment was filed in the New York Supreme Court by Miss Jane Kaye, whose daughter was going to attend City College.

With more zeal than accuracy, the prosecuting lawyer in the trial described Russell's books as ". . . lecherous, salacious, libidinous, lustful, venerous, erotomanic, aphrodisiac, atheistic, irreverent, narrow-minded, bigoted, untruthful . . . and bereft of moral fiber."[42] Russell, he maintained, had written salacious poetry, conducted a nudist colony in England, and condoned homosexuality. The judge, a Roman Catholic, delivered the historic verdict: Russell's appointment was to be annulled on three grounds: (1) Russell was not an American; (2) he had not been given a competitive examination on logic and mathematics, and (3) his books were immoral and full of filth.[43]

Russell was never allowed to offer a defense in the proceedings or to be a party to the case. Hundreds of eminent people rallied to Russell's defense but to no avail. Albert Einstein wrote to Russell stating that "great spirits have always encountered violent opposition from mediocre minds. . . ."[44] After this historic case, Russell found it very difficult to obtain teaching positions and subsequently endured a long period of financial hardship. Ten years later, in 1950, the judge in the case, the prosecuting lawyer, and the woman who had initially filed suit were strangely silent when Russell was awarded the Nobel Prize for Literature in recognition of his "philosophical works . . . of service to moral civilization."[45]

A few months after the bombing of Hiroshima and Nagasaki in 1945, Russell was one of the first to speak out on the dangers of nuclear war. He forecast and explained the making of nuclear bombs of far greater power than those used on the Empire of Japan, namely, the much more destructive fusion bombs. Everybody applauded his speech; not a single peer said that his fears were excessive. But they all agreed that it was a problem for their grandchildren. When Russell learned that Russia had exploded its own atomic weapon, his interests increasingly turned toward world government as the only solution if a total nuclear holocaust was to be avoided.

Now, by the early part of 1950, Russell had become so respectable in the eyes of the Establishment that members of Parliament felt that he should be given the Order of Merit, England's highest honor to a civilian. Russell recalls the event: "I had to go to Buckingham Palace for the official bestowal of it. The King [George VI] was affable, but somewhat embarrassed at having to behave so graciously to so queer a fellow, a convict to boot. He remarked, 'You have sometimes behaved in a way which would not do if generally adopted.' I have been glad ever since that I did not make the reply that sprang to my mind, 'Like your brother?' . . . I did not feel that I could let this remark pass in silence, so I said, 'How a man should behave depends on his profession. A postman, for instance, should knock at all the doors in a street at which he has letters to deliver, but if anyone else knocked on all the doors, he would be considered a public nuisance.' The King, to avoid answering, abruptly changed the subject."[46]

The next year, Russell was awarded the Nobel Prize for Literature. This period marked the height of Russell's respectability. He later remarked: "It is true that I began to feel slightly uneasy, fearing that this might mean the onset of blind orthodoxy. I have always held that no one can be respectable without being wicked, but so blunted was my moral sense that I could not see in what way I had sinned."[47]

In the following years Russell devoted his life to professing the inherent dangers of nuclear weapons. He gave an enormously successful broadcast on December 23, 1954, entitled, "Man's Peril." In his closing words he starkly presented the alternatives for his listeners: "I cannot believe that this is to be the end. I would have men forget their quarrels for a moment and reflect that, if they will allow themselves to survive, there is every reason to expect the triumphs of the future to exceed immeasurably the triumphs of the past. There lies before us, if we choose, continual progress in happiness, knowledge, and wisdom. Shall we, instead, choose death, because we cannot forget our quarrels? I appeal, as a human being to human beings: remember your humanity and forget the rest. If you can do so, the way lies open to a new Paradise; if you cannot, nothing lies before you but universal death."[48]

"Man's Peril" was a turning point in Russell's life. It led to his collaboration with Albert Einstein to gather the world's leading scientists from both the East and the West to issue a solemn statement to the world on July 9, 1955, just prior to the Summit Meeting of the Big Four nations in Geneva, on the necessity of avoiding a nuclear war. The path to this famous Einstein-Russell Declaration started with a letter to Russell's good friend Albert Einstein. Russell wrote: "In common with every other thinking person, I am profoundly disquieted by the armaments race in nuclear weapons. You have on various occasions given expression to feelings and opinions with which I am in close agreement. I think that eminent men of science ought to do something dramatic to bring home to the public and governments the disasters that may occur. Do you think it would be possible to get, say, six men of the very highest scientific repute, headed by yourself, to make a very solemn statement about the imperative necessity of avoiding war? These men should be so diverse in their politics that any statement signed by all of them would be obviously free from pro-Communist or anti-Communist bias. I have had a letter form Joliot-Curie which I found encouraging since the fact that he is a Communist and I am not did not prevent agreement in this matter. . . . My own belief is that there should be an appeal to neutral powers. I should like to see one or more of the neutral powers appointing small commissions of their own nationals. . . ."[49]

Einstein replied within the week. "Dear Bertrand Russell, I agreed with every word in your letter. . . ."[50] Russell then prepared a draft of the statement and sent it to Einstein, who replied promptly on April 11, 1955: "Thank you for your letter of April 5. I am gladly willing to sign your excellent statement. I also agree with your choice of prospective signers."[51] This letter and Russell's statement were the last two documents Einstein signed before his death. Two days later, after signing the declaration, Einstein was fatally stricken. Hence the statement came to be known as the Einstein-Russell Declaration. The Declaration was also signed by such prominent scientists as Linus Pauling, Max Born, Niels Bohr, Joliot-Curie, and Hideki Yukawa.

The success of the Einstein-Russell Declaration provided Russell with the necessary momentum to launch the Pugwash Movement. This movement was to gather the world's leading scientists together to bring to their respective governments the disinterested ways and means to avert a nuclear disaster. The Pugwash Movement, which still flourishes today, was partly responsible for the signing of the multinational test-ban treaty in 1962 and the subsequent nuclear nonproliferation treaty.

This in turn made Russell the natural choice as president of the Campaign for Nuclear Disarmament when it was founded in 1958, and his work in the CND led almost inexorably to the more radical Committee of 100 and his imprisonment for civil disobedience. It was through the CND that he led the famous Aldermaston marches. At one of these marches, during Easter, Russell introduced the symbol for total nuclear disarmament that latter became the universal peace symbol. In 1961 he led a rally in Trafalgar Square in which more than 20,000 people took part.

In 1961, Russell and his fourth wife, Edith, were charged, under an Act of 1361, with inciting the public to disobedience, as were thirty-six other members of the Committee of 100. During the trial, Russell made one of the best short speeches of his life, in which he cogently pointed out that civil disobedience had been started with great reluctance and only as a last resort. "Patriotism and humanity alike urged us to see some way of saving our country and the world," he argued. "No-one can desire the slaughter of our families, friends, our compatriots, and a majority of the human race, in a contest in which there will be only vanquished and no victors."[52] The judge offered Russell and his wife freedom from prosecution if he promised to behave himself. The eighty-nine-year-old Russell refused to behave himself, so he and his wife were sentenced to two months in prison, later commuted to seven days on medical grounds.

At the time of the Cuban Missile Crisis of October 1962 and the Sino-Indian border dispute a few months later, Russell exerted whatever influence he could to bring about peaceful settlements. He had enough of an impact on Soviet Premier Khrushchev during the Cuban Missile Crisis, that the Soviet leader first signaled compromise through a letter addressed to Russell and published through the TASS news agency. Secretary General U Thant of the United Nations wrote of the crisis in his memoirs: "I am writing at some length concerning Bertrand Russell's activities during the Cuban

Missile Crisis, because I felt at that time, and still feel, that Khrushchev's positive reply was due, at least in part, to Earl Russell's constant pleadings to him and his congratulating him on his courageous stand for sanity."[53] In a private letter sent to President Kennedy, just after the resolution of the crisis, Khrushchev had this to say: "We welcome all forces which stand on positions of peace. Consequently, I expressed gratitude to Mr. Bertrand Russell, too, who manifests alarm and concern for the fate of the world, and I readily responded to the Appeal of the Acting Secretary of United Nations, U. Thant."[54]

In 1963, Russell formed an international body for seeking peaceful solutions, The Bertrand Russell Peace Foundation, which included in its list of sponsors such eminent men as Albert Schweitzer, Linus Pauling, Max Born, and Prime Minister Nehru, as well as many other distinguished patrons. Russell was, of course, aware that the task undertaken by the foundation ought to have been the responsibility of the United Nations, but he saw the exclusion of Communist China and the existence of undemocratic veto powers in the Security Council as barriers to any successful functioning of the United Nations.

During his final years, Russell took up the cause of political prisoners in Brazil, Burma, the Congo, Greece, the Philippines, and Iraq. He also appealed on behalf of Jewish and political prisoners in Russia and protested, as strongly as any irate conservative politician could, against Russia's testing of even more destructive nuclear weapons. This fact is frequently overlooked.

After the assassination of President Kennedy, Russell headed the British "Who Killed Kennedy?" Committee, which denounced the Warren Report as a massive cover-up.

During the 1960s, Russell's fears of nuclear disaster tended to be overshadowed by the war in Vietnam. One reason for this was probably his belief that as both sides had drawn back from the brink during the Cuban Missile Crisis, the prospect of nuclear war had diminished; if this were so, Vietnam should, for the time being, take priority. He had been suspicious about Vietnam long before most people in Britain were prepared to be. Many of these suspicions were later found to be justified, and it is curious that his book, *War Crimes in Vietnam,* and the work of the War Crimes Tribunal, which he set up, should have been so counterproductive. No doubt one reason was the strength of his horror and the knowledge that, in his nineties, he had no time to waste. In the book he abandoned the calculated rapier-like attack that served him so well for so long.

Russell's inner toughness, the outcome of his inheritance and his experiences at Pembroke Lodge, still enabled him even at ninety-seven to keep at bay most of the illnesses of old age. It was an alert Russell who on the afternoon of January 31, 1971, dictated a message to be read to the International Conference of Parliamentarians in Cairo. Vintage Russell, it condemned Israel for bombing Egypt, and noted that to "invoke the horrors of the past to justify those of the present is gross hypocrisy."[55]

Two days later, he felt ill in the morning and retired to his bed. He was dead within an hour. In accordance with his wishes, he was buried without a religious ceremony. A fitting epitaph can be found in something Russell wrote late in life, probably while contemplating the richness of his many years:

Some old people are oppressed by the fear of death. In the young there is justification for this feeling. Young men who have reason to fear that they will be killed in battle may justifiably feel bitter in the thought that they have been cheated of the best things that life has to offer. But in an old man who has known human joys and sorrows, and has achieved whatever work it was in him to do, the fear of death is somewhat abject and ignoble. The best way to overcome it—so at least it seems to me—is to make your interests gradually wider and more impersonal, until bit by bit the walls of the ego recede, and your life becomes increasingly merged in the universal life. An individual human experience should be like a river—small at first, narrowly contained within its banks, and rushing passionately past boulders and over waterfalls. Gradually the river grows wider, the banks recede, the waters flow more quietly, and in the end, without any visible break, they become merged in the sea, and painlessly lose their individual beings. The man who, in old age, can see his life in this way, will not suffer from the fear of death, since the things he cares for will continue. And if, with the decay of vitality, weariness increases, the thought of rest will not be unwelcome. The wise man should wish to die while still at work, knowing that others will carry on what he can no longer do, and content in the thought that what was possible has been done."[56]

NOTES

1. Bertrand Russell, *The Autobiography of Bertrand Russell: 1872-1914* (Boston: Atlantic Monthly Press, 1967), pp. 3-4.
2. D. E. Pears, (ed.), *Bertrand Russell: A Collection of Critical Essays* (New York: Anchor Books, 1972), p. 1.
3. Anon., *Into the 10th Decade: Tribute to Bertrand Russell* (London: Malvern Press, 1962), p. 34.
4. Bertrand Russell, *Principles of Social Reconstruction* (London: George and Allen Unwin, 1916), pp. 165-166.
5. Russell, *Autobiography, 1872-1914,* p. 10.
6. Alan Wood, *Bertrand Russell: The Passionate Skeptic* (New York: Simon and Schuster, 1958), p. 16.
7. Bertrand Russell, *Portraits From Memory* (London: George and Allen Unwin, 1956), p. 9.
8. Russell, *Autobiography, 1872-1914,* p. 18.
9. Russell, *Portraits,* p. 19.
10. Bertrand Russell, *My Philosophical Development* (London: George and Allen Unwin, 1959), p. 11.
11. Ronald Clark, *The Life of Bertrand Russell* (New York: Alfred Knopf Press, 1976), p. 32.
12. Ibid., pp. 32-33.
13. Russell, *Autobiography, 1872-1914,* pp. 99-100.
14. Clark, op. cit., p. 47.
15. Ibid., p. 53.
16. Bertrand Russell, *An Introduction to Mathematical Philosophy* (London: George and Allen Unwin, 1919), p. 184.
17. Ibid., pp. 15-16.
18. Ibid., p. 18.
19. Russell, *Portraits,* p. 35.
20. Russell, *Autobiography 1872-1914,* p. 231.
21. Russell, *My Philosophical Development,* p. 212.
22. Bertrand Russell, *The Autobiography of Bertrand Russell: 1914- 1944* (Boston: Atlantic Monthly Press, 1968), p. 7.
23. Russell, *Portraits,* p. 12.
24. Paul Edwards, *The Encyclopedia of Philosophy, Vol. 7* (New York: Macmillan Publishing Co., 1967), p. 237.
25. Ronald Clark, *Bertrand Russell and His World* (New York: Thames and Hudson, 1981), p. 51.
26. Russell, *Autobiography, 1914-1944,* p. 79.
27. Ibid., pp. 104-105.
28. Wood, op. cit., p. 112.
29. Russell, *Autobiography, 1914-1944,* p. 30.

30. Ibid., p. 35.

31. Clark, *The Life of Bertrand Russell,* op. cit., p. 166.

32. *Russell Society News,* No. 35 (August, 1982):7.

33. Ibid.

34. Russell, *Portraits,* pp. 13–14.

35. Bertrand Russell, *Marriage and Morals* (New York: Horace Liveright, 1929), p. 319.

36. Bertrand Russell, *Bertrand Russell Speaks His Mind* (New York: World Publishing Co., 1960), p. 66.

37. Russell, *Marriage and Morals,* p. 311.

38. Russell, *Autobiography: 1914–1944,* pp. 222–223.

39. David Harley, "Beacon Hill School," in *Russell: The Journal of the Bertrand Russell Archives.* Vols. 35–36. (1979–1980), p. 5.

40. Russell, *Autobiography: 1914–1944,* p. 304.

41. John Dewey, *The Bertrand Russell Case* (New York: Viking Press, 1941), p. 19.

42. Barry Feinberg and Ronald Kasrils (eds.), *Bertrand Russell's America: 1896–1945* (London: George and Allen Unwin, 1973), p. 153.

43. Dewey, op. cit., pp. 213–225.

44. Bertrand Russell, *Why I Am Not A Christian and Other Essays on Religion and Related Subjects* (New York: Simon and Schuster, 1957), p. 215.

45. Clark, *The Life of Bertrand Russell,* op. cit., pp. 512–513.

46. Bertrand Russell, *The Autobiography of Bertrand Russell: 1945–1969* (New York: Simon and Schuster, 1969), p. 19.

47. Russell, *Autobiography: 1944–1969,* p. 26.

48. Bertrand Russell, *The Basic Writings of Bertrand Russell* (New York: Simon and Schuster, 1961), p. 732.

49. Otto Nathan and Heinz Nolan (eds.), *Einstein on Peace* (New York: Avenel Books, 1981), pp. 623–625.

50. Ibid., p. 625.

51. Ibid., p. 631.

52. Clark, *The Life of Bertrand Russell,* op. cit., p. 590.

53. U. Thant, *View From the UN: The Memoirs of U Thant* (New York: Doubleday & Co., Inc., 1978), pp. 171–172.

54. Ibid., p. 172.

55. Clark, *The Life of Bertrand Russell,* op. cit., p. 638.

56. Russell, *Portraits,* p. 52.

Part One

1

My Religious Reminiscences

My parents, Lord and Lady Amberley, were considered shocking in their day on account of their advanced opinions in politics, theology, and morals. When my mother died in 1874 she was buried without any religious ceremony in the grounds of their house in the Wye Valley. My father intended to be buried there also, but when he died in 1876 his wishes were disregarded, and both were removed to the family vault at Chenies. By my father's will my brother and I were to have been in the guardianship of two friends of his who shared his opinions, but the will was set aside and we were placed by the Court of Chancery in the care of my grandparents. My grandfather, the statesman, died in 1878, and it was his widow who decided the manner of my education. She was a Scotch Presbyterian, who gradually became a Unitarian. I was taken on alternate Sundays to the Parish Church and to the Presbyterian Church, while at home I was taught the tenets of Unitarianism. Eternal punishment and the literal truth of the Bible were not inculcated, and there was no Sabbatarianism beyond a suggestion of avoiding cards on Sunday for fear of shocking the servants. But in other respects morals were austere, and it was held to be certain that conscience, which is the voice of God, is an infallible guide in all practical perplexities.

My childhood was solitary, as my brother was seven years older than I was, and I was not sent to school. Consequently I had abundant leisure for reflection, and when I was about fourteen my

First published in *The Rationalist Annual* (1938) by Watts & Company for the Rationalist Press Association, and reprinted by permission of the Rationalist Press Association.

thoughts turned to theology. During the four following years I rejected, successively, free will, immortality, and belief in God, and believed that I suffered much pain in the process, though when it was completed I found myself far happier than I had been while I remained in doubt. I think, in retrospect, that loneliness had much more to do with my unhappiness than theological difficulties, for throughout the whole time I never said a word about religion to anyone, with the brief exception of an agnostic tutor, who was soon sent away, presumably because he did not discourage my unorthodoxy.

What kept me silent was mainly the fear of ridicule. At the age of fourteen I became convinced that the fundamental principle of ethics should be the promotion of human happiness, and at first this appeared to me so self-evident that I supposed it must be the universal opinion. Then I discovered, to my surprise, that it was a view regarded as unorthodox, and called Utilitarianism. I announced, no doubt with a certain pleasure in the long word, that I was a Utilitarian; but the announcement was received with derision. My grandmother for a long time missed no opportunity of ironically submitting ethical conundrums to me, and challenging me to solve them on Utilitarian principles. To my surprise I discovered, in preparing the Amberley Papers, that she had subjected an uncle of mine, in his youth, to the same treatment on the same topic. The result in my case was a determination to keep my thoughts to myself; no doubt in his it was similar. Ridicule, nominally amusing but really an expression of hostility, was the favorite weapon—the worst possible, short of actual cruelty, in dealing with young people. When I became interested in philosophy—a subject which, for some reason, was anathema—I was told that the whole subject could be summed up in the saying: "What is mind?—No matter. What is matter?—Never mind." At the fifteenth or sixteenth repetition of this remark it ceased to be amusing.

Nevertheless on most topics the atmosphere was liberal. For instance, Darwinism was accepted as a matter of course. I had at one time, when I was thirteen, a very orthodox Swiss tutor, who, in consequence of something I had said, stated with great earnestness: "If you are a Darwinian I pity you, for one cannot be a Darwinian and a Christian at the same time." I did not then believe in the incompatibility, but I was already clear that, if I had to choose, I would choose Darwin.

Until I went to Cambridge I was almost wholly unaware of

contemporary movements of thought. I was influenced by Darwin, and then by John Stuart Mill, but more than either by the study of dynamics; my outlook, in fact, was more appropriate to a seventeenth- or eighteenth-century Cartesian than to a post-Darwinian. It seemed to me that all the motions of matter were determined by physical laws, and that in all likelihood this was true of the human body as well as of other matter. Being passionately interested in religion and unable to speak about it, I wrote down my thoughts in Greek letters in a book which I headed "Greek Exercises," in which, to make concealment more complete, I adopted an original system of phonetic spelling. In this book, when I was fifteen, I wrote: "Taking free will first to consider, there is no clear dividing line between man and the protozoon. Therefore, if we give free will to man we must give it also to the protozoon. This is rather hard to do. Therefore, unless we are willing to give free will to the protozoon we must not give it to man. This, however, is possible, but it is difficult to imagine. If, as seems to me probable, protoplasm only came together in the ordinary course of nature without any special Providence from God, then we and all animals are simply kept going by chemical forces and are nothing more wonderful than a tree (which no one pretends has free will), and if we had a good enough knowledge of the forces acting on any one at any time, the motives pro and con, the constitution of his brain at any time, then we could tell exactly what he would do."

Until the age of eighteen I continued to believe in a Deist's God, because the First-Cause argument seemed to me irrefutable. Then in John Stuart Mill's *Autobiography* I found that James Mill had taught him the refutation of that argument—namely, that it gives no answer to the question "Who made God?" It is curious that Mill should have had so much influence on me, for he was my father's and mother's close friend and the source of many of their opinions, but I did not know this until a much later date. Without being aware that I was following in my father's footsteps, I read, before I went to Cambridge, Mill's *Logic* and *Political Economy,* and made elaborate notes in which I practiced the art of expressing the gist of each paragraph in a single sentence. I was already interested in the principles of mathematics, and was profoundly dissatisfied with his assimiliation of pure mathematics to empirical science—a view which is now universally abandoned.

Throughout adolescence I read widely, but as I depended mainly on my grandfather's library few of the books I read belonged to my own time. They were a curious collection. I remember, as having been important to me, Milman's *History of Christianity,* Gibbon, Comte, Dante, Machiavelli, Swift, and Carlyle; but above all Shelley—whom, however, though born in the same month as my grandfather, I did not find on his shelves.

It was only at Cambridge that I became aware of the modern world—I mean the world that was modern in the early 'nineties: Ibsen and Shaw, Flaubert and Pater, Walt Whitman, Nietzsche, etc. But I do not think any of these men had much influence on me, with the possible exception of Ibsen. The men who changed my opinions at that time were two: first McTaggart in one direction, and then, after I had become a Fellow, G. E. Moore in the opposite direction. McTaggart made me a Hegelian, and Moore caused me to revert to the opinions I had had before I went to Cambridge. Most of what I learnt at Cambridge had to be painfully unlearnt later; on the whole, what I had learnt for myself from being left alone in an old library had proved more solid.

The influence of German idealism in England has never gone much beyond the universities, but in them, when I was young, it was almost completely dominant. Green and Caird converted Oxford, and Bradley and Bosanquet—the leading British philosophers in the 'nineties—were more in agreement with Hegel than with anyone else, though, for some reason unknown to me, they hardly ever mentioned him. In Cambridge Henry Sidgwick still represented the Benthamite tradition, and James Ward was a Kantian; but the younger men—Stout, Mackenzie, and McTaggart—were, in varying degrees, Hegelians.

Very different attitudes towards Christian dogma were compatible with acceptance of Hegel. In his philosophy nothing is held to be quite true, and nothing quite false; what can be uttered has only a limited truth, and, since men must talk, we cannot blame them for not speaking the whole truth and nothing but the truth. The best we can do, according to Bradley, is to say things that are "not intellectually corrigible"—further progress is only possible through a synthesis of thought and feeling, which, when achieved, will lead to our saying nothing. Ideas have degrees of truth, greater or less according to the stage at which they come in the dialectic. God has a good deal of truth, since He comes rather late in the dialectic; but He has not complete truth, since He is swallowed up in the Absolute Idea. The right wing among Hegelians emphasized the truth in the concept of God, the left wing the falsehood, and each wing was true to the Master. A German Hegelian, if he was taking orders, remembered how much truer the concept of God is than, e.g., that of gods; if he was becoming a civil servant, he remembered the even greater truth of the Abolute Idea, whose earthly copy was the Prussian State.

In England teachers of philosophy who were Hegelians almost all belonged to the left wing. "Religion," says Bradley, "is practical, and therefore still is dominated by the idea of the Good; and in the essence of this idea is contained an unsolved contradiction. Religion is still forced to maintain unreduced aspects, which, as such, cannot be united; and it exists, in short, by a kind of perpetual oscillation and compromise." Neither Bradley nor Bosanquet believed in personal immortality. Mackenzie, while I was reading philosophy, stated in a paper which I heard that "a personal God is, in a sense, a contradiction in terms": he was subsequently one of my examiners. The attitude of these men to religion was thus not one of which the orthodox could approve, but it was by no means one of hostility: they held religion to be an essential ingredient in the truth, and defective only when taken as the whole truth. The sort of view that I had previously held, "either there is a God or there is not, and probably the latter," seemed to them very crude; the correct opinion, they would say, was that from one point of view there is a God and from another there is not, but from the highest point of view there neither is nor is not. Being myself naturally "crude," I never succeeded in reaching this pitch of mellowness.

McTaggart, who dominated the philosophical outlook of my generation at Cambridge, was peculiar among Hegelians in various ways. He was more faithful than the others to the dialectic method, and would defend even its details. Unlike some of the school, he was definite in asserting certain things and denying others; he called himself an Atheist, but firmly believed in personal immortality, of which he was convinced that he possessed a logical demonstration. He was four years senior to me, and in my first term was President of the Union. He and I were both so shy that when, about a fortnight after I came up, he called on me, he had not the courage to come in and I had not the courage to ask him in, so that he remained in the doorway about five minutes. Soon, however, the conversation got on to philosophy, and his shyness ceased. I found that all I had thought about ethics and logic and metaphysics was considered to be refuted by an abstruse technique that completely baffled me; and by this same technique it was to be proved that I should live forever. I found that the old thought this nonsense, but the young thought it good sense, so I determined to study it sympathetically, and for a time I more or less believed it. So, for a short time, did G. E. Moore. But he found the Hegelian philosophy inapplicable to chairs and tables, and I found it inapplicable to mathematics, so with his help I climbed out of it, and back to common sense tempered by mathematical logic.

The intellectual temper of the 'nineties was very different from that of my father's youth: in some ways better, but in many ways worse. There was no longer, among the abler young men, any preoccupation with the details of the Christian faith; they were almost all Agnostics, and not interested in discussions as to the divinity of Christ, or in the details of Biblical criticism. I remember a feeling of contempt when I learned that Henry Sidgwick as a young man, being desirous of knowing whether God exists, thought it necessary, as a first step, to learn Semitic languages, which seemed to me to show an insufficient sense of logical relevance. But I was willing, as were most of my friends, to listen to a metaphysical argument for or against God or immortality or free will; and it was only after acquiring a new logic that I ceased to think such arguments worth examining.

The nonacademic heroes of the 'nineties—Ibsen, Strindberg, Nietzsche, and (for a time) Oscar Wilde—differed very greatly from those of the previous generation. The great men of the 'sixties were all "good" men: they were patient, painstaking, in favor of change only when a detailed and careful investigation had persuaded them that it was necessary in some particular respect. They advocated reforms, and in general their advocacy was successful, so that the world improved very fast; but their temper was not that of rebels. I do not mean that no great rebels existed; Marx and Dostoievsky, to mention only two, did most of their best work in the 'sixties. But these men were almost unknown among cultured people in their own day, and their influence belongs to a much later date. The men who commanded respect in England in the 'sixties—Darwin, Huxley, Newman, the authors of *Essays and Reviews,* etc.—were not fundamentally at war with society; they could meet, as they did in the "Metaphysical Society," to discuss urbanely whether there is a God. At the end they divided; and Sir Mountstuart Grant Duff, on being asked afterwards whether there is a God, replied: "Yes, we had a very good majority." In those days democracy ruled even over Heaven.

But in the 'nineties young men desired something more sweeping and passionate, more bold and less bland. The impulse towards destruction and violence which has swept over the world began in the sphere of literature. Ibsen, Strindberg, and Nietzsche were angry men—not primarily angry about this or that, but just angry. And so they each found an outlook on life that justified anger. The young admired their passion, and found in it an outlet for their own feelings of revolt against parental authority. The assertion of freedom seemed sufficiently noble to justify violence; the violence duly ensued, but freedom was lost in the process.

2

First Efforts

I began thinking about philosophical questions at the age of fifteen. From then until I went to Cambridge, three years later, my thinking was solitary and completely amateurish, since I read no philosophical books, until I read Mill's *Logic* in the last months before going to Trinity. Most of my time was taken up by mathematics, and mathematics largely dominated my attempts at philosophical thinking, but the emotional drive which caused my thinking was mainly doubt as to the fundamental dogmas of religion. I minded my theological doubts, not only because I had found comfort in religion, but also because I felt that these doubts, if I revealed them, would cause pain and bring ridicule, and I therefore became very isolated and solitary. Just before and just after my sixteenth birthday, I wrote down my beliefs and unbeliefs, using Greek letters and phonetic spelling for purposes of concealment. The following are some extracts from these reflections.

Eighteen eighty-eight. March three. I shall write about some subjects, especially religious ones, which now interest me. I have, in consequence of a variety of circumstances, come to look into the very foundations of the religion in which I have been brought up. On some points my conclusions have been to confirm my former creed, while on others I have been irresistibly led to such conclusions as would not only shock my people, but have given me much pain. I have arrived at certainty in few things, but my opinions,

From Bertrand Russell, *My Philosophical Development*, pp. 28–36. Copyright © 1959 by George and Allen Unwin. Reprinted by permission of the publisher.

even where not convictions, are on some things nearly such. I have not the courage to tell my people that I scarcely believe in immortality. . . .

19th. I mean today to put down my grounds for belief in God. I may say to begin with that I do believe in God, and that I should call myself a theist if I had to give my creed a name. Now in finding reasons for believing in God I shall only take account of scientific arguments. This is a vow I have made, which costs me much to keep, and to reject all sentiment. To find the scientific grounds for a belief in God we must go back to the beginning of all things. We know that, if the present laws of nature have always been in force, the exact quantity of matter and energy now in the universe must always have been in existence, but the nebular hypothesis points to no distant date for the time when the whole universe was filled with undifferentiated nebulous matter. Hence it is quite possible that the matter and force now in existence may have had a creation which clearly could be only by divine power. But even granting that they have always been in existence, yet whence comes the cause which regulates the action of force on matter? I think they are only attributable to a divine controlling power which I accordingly call God.

March twenty-two. In my last exercise I proved the existence of God by the uniformity of nature and the persistence of certain laws in all her ways. Now let us look into the reasonableness of the reasoning. Let us suppose that the universe we now see has, as some suppose, grown by mere chance. Should we then expect every atom to act in any given conditions precisely similarly to another atom? I think, if atoms be lifeless, there is no reason to expect them to do anything without a controlling power. If, on the other hand, they be endowed with free will, we are forced to the conclusion that all atoms in the universe have combined in the commonwealth and have made laws which none of them ever break. This is clearly an absurd hypothesis, and therefore we are forced to believe in God. But this way of proving his existence at the same time disproves miracles and other supposed manifestations of divine power. It does not, however, disprove their possibility, for, of course, the maker of laws can also unmake them. We may arrive in another way at a disbelief in miracles, for, if God is the maker of the laws, surely it would imply an imperfection in the law if it had to be altered occasionally, and such imperfection we can never impute to the divine nature, as in the bible God repented him of the work.

April second. I now come to the subject which personally interests us poor mortals more, perhaps, than any other. I mean the question of immortality. This is the one in which I have been most disappointed and pained by thought. There are two ways of looking at it. First, by evolution and comparing man to animals. Second, by comparing man with God. The first is the more scientific, for we know all about the animals but not about God. Well, I hold that, taking free will first to consider, there is no clear dividing line between man and the protozoon. Therefore, if we give free will to man, we must give it also to the protozoon. This is rather hard to do. Therefore, unless we are willing to give free will to the protozoon, we cannot give it to man. This, however, is possible, but it is difficult to imagine if, as seems to me probable, protoplasm only came together in the ordinary course of nature without any special providence from God. Then we and all living things are simply kept going by chemical forces and are nothing more wonderful than a tree, which no one pretends has free will, and, even if we had a good enough knowledge of the forces acting on anyone at any time, the motives pro and con, the constitution of his brain, at any time, then we could tell exactly what he will do. Again, from the religious point of view, free will is a very arrogant thing for us to claim, for of course it is an interruption of God's laws, for by his ordinary laws all our actions would be fixed as the stars. I think we must leave to God the primary establishment of laws which are never broken and determine everybody's doings. And not having free will we cannot have immortality.

Monday, April 9. . . . I do wish I believed in life eternal, for it makes me quite miserable to think man is merely a kind of machine endowed, unhappily for himself, with consciousness. But no other theory is consistent with the complete omnipotence of God of which science I think gives ample manifestations. Thus, I must either be an atheist or disbeliever in immortality. Finding the first impossible, I accept the second and let no one know. I think, however disappointing may be this view of man, it does give us a wonderful idea of God's greatness to think that he can, in the beginning, create laws which, by acting on a mere mass of nebulous matter, perhaps merely ether diffused through this part of the universe, will produce creatures like ourselves, conscious not only of our existence but even able to fathom to a certain extent God's mysteries! All this

with no more intervention on his part! Now let us think whether
this doctrine of want of free will is so absurd. If we talk about it to
anyone they kick their legs or something of that sort. But perhaps
they cannot help it, for they have something to prove and therefore
that supplies a motive to them to do it. Thus, in anything we do we
always have motives which determine us. Also, there is no line of
demarcation between Shakespeare or Herbert Spencer and a Papuan. But between them and a Papuan there seems as much difference as between a Papuan and a monkey.

April 14th. Yet there are great difficulties in the way of the
doctrine that man has not immortality nor free will nor a soul, in
short that he is nothing more than a species of ingenious machine
endowed with consciousness. For consciousness, in itself, is a quality quite distinguishing men from dead matter, and if they have
one thing different from dead matter why not another, free will? By
free will I mean that they do not, for example, obey the first law of
motion, or at least that the direction in which the energy they
contain is employed depends not entirely on external circumstances.
Moreover, it seems impossible to imagine that man, the great Man,
with his reason, his knowledge of the universe and his ideas of
right and wrong, Man with his emotions, his love and hate, and
his religion, that this Man should be a more perishable chemical
compound, whose character and his influence for good or for evil
depends solely and entirely on the particular notions of the molecules of his brain and that all the greatest men have been great by
reason of some one molecule hitting up against some other a little
oftener than in other men! Does this not seem utterly incredible,
and must not any one be mad who believes in such an absurdity?
But what is the alternative? That, accepting the evolution theory
which is practically proved, apes have gradually increased in intelligence, God suddenly by a miracle endowed one with that wonderful reason which it is a mystery how we possess. Then is man,
truly called the glorious work of God, is man destined to perish
utterly after he has been so many ages in evolving? We cannot say,
but I prefer that idea to God's having needed a miracle to produce
man and now leaving him to do as he likes.

April eighteenth. Accepting, then, the theory that man is mortal
and destitute of free will, which is as much as ever a mere theory,
as of course all these kinds of things are mere speculations, what
idea can we form of right and wrong? Many say, if you make any

mention of such an absurd doctrine as predestination, which comes to much the same thing though persons don't think so, why what becomes of conscience, etc. (which they think has been directly implanted in man by God)? Now my idea is that our conscience is in the first place due to evolution which would of course form instincts of self-preservation, and in the second place to civilization and education, which introduces great refinements of the idea of self-preservation. Let us take, for example, the ten commandments as illustrative of primitive morality. Many of them are conducive to the quiet living of the community which is best for the preservation of the species. Thus, what is always considered the worst possible crime, and the one for which most remorse is felt, is murder, which is direct annihilation of the species. Again, as we know, among the Hebrews it was thought a mark of God's favor to have many children, while the childless were considered as cursed of God. Among the Romans, also, widows were hated and, I believe, forbidden to remain unmarried in Rome more than a year. Now why these peculiar ideas? Were they not simply because these objects of pity or dislike did not bring forth fresh human beings? We can well understand how such ideas might grow up when men become rather sensible, for, if murder and suicide were common in a tribe, that tribe would die out, and hence one which held such acts in abhorrence would have a great advantage. Of course, among more educated societies, these ideas are rather modified. My own, I mean to give next time.

April twentieth. Thus I think that primitive morality always originates in the idea of the preservation of the species. But is this a rule which a civilized community ought to follow? I think not. My rule of life which I guide my conduct by, and a departure from which I consider as a sin, is to act in the manner which I believe to be most likely to produce the greatest happiness considering both the intensity of the happiness and the number of people made happy. I know that my grandmother considers this an impractical rule of life and says that, since you can never know the thing which will produce greatest happiness, you do much better in following the inner voice. The conscience, however, can easily be seen to depend mostly upon education (as, for example, common Irishmen do not consider lying wrong) which fact alone seems to me quite sufficient to disprove the divine nature of conscience. And, since, as I believe, conscience is merely the combined product of evolution and education, then obviously it is an absurdity to follow that rather than reason. And my reason tells me that it is better to act so as to produce maximum of happiness than in any other way. For I have tried to see what other object I could set before me, and I have failed. Not my own individual happiness in particular, but everybody's equally, making no distinction between myself, relations, friends, or perfect strangers. In real life it makes very little difference to me as long as others are not of my opinion, for obviously where there is any chance of being found out, it is better to do what one's people consider right. My reason for this view is, first, that I can find no other, having been forced as everybody must who seriously thinks about evolution to give up the old idea of asking one's conscience; next, that it seems to me that happiness is the great thing to seek after and which practically all honest public men do seek after. As an application of the theory to practical life, I will say that in a case where nobody but myself was concerned (if indeed such a case exist) I should of course act entirely selfishly to please myself. Suppose, for another instance, that I had the chance of saving a man whom I knew to be a bad man who would be better out of the world, obviously I should consult my own happiness better by plunging in after him. For, if I lost my life, that would be a very neat way of managing it, and, if I saved him, I should have the pleasure of no end of praise. But if I let him drown, I should have lost an opportunity of death and should have the misery of much blame, but the world would be better for his loss and, as I have some slight hope, for my life.

April 29. In all things I have made the vow to follow reason, not the instincts inherited partly from my ancestors and gained gradually by selection and partly due to my education. How absurd it would be to follow these in the questions of right and wrong. For as I observed before, the inherited part can only be principles leading to the preservation of the species, or of that particular section of the species to which I belong. The part due to education is good or bad according to the individual education. Yet this inner voice, this God-given conscience which made Bloody Mary burn the Protestants, this is what we reasonable beings are to follow. I think this idea mad, and I endeavor to go by reason as far as possible. What I take as my ideal is that which ultimately produces greatest happiness of greatest number. Then I can apply reason to find out the course most conducive to this, and in my individual case however I can also go more or less by conscience owing to the excellence of my education. But it is curious how people dislike the abandonment of brutish impulse for reason. . . .

May three. . . . There is another very strong argument which I did not insert in its place, namely, that the soul here below seems so inseparably bound up with the body, growing with it, weakened with it, sleeping with it and affecting the brain and affected in return by anything abnormal in the brain. Wordsworth's *Intimations* are humbug, for it is obvious how the soul grows with the body, not as he says perfect from the first.

June third. It is extraordinary how few principles or dogmas I have been able to become convinced of. One after another I find my former undoubted beliefs slipping from me into the region of doubt. For example, I used never for a moment to doubt that truth was a good thing to get hold of. But now I have the greatest doubt and uncertainty. For the search for truth has led me to these results I have put in this book, whereas, had I been content to accept the teachings of my youth, I should have remained comfortable. The search for truth has shattered most of my old beliefs and has made me commit what are probably sins where otherwise I should have kept clear of them. I do not think it has in any way made me happier; of course it has given me a deeper character, a contempt for trifles or mockery, but at the same time it has taken away cheerfulness and made it much harder to make bosom friends and, worst of all, it has debarred me from free intercourse with my people, and thus made them strangers to some of my deepest thoughts which, if by any mischance I do let them out, immediately become the subject for mockery which is inexpressibly bitter to me though not unkindly meant. Thus, in my individual case, I should say the effects of a search for truth have been more bad than good. But the truth which I accept as such may be said not to be truth, and I may be told that if I get at real truth I shall be made happier by it, but this is a very doubtful proposition. Hence I have great doubts of the unmixed advantages of truth. Certainly, truth in biology lowers one's idea of man, which must be painful. Moreover, truth estranges former friends and prevents the making of new ones, which is also a bad thing. One ought perhaps to look upon all these things as a martyrdom, since very often truth attained by one man may lead to the increase in the happiness of many others, though not to his own. On the whole I am inclined to pursue truth, though truth of the kind in this book (if that indeed be truth) I have no desire to spread, but rather to prevent from spreading.

My mind at this time was in a state of confusion derived from an attempt to combine points of view and ways of feeling belonging to three different centuries. As the above extracts show, my thinking was, in a crude form, along lines very similar to that of Descartes. I was familiar with the *name* of Descartes, but I knew him only as the inventor of Cartesian co-ordinates, and was not aware that he had written philosophy. My rejection of free will on the ground that it infringed God's omnipotence might have led me on to a philosophy like that of Spinoza. I was led to this seventeenth-century point of view by the same causes which had originally produced it: namely, familiarity with the laws of dynamics and belief that they accounted for all the movements of matter. After a time, however, I came to disbelieve in God, and advanced to a position much more like that of the eighteenth-century French *Philosophes*. I agreed with them in being a passionate believer in rationalism; I liked Laplace's calculator; I hated what I considered superstition; and I believed profoundly in the perfectibility of man by a combination of reason and machinery. All this was enthusiastic, but not essentially sentimental. I had, however, alongside of this, a very vivid emotional attitude for which I could find no intellectual support. I regretted my loss of religious belief; I loved natural beauty with a wild passion; and I read with sympathetic feeling, though with very definite intellectual rejection, the sentimental apologies for religion of Wordsworth, Carlyle and Tennyson. I did not come across any books, except Buckle, until I read Mill's *Logic* which seemed to me to possess intellectual integrity. But, nonetheless, I was moved by rhetoric which I could not accept. Carlyle's "Everlasting No" and "Everlasting Yea" seemed to me very splendid, in spite of my thinking that at bottom they were nonsense. Only Shelley, among the writers whom I knew at that time, was wholly congenial to me. He was congenial to me not only in his merits, but also in his faults. His self-pity and his atheism, alike, consoled me. I was quite unable to combine into a harmonious total seventeenth-century knowledge, eighteenth-century beliefs and nineteenth-century enthusiasms.

It was not only as to theology that I had doubts, but also as to mathematics. Some of Euclid's proofs, especially those that used the method of superposition, appeared to me very shaky. One of my tutors spoke to me of non-Euclidean geometry. Although I knew nothing of it, except the bare fact of its existence, until many years later, I found the knowledge that there was such a subject very exciting, intellectually delightful, but a source of disquieting geometrical doubt. Those who taught me the infinitesimal Calculus did not know the valid proofs of its fundamental theorems and tried to persuade me to accept the official sophistries as an act of faith. I realized that the calculus works in practice, but I was at a loss to understand why it should do so. However, I found so much pleasure in the acquisition of technical skill that at most times I forgot my doubts. And, to some extent, they were laid to rest by a book which greatly delighted me: W. K. Clifford's *Common Sense of the Exact Sciences.*

Although filled with adolescent misery, I was kept going in these years by the desire for knowledge and for intellectual achievement. I thought that it should be possible to clear away muddles, and that then everybody would be happy in a world where machines would do the work and justice would regulate distribution. I hoped sooner or later to arrive at a perfected mathematics which should leave no room for doubts, and bit by bit to extend ths sphere of certainty from mathematics to other sciences. Gradually during these three years my interest in theology grew less, and it was with a genuine sense of relief that I discarded the last vestiges of theological orthodoxy.

3

Why I Am Not A Christian

As your Chairman has told you, the subject about which I am going to speak to you tonight is "Why I Am Not A Christian." Perhaps it would be as well, first of all, to try to make out what one means by the word "Christian." It is used in these days in a very loose sense by a great many people. Some people mean no more by it than a person who attempts to live a good life. In that sense I suppose there would be Christians in all sects and creeds; but I do not think that that is the proper sense of the word, if only because it would imply that all the people who are not Christians—all the Buddhists, Confucians, Mohammedans, and so on—are not trying to live a good life. I do not mean by a Christian any person who tries to live decently according to his lights. I think that you must have a certain amount of definite belief before you have a right to call yourself a Christian. The word does not have quite such a full-blooded meaning now as it had in the times of St. Augustine and St. Thomas Aquinas. In those days, if a man said that he was a Christian it was known what he meant. You accepted a whole collection of creeds which were set out with great precision, and every single syllable of those creeds you believed with the whole strength of your convictions.

First published in The Rationalist Annual (1927) by Watts & Company for the Rationalist Press Association, and reprinted by permission of the Rationalist Press Association.

WHAT IS A CHRISTIAN?

Nowadays it is not quite that. We have to be a little more vague in our meaning of Christianity. I think, however, that there are two different items which are quite essential to anybody calling himself a Christian. The first is one of a dogmatic nature—namely, that you must believe in God and in immortality. If you do not believe in those two things, I do not think that you can properly call yourself a Christian. Then, further than that, as the name implies, you must have some kind of belief about Christ. The Mohammedans, for instance, also believe in God and in immortality, and yet they would not call themselves Christians. I think you must have at the very lowest the belief that Christ was, if not divine, at least the best and the wisest of men. If you are not going to believe that much about Christ, I do not think that you have any right to call yourself a Christian. Of course there is another sense which you find in *Whitaker's Almanack* and in geography books, where the population of the world is said to be divided into Christians, Mohammedans, Buddhists, fetish worshippers, and so on; and in that sense we are all Christians. The geography books count us all in, but that is a purely geographical sense, which I suppose we can ignore. Therefore I take it that when I tell you why I am not a Christian I have to tell you two different things: first, why I do not believe in God and in immortality; and, secondly, why I do not think that Christ was the best and the wisest of men, although I grant him a very high degree of moral goodness.

But for the successful efforts of unbelievers in the past, I could not take so elastic a definition of Christianity as that. As I said before, in olden days it had a much more full-blooded sense. For instance, it included the belief in hell. Belief in eternal hell fire was an essential item of Christian belief until pretty recent times. In this country, as you know, it ceased to be an essential item because of a decision of the Privy Council, and from that decision the Archbishop of Canterbury and the Archbishop of York dissented; but in this country our religion is settled by Act of Parliament, and therefore the Privy Council was able to override their Graces, and hell was no longer necessary to a Christian. Consequently I shall not insist that a Christian must believe in hell.

THE EXISTENCE OF GOD

To come to this question of the existence of God, it is a large and serious question, and if I were to attempt to deal with it in any adequate manner I should have to keep you here until Kingdom Come, so that you will have to excuse me if I deal with it in a somewhat summary fashion. You know, of course, that the Catholic Church has laid it down as a dogma that the existence of God can be proved by the unaided reason. That is a somewhat curious dogma, but it is one of their dogmas. They had to introduce it because at one time the Freethinkers adopted the habit of saying that there were such and such arguments which mere reason might urge against the existence of God, but of course they knew as a matter of faith that God did exist. The arguments and the reasons were set out at great length, and the Catholic Church felt that they must stop it. Therefore they laid it down that the existence of God can be proved by the unaided reason, and they had to set up what they considered were arguments to prove it. There are, of course, a number of them, but I shall take only a few.

The First Cause Argument

Perhaps the simplest and easiest to understand is the argument of the First Cause. It is maintained that everything we see in this world has a cause, and as you go back in the chain of causes further and further you must come to a First Cause, and to that First Cause you give the name God. That argument, I suppose, does not carry very much weight nowadays, because, in the first place, cause is not quite what it used to be. The philosophers and the men of science have got going on cause, and it has not anything like the vitality that it used to have; but, apart from that, you can see that the argument that there must be a First Cause is one that cannot have any validity. I may say that when I was a young man, and was debating these questions very seriously in my mind, I for a long time accepted the argument of the First Cause, until one day, at the age of eighteen, I read John Stuart Mill's *Autobiography,* and I there found this sentence: "My father taught me that the question, Who made me? cannot be answered, since it immediately suggests the further question, Who made God?" That very simple sentence showed me, as I still think, the fallacy in the argument of the First Cause. If everything must have a cause, then God must have a cause. If there can be anything without a cause, it may just as well be the world as God, so that there cannot be any validity in that argument. It is exactly of the same nature as the Indian's view, that the world rested upon an elephant and the elephant rested upon a tortoise; and when they said, "How about the tortoise?" the Indian said, "Suppose we change the subject." The argument is really no better than that. There is no reason why the world could not have come into being without a cause; nor, on the other hand, is there any reason why it should not have always existed. There is no reason to suppose that the world had a beginning at all. The idea that things must have a beginning is really due to the poverty of our imagination. Therefore, perhaps, I need not waste any more time upon the argument about the First Cause.

The Natural Law Argument

Then there is a very common argument from natural law. That was a favorite argument all through the eighteenth century, especially under the influence of Sir Isaac Newton and his cosmogony. People observed the planets going round the sun according to the law of gravitation, and they thought that God had given a behest to these planets to move in that particular fashion, and that was why they did so. That was, of course, a convenient and simple explanation that saved them the trouble of looking any further for explanations of the law of gravitation. Nowadays we explain the law of gravitation in a somewhat complicated fashion that Einstein has introduced. I do not propose to give you a lecture on the law of gravitation, as interpreted by Einstein, because that again would take some time; at any rate, you no longer have the sort of natural law that you had in the Newtonian system, where, for some reason that nobody could understand, nature behaved in a uniform fashion. We now find that a great many things that we thought were natural laws are really human conventions. You know that even in the remotest depths of stellar space there are still three feet to a yard. That is, no doubt, a very remarkable fact, but you would hardly call it a law of nature. And a great many things that have been regarded as laws of nature are of that kind. On the other hand, where you can get down to any knowledge of what atoms actually do, you find that they are much less subject to law than people thought, and that the laws at which you arrive are statistical averages of just the sort that would emerge from chance. There is, as we all know, a law that if you throw dice you will get double sixes only about once in thirty-six times, and we do not regard that as evidence that the fall of the dice is regulated by design; on the contrary, if the double sixes came every time we should think that there was design. The laws of nature are of that sort as regards a great many of them. They are statistical averages such as would emerge from the laws of chance; and that makes this whole business of natural law much less impressive than it formerly was. Quite apart from that, which represents the momentary state of science that may change tomorrow, the whole idea that natural laws imply a lawgiver is due to a confusion between natural and human laws. Human laws are behests commanding you to behave in a certain way, in which way you may choose to behave, or you may choose not to behave; but natural laws are a description of how things do in fact behave, and, being a mere description of what they in fact do, you cannot argue that there must be somebody who told them to do that, because even supposing that there were you are then faced with the question, Why did God issue just those natural laws and no others? If you say that he did it simply from his own good pleasure, and without any reason, you then find that there is something which is not subject to law, and so your train of natural law is interrupted. If you say, as more orthodox theologians do, that in all the laws which God issued he had a reason for giving those laws rather than others—the reason, of course, being to create the best universe, although you would never think it to look at it—if there was a reason for the laws which God gave, then God himself was subject to law, and therefore you do not get any advantage by introducing God as an intermediary. You have really a law outside and anterior to the divine edicts, and God does not serve your purpose, because he is not the ultimate lawgiver. In short, this whole argument about natural law no longer has anything like the strength that it used to have. I am travelling on in time in my review of the arguments. The arguments that are used for the existence of God change their character as time goes on. They were at first hard intellectual arguments embodying certain quite definite fallacies. As we come to modern times they become less respectable intellectually and more and more affected by a kind of moralizing vagueness.

The Argument from Design

The next step in this process brings us to the argument from design.

You all know the argument from design: everything in the world is made just so that we can manage to live in the world, and if the world was ever so little different we could not manage to live in it. That is the argument from design. It sometimes takes rather a curious form; for instance, it is argued that rabbits have white tails in order to be easy to shoot. I do not know how rabbits would view that application. It is an easy argument to parody. You all know Voltaire's remark, that obviously the nose was designed to be such as to fit spectacles. That sort of parody has turned out to be not nearly so wide of the mark as it might have seemed in the eighteenth century, because since the time of Darwin we understand much better why living creatures are adapted to their environment. It is not that their environment was made to be suitable to them, but that they grew to be suitable to it, and that is the basis of adaptation. There is no evidence of design about it.

When you come to look into this argument from design, it is a most astonishing thing that people can believe that this world, with all the things that are in it, with all its defects, should be the best that omnipotence and omniscience has been able to produce in millions of years. I really cannot believe it. Do you think that, if you were granted omnipotence and omniscience and millions of years in which to perfect your world, you could produce nothing better than the Ku Klux Klan, the Fascisti, and Mr. Winston Churchill?* Really I am not much impressed with the people who say: "Look at me: I am such a splendid product that there must have been design in the universe." I am not very much impressed by the splendor of those people. Therefore I think that this argument of design is really a very poor argument indeed. Moreover, if you accept the ordinary laws of science, you have to suppose that human life and life in general on this planet will die out in due course: it is merely a flash in the pan; it is a stage in the decay of the solar system; at a certain stage of decay you get the sort of conditions of temperature and so forth which are suitable to protoplasm, and there is life for a short time in the life of the whole solar system. You see in the moon the sort of thing to which the earth is tending—something dead, cold, and lifeless.

I am told that that sort of view is depressing, and people will sometimes tell you that if they believed that they would not be able to go on living. Do not believe it; it is all nonsense. Nobody really

*Russell removed Winston Churchill's name from all later editions of this essay. —*Ed.*

worries much about what is going to happen millions of years hence. Even if they think they are worrying much about that, they are really deceiving themselves. They are worried about something much more mundane, or it may merely be a bad digestion; but nobody is really seriously rendered unhappy by the thought of something that is going to happen to this world millions and millions of years hence. Therefore, although it is of course a gloomy view to suppose that life will die out—at least I suppose we may say so, although sometimes when I contemplate the things that people do with their lives I think it is almost a consolation—it is not such as to render life miserable. It merely makes you turn your attention to other things.

The Moral Arguments for Deity

Now we reach one stage further in what I shall call the intellectual descent that the Theists have made in their argumentations, and we come to what are called the moral arguments for the existence of God. You all know, of course, that there used to be in the old days three intellectual arguments for the existence of God, all of which were disposed of by Immanuel Kant in the *Critique of Pure Reason;* but no sooner had he disposed of those arguments than he invented a new one, a moral argument, and that quite convinced him. He was like many people: in intellectual matters he was skeptical, but in moral matters he believed implicitly in the maxims that he had imbibed at his mother's knee. That illustrates what the psychoanalysts so much emphasize—the immensely stronger hold upon us that our very early associations have than those of later times.

Kant, as I say, invented a new moral argument for the existence of God, and that in varying forms was extremely popular during the nineteenth century. It has all sorts of forms. One form is to say that there would be no right or wrong unless God existed. I am not for the moment concerned with whether there is a difference between right and wrong, or whether there is not: that is another question. The point I am concerned with is that, if you are quite sure there is a difference between right and wrong, you are then in this situation: Is that difference due to God's fiat or is it not? If it is due to God's fiat, then for God himself there is no difference between right and wrong, and it is no longer a significant statement to say that God is good. If you are going to say, as theologians do, that God is good, you must then say that right and wrong have some meaning which is independent of God's fiat, because God's fiats are good and not bad independently of the mere fact that he made them. If you are going to say that, you will then have to say that it is not only through God that right and wrong come into being, but that they are in their essence logically anterior to God. You could, of course, if you liked, say that there was a superior deity who gave orders to the God who made this world, or you could take up the line that some of the gnostics took up—a line which I often thought was a very plausible one—that as a matter of fact this world that we know was made by the devil at a moment when God was not looking. There is a good deal to be said for that, and I am not concerned to refute it.

The Argument for the Remedying of Injustice

Then there is another very curious form of moral argument, which is this: they say that the existence of God is required in order to bring justice into the world. In the part of this universe that we know there is great injustice, and often the good suffer, and often the wicked prosper, and one hardly knows which of those is the more annoying; but if you are going to have justice in the universe as a whole you have to suppose a future life to redress the balance of life here on earth, and so they say that there must be a God, and there must be heaven and hell in order that in the long run there may be justice. That is a very curious argument. If you looked at the matter from a scientific point of view, you would say: "After all, I know only this world. I do not know about the rest of the universe, but so far as one can argue at all on probabilities one would say that probably this world is a fair sample, and if there is injustice here the odds are that there is injustice elsewhere also." Supposing you got a crate of oranges that you opened, and you found all the top layer of oranges bad, you would not argue: "The underneath ones must be good, so as to redress the balance." You would say: "Probably the whole lot is a bad consignment"; and that is really what a scientific person would argue about the universe. He would say: "Here we find in this world a great deal of injustice, and so far as that goes that is a reason for supposing that justice does not rule in the world; and therefore so far as it goes it affords a moral argument against a deity and not in favor of one." Of course I know that the sort of intellectual arguments that I have been talking to you about are not what really moves people. What really moves people to believe in God is not any intellectual argument at all. Most people believe in God because they have been taught from early infancy to do it, and that is the main reason.

Then I think that the next most powerful reason is the wish for safety, a sort of feeling that there is a big brother who will look after you. That plays a very profound part in influencing people's desire for a belief in God.

THE CHARACTER OF CHRIST

I now want to say a few words upon a topic which I often think is not quite sufficiently dealt with by Rationalists, and that is the question whether Christ was the best and the wisest of men. It is generally taken for granted that we should all agree that that was so. I do not myself. I think that there are a good many points upon which I agree with Christ a great deal more than the professing Christians do. I do not know that I could go with him all the way, but I could go with him much further than most professing Christians can. You will remember that he said: "Resist not evil, but whosoever shall smite thee on thy right cheek, turn to him the other also." That is not a new precept or a new principle. It was used by Lao-Tse and Buddha some 500 or 600 years before Christ, but it is not a principle which as a matter of fact Christians accept. I have no doubt that the present Prime Minister, for instance, is a most sincere Christian, but I should not advise any of you to go and smite him on one cheek. I think that you might find that he thought this text was intended in a figurative sense.

Then there is another point which I consider is excellent. You will remember that Christ said: "Judge not lest ye be judged." That principle I do not think you would find was popular in the law courts of Christian countries. I have known in my time quite a number of judges who were very earnest Christians, and they none of them felt that they were acting contrary to Christian principles in what they did. Then Christ says: "Give to him that asketh of thee, and from him that would borrow of thee turn not thou away." That is a very good principle. Your Chairman has reminded you that we are not here to talk politics, but I cannot help observing that the last General Election was fought on the question of how desirable it was to turn away from him that would borrow of thee, so that one must assume that the Liberals and Conservatives of this country are composed of people who do not agree with the teaching of Christ, because they certainly did very emphatically turn away on that occasion.

Then there is one other maxim of Christ which I think has a great deal in it, but I do not find that it is very popular among some of our Christian friends. He says: "If thou wilt be perfect, go and sell that which thou hast, and give to the poor." That is a very excellent maxim, but, as I say, it is not much practiced. All these, I think, are good maxims, although they are a little difficult to live up to. I do not profess to live up to them myself; but then, after all, I am not by way of doing so, and it is not quite the same thing as for a Christian.

DEFECTS IN CHRIST'S TEACHING

Having granted the excellence of these maxims, I come to certain points in which I do not believe that one can grant either the superlative wisdom or the superlative goodness of Christ as depicted in the Gospels; and here I may say that one is not concerned with the historical question. Historically it is quite doubtful whether Christ ever existed at all, and if he did we do not know anything about him, so that I am not concerned with the historical question, which is a very difficult one. I am concerned with Christ as he appears in the Gospels, taking the Gospel narrative as it stands, and there one does find some things that do not seem to be very wise. For one thing, he certainly thought that his second coming would occur in clouds of glory before the death of all the people who were living at that time. There are a great many texts that prove that. He says, for instance: "Ye shall not have gone over the cities of Israel till the Son of Man be come." Then he says: "There are some standing here which shall not taste death till the Son of Man come into his kingdom"; and there are a lot of places where it is quite clear that he believed that his second coming would happen during the lifetime of many then living. That was the belief of his earlier followers, and it was the basis of a good deal of his moral teaching. When he said, "Take no thought for the morrow," and things of that sort, it was very largely because he thought that the second coming was going to be very soon, and that all ordinary mundane affairs did not count. I have, as a matter of fact, known some Christians who did believe that the second coming was imminent. I knew a parson who frightened his congregation terribly by telling them that the second coming was very imminent indeed, but they were much consoled when they found that he was planting trees in his garden. The early Christians did really believe it, and they did abstain from such things as planting trees in their gardens, because they did accept from Christ the belief that the second coming was imminent. In that respect clearly he was not so wise as some other people have been, and he was certainly not superlatively wise.

THE MORAL PROBLEM

Then you came to moral questions. There is one very serious defect to my mind in Christ's moral character, and that is that he believed in hell. I do not myself feel that any person who is really profoundly humane can believe in everlasting punishment. Christ certainly as depicted in the Gospels did believe in everlasting punishment, and one does find repeatedly a vindictive fury against those people who would not listen to his preaching—an attitude which is not uncommon with preachers, but which does somewhat detract from superlative excellence. You do not, for instance, find that attitude in Socrates. You find him quite bland and urbane towards the people who would not listen to him; and it is, to my mind, far more worthy of a sage to take that line than to take the line of indignation. You probably all remember the sort of things that Socrates was saying when he was dying, and the sort of things that he generally did say to people who did not agree with him.

You will find that in the Gospels Christ said: "Ye serpents, ye generation of vipers, how can ye escape the damnation of hell." That was said to people who did not like his preaching. It is not really to my mind quite the best tone, and there are a great many of these things about hell. There is, of course, the familiar text about the sin against the Holy Ghost: "Whosoever speaketh against the Holy Ghost it shall not be forgiven him neither in this world nor in the world to come." That text has caused an unspeakable amount of misery in the world, for all sorts of people have imagined that they have committed the sin against the Holy Ghost, and thought that it would not be forgiven them either in this world or in the world to come. I really do not think that a person with a proper degree of kindliness in his nature would have put fears and terrors of that sort into the world.

Then Christ says: "The Son of Man shall send forth his angels, and they shall gather out of his kingdom all things that offend, and them which do iniquity, and shall cast them into a furnace of fire; there shall be wailing and gnashing of teeth"; and he goes on about the wailing and gnashing of teeth. It comes in one verse after another, and it is quite manifest to the reader that there is a certain pleasure in contemplating wailing and gnashing of teeth, or else it would not occur so often. Then you all, of course, remember about the sheep and the goats; how at the second coming he is going to divide the sheep from the goats, and he is going to say to the goats: "Depart from me, ye cursed, into everlasting fire." He continues: "And these shall go away into everlasting fire." Then he says again: "If thy hand offend thee, cut it off; it is better for thee to enter into life maimed, than having two hands to go into hell, into the fire that never shall be quenched; where their worm dieth not and the fire is not quenched." He repeats that again and again also. I must say that I think all this doctrine, that hell fire is a punishment for sin, is a doctrine of cruelty. It is a doctrine that put cruelty into the world and gave the world generations of cruel torture; and the Christ of the Gospels, if you could take him as his chroniclers represent him, would certainly have to be considered partly responsible for that.

There are other things of less importance. There is the instance of the Gadarene swine, where it certainly was not very kind to the pigs to put the devils into them and make them rush down the hill to the sea. You must remember that he was omnipotent, and he could have made the devils simply go away; but he chooses to send them into the pigs. Then there is the curious story of the fig-tree, which always rather puzzled me. You remember what happened about the fig-tree. "He was hungry; and seeing a fig-tree afar off having leaves; he came if haply he might find anything thereon; and when he came to it he found nothing but leaves, for the time of figs was not yet. And Jesus answered and said unto it: 'No man eat fruit of thee hereafter for ever'. . . and Peter . . . saith unto him: 'Master, behold the fig-tree which thou cursedst is withered away.'" That is a very curious story, because it was not the right time of year for figs, and you really could not blame the tree. I cannot myself feel that either in the matter of wisdom or in the matter of virtue Christ stands quite as high as some other people known to history. I think I should put Buddha and Socrates above him in those respects.

THE EMOTIONAL FACTOR

As I said before, I do not think that the real reason why people accept religion is anything to do with argumentation. They accept religion on emotional grounds. One is often told that it is a very wrong thing to attack religion, because religion makes men virtuous. So I am told; I have not noticed it. You know, of course, the parody of that argument in Samuel Butler's book, *Erewhon Revisited.* You will remember that in *Erewhon* there is a certain Higgs who arrives in a remote country, and after spending some time there he escapes from that country in a balloon. Twenty years later he comes back to that country and finds a new religion, in which he is worshipped under the name of the "Sun Child"; and it is said that he ascended into heaven. He finds that the Feast of the Ascension is about to be celebrated, and he hears Professors Hanky and Panky say to each other that they never set eyes on the man Higgs, and they hope they never will; but they are the high priests of the religion of the Sun Child. He is very indignant, and he comes up to them, and he says: "I am going to expose all this humbug and tell the people of Erewhon that it was only I, the man Higgs, and I went up in a balloon." He was told: "You must not do that, because all the morals of this country are bound round his myth, and if they once know that you did not ascend into heaven they will all become wicked"; and so he is persuaded of that, and he goes away quite quietly.

That is the idea—that we should all be wicked if we did not hold to the Christian religion. It seems to me that the people who have held to it have been for the most part extremely wicked. You find this curious fact, that the more intense has been the religion of any period and the more profound has been the dogmatic belief, the greater has been the cruelty and the worse has been the state of affairs. In the so-called ages of faith, when men really did believe the Christian religion in all its completeness, there was the Inquisition, with its tortures; there were millions of unfortunate women burnt as witches; and there was every kind of cruelty practiced upon all sorts of people in the name of religion.

You find as you look round the world that every single bit of progress in humane feeling, every improvement in the criminal law, every step towards the diminution of war, every step towards better treatment of the colored races, or every mitigation of slavery, every moral progress that there has been in the world, has been consistently opposed by the organized Churches of the world. I say quite deliberately that the Christian religion, as organized in its Churches, has been and still is the principal enemy of moral progress in the world.

HOW THE CHURCHES HAVE RETARDED PROGRESS

You may think that I am going too far when I say that that is still so. I do not think that I am. Take one fact. You will bear with me if I mention it. It is not a pleasant fact, but the Churches compel one to mention facts that are not pleasant. Supposing that in this world that we live in today an inexperienced girl is married to a syphilitic man, in that case the Catholic Church says: "This is an indissoluble sacrament. You must stay together for life," and no steps of any sort must be taken by that women to prevent herself from giving birth to syphilitic children. That is what the Catholic Church says. I say that that is fiendish cruelty, and nobody whose natural sympathies have not been warped by dogma, or whose moral nature was not absolutely dead to all sense of suffering, could maintain that it is right and proper that that state of things should continue.

That is only an example. There are a great many ways in which at the present moment the Church, by its insistence upon what it chooses to call morality, inflicts upon all sorts of people undeserved and unnecessary suffering. And of course, as we know, it is in its major part an opponent still of progress and of improvement in all the ways that diminish suffering in the world, because it has chosen to label as morality a certain narrow set of rules of conduct which have nothing to do with human happiness; and when you say that this or that ought to be done because it would make for human happiness, they think that has nothing to do with the matter at all. "What has human happiness to do with morals? The object of morals is not to make people happy. It is to fit them for heaven." It certainly seems to unfit them for this world.

FEAR FOR THE FOUNDATION OF RELIGION

Religion is based, I think, primarily and mainly upon fear. It is partly the terror of the unknown, and partly, as I have said, the wish to feel that you have a kind of elder brother who will stand by you in all your troubles and disputes. Fear is the basis of the whole thing—fear of the mysterious, fear of defeat, fear of death. Fear is the parent of cruelty, and therefore it is no wonder if cruelty and religion have gone hand-in-hand. It is because fear is at the basis of those two things. In this world we can now begin a little to understand things, and a little to master them by the help of science, which has forced its way step by step against the Christian religion, against the Churches, and against the opposition of all the old precepts. Science can help us to get over this craven fear in which mankind has lived for so many generations. Science can teach us, and I think our own hearts can teach us, no longer to look round for imaginary supports, no longer to invent allies in the sky, but rather to look to our own efforts here below to make this world a fit place to live in, instead of the sort of place that the Churches in all these centuries have made it.

WHAT WE MUST DO

We want to stand upon our own feet and look fair and square at the world—its good facts, its bad facts, its beauties, and its ugliness; see the world as it is, and be not afraid of it. Conquer the world by intelligence, and not merely by being slavishly subdued by the terror that comes from it. The whole conception of God is a conception derived from the ancient Oriental despotisms. It is a conception quite unworthy of free men. When you hear people in church debasing themselves and saying that they are miserable sinners, and all the rest of it, it seems contemptible and not worthy of self-respecting human beings. We ought to stand up and look the world frankly in the face. We ought to make the best we can of the world, and if it is not so good as we wish, after all it will still be better than what these others have made of it in all these ages. A good world needs knowledge, kindliness, and courage; it does not need a regretful hankering after the past, or a fettering of the free intelligence by the words uttered long ago by ignorant men. It needs a fearless outlook and a free intelligence. It needs hope for the future, not looking back all the time towards a past that is dead, which we trust will be far surpassed by the future that our intelligence can create.

4

What Is an Agnostic?

Are agnostics atheists?

No. An atheist, like a Christian, holds that we *can* know whether or not there is a God. The Christian holds that we can know there is a God; the atheist, that we can know there is not.* The agnostic suspends judgment, saying that there are not sufficient grounds either for affirmation or for denial. At the same time, an agnostic may hold that the existence of God, though not impossible, is very improbable; he may even hold it so improbable that it is not worth considering in practice. In that case, he is not far removed from atheism. His attitude may be that which a careful philosopher would have toward the gods of ancient Greece. If I were asked to *prove* that Zeus and Poseidon and Hera and the rest of the Olympians do not exist, I should be at a loss to find conclusive arguments. An agnostic may think the Christian God as improbable as the Olympians; in that case, he is, for practical purposes, at one with the atheists.

Since you deny "God's law," what authority do you accept as a guide to conduct?

An agnostic does not accept any "authority" in the sense in which religious people do. He holds that a man should think out questions

---

From *Look Magazine,* copyright © 1953 by Cowles Magazine Inc.,

*Many freethinkers do not accept this definition. For them atheism means without theism or without a belief in a god or gods. —*Ed.*

of conduct for himself. Of course, he will seek to profit by the wisdom of others, but he will have to select for himself the people he is to consider wise, and he will not regard even what they say as unquestionable. He will observe that what passes as "God's law" varies from time to time. The Bible says both that a woman must not marry her deceased husband's brother, and that, in certain circumstances, she must do so. If you have the misfortune to be a childless widow with an unmarried brother-in-law, it is logically impossible for you to avoid disobeying "God's law."

How do you know what is good and what is evil?
What does an agnostic consider a sin?

The agnostic is not quite so certain as some Christians are as to what is good and what is evil. He does not hold, as most Christians in the past held, that people who disagree with the government on abstruse points of theology ought to suffer a painful death. He is against persecution, and rather chary of moral condemnation.

As for "sin," he thinks it not a useful notion. He admits, of course, that some kinds of conduct are desirable and some undesirable, but he holds that the punishment of undesirable kinds is only to be commended when it is deterrent or reformatory, not when it is inflicted because it is thought a good thing on its own account that the wicked should suffer. It was this belief in vindictive punishment that made men accept hell. This is part of the harm done by the notion of "sin."

Does an agnostic do whatever he pleases?

In one sense, no; in another sense, everyone does whatever he pleases. Suppose, for example, you hate someone so much that you would like to murder him. Why do you not do so? You may reply: "Because religion tells me that murder is a sin." But as a statistical fact, agnostics are not more prone to murder than other people, in fact, rather less so. They have the same motives for abstaining from murder as other people have. Far and away the most powerful of these motives is the fear of punishment. In lawless conditions, such as a gold rush, all sorts of people will commit crimes, although in ordinary circumstances they would have been law-abiding. There is not only actual legal punishment; there is the discomfort of dreading discovery, and the lonelines of knowing that, to avoid being hated, you must wear a mask even with your closest intimates. And there is also what may be called "conscience": If you ever contemplated a murder, you would dread the horrible memory of your victim's last moments or lifeless corpse. All this, it is true, depends upon your living in a law-abiding community, but there are abundant secular reasons for creating and preserving such a community.

I said that there is another sense in which every man does as he pleases. No one but a fool indulges every impulse, but what holds a desire in check is always some other desire. A man's anti-social wishes may be restrained by a wish to please God, but they may also be restrained by a wish to please his friends, or to win the respect of his community, or to be able to contemplate himself without disgust. But if he has no such wishes, the mere abstract precepts of morality will not keep him straight.

How does an agnostic regard the Bible?

An agnostic regards the Bible exactly as enlightened clerics regard it. He does not think that it is divinely inspired; he thinks its early history legendary, and no more exactly true than that in Homer; he thinks its moral teaching sometimes good, but sometimes very bad. For example: Samuel ordered Saul, in a war, to kill not only every man, woman, and child of the enemy, but also all the sheep and cattle. Saul, however, let the sheep and cattle live, and for this we are told to condemn him. I have never been able to admire Elisha for cursing the children who laughed at him, or to believe (what the Bible asserts) that a benevolent Deity would send two she-bears to kill the children.

How does an agnostic regard Jesus,
the Virgin Birth, and the Holy Trinity?

Since an agnostic does not believe in God, he cannot think that Jesus was God. Most agnostics admire the life and moral teachings of Jesus as told in the Gospels, but not necessarily more than those of certain other men. Some would place him on a level with Buddha, some with Socrates and some with Abraham Lincoln. Nor do they think that what He said is not open to question, since they do not accept any authority as absolute.

They regard the Virgin Birth as a doctrine taken over from pagan mythology, where such births were not uncommon. (Zoroaster was said to have been born of a virgin; Ishtar, the Babylonian goddess, is called the Holy Virgin.) They cannot give credence to it, or to the doctrine of the Trinity, since neither is possible without belief in God.

Can an agnostic be a Christian?

The word "Christian" has had various different meanings at different times. Throughout most of the centuries since the time of Christ, it has meant a person who believed in God and immortality and held that Christ was God. But Unitarians call themselves Christians, although they do not believe in the divinity of Christ, and many people nowadays use the word "God" in a much less precise sense than that which it used to bear. Many people who say they believe in God no longer mean a person, or a trinity of persons, but only a vague tendency or power or purpose immanent in evolution. Others, going still further, mean by "Christianity" merely a system of ethics which, since they are ignorant of history, they imagine to be characteristic of Christians only.

When, in a recent book, I said that what the world needs is "love, Christian love, or compassion," many people thought this showed some changes in my views, although, in fact, I might have said the same thing at any time. If you mean by a "Christian" a man who loves his neighbor, who has wide sympathy with suffering, and who ardently desires a world freed from the cruelties and abominations which at present disfigure it, then, certainly, you will be justified in calling me a Christian. And, in this sense, I think you will find more "Christians" among agnostics than among the orthodox. But, for my part, I cannot accept such a definition. Apart from other objections to it, it seems rude to Jews, Buddhists, Mohammedans, and other non-Christians, who, so far as history shows, have been at least as apt as Christians to practice the virtues which some modern Christians arrogantly claim as distinctive of their own religion.

I think also that all who called themselves Christians in an earlier time, and a great majority of those who do so at the present day, would consider that belief in God and immortality is essential to a Christian. On these grounds, I should not call myself a Christian, and I should say that an agnostic cannot be a Christian. But, if the word "Christianity" comes to be generally used to mean merely a kind of morality, then it will certainly be possible for an agnostic to be a Christian.

Does an agnostic deny that man has a soul?

This question has no precise meaning unless we are given a definition of the word "soul." I suppose what is meant is, roughly, something nonmaterial which persists throughout a person's life and even, for those who believe in immortality, throughout all future time. If this is what is meant, an agnostic is not likely to believe that man has a soul. But I must hasten to add that this does not mean that an agnostic must be a materialist. Many agnostics (including myself) are quite as doubtful of the body as they are of the soul, but this is a long story taking one into difficult metaphysics. Mind and matter alike, I should say, are only convenient symbols in discourse, not actually existing things.

Does an agnostic believe in a hereafter, in heaven or hell?

The question whether people survive death is one as to which evidence is possible. Psychical research and spiritualism are thought by many to supply such evidence. An agnostic, as such, does not take a view about survival unless he thinks that there is evidence one way or the other. For my part, I do not think there is any good reason to believe that we survive death, but I am open to conviction if adequate evidence should appear.

Heaven and hell are a different matter. Belief in hell is bound up with the belief that the vindictive punishment of sin is a good thing, quite independently of any reformative or deterrent effect that it may have. Hardly an agnostic believes this. As for heaven, there might conceivably someday be evidence of its existence through spiritualism, but most agnostics do not think that there is such evidence, and therefore do not believe in heaven.

*Are you never afraid of God's judgment
in denying him?*

Most certainly not. I also deny Zeus and Jupiter and Odin and Brahma, but this causes me no qualms. I observe that a very large portion of the human race does not believe in God and suffers no visible punishment in consequence. And if there were a God, I think it very unlikely that He would have such an uneasy vanity as to be offended by those who doubt His existence.

*How do agnostics explain the beauty
and harmony of nature?*

I do not understand where this "beauty" and "harmony" are supposed to be found. Throughout the animal kingdom, animals ruthlessly prey upon each other. Most of them are either cruelly killed by other animals or slowly die of hunger. For my part, I am unable to see any very great beauty or harmony in the tapeworm. Let it not be said that this creature is sent as a punishment for our sins, for it is more prevalent among animals than among humans. I suppose the questioner is thinking of such things as the beauty of the starry heavens. But one should remember that stars every now and again explode and reduce everything in their neighborhood to a vague mist. Beauty, in any case, is subjective and exists only in the eye of the beholder.

*How do agnostics explain miracles and other
revelations of God's omnipotence?*

Agnostics do not think that there is any evidence of "miracles" in the sense of happenings contrary to natural law. We know that faith healing occurs and is in no sense miraculous. At Lourdes, certain diseases an be cured and others cannot. Those that can be cured at Lourdes can probably be cured by any doctor in whom the patient has faith. As for the records of other miracles, such as Joshua commanding the sun to stand still, the agnostic dismisses them as legends and points to the fact that all religions are plentifully supplied with such legends. There is just as much miraculous evidence for the Greek gods in Homer as for the Christian God in the Bible.

*There have been base and cruel passions, which
religion opposes. If you abandon religious
principles, could mankind exist?*

The existence of base and cruel passions is undeniable, but I find no
evidence in history that religion has opposed these passions. On the
contrary, it has sanctified them, and enabled people to indulge them
without remorse. Cruel persecutions have been commoner in Christendom than anywhere else. What appears to justify persecution is
dogmatic belief. Kindliness and tolerance only prevail in proportion
as dogmatic belief decays. In our day, a new dogmatic religion,
namely, communism, has arisen. To this, as to other systems of
dogma, the agnostic is opposed. The persecuting character of present-
day communism is exactly like the persecuting character of Christianity in earlier centuries. In so far as Christianity has become less
persecuting, this is mainly due to the work of freethinkers who have
made dogmatists rather less dogmatic. If they were as dogmatic
now as in former times, they would still think it right to burn
heretics at the stake. The spirit of tolerance which some modern
Christians regard as essentially Christian is, in fact, a product of
the temper which allows doubt and is suspicious of absolute cer-
tainties. I think that anybody who surveys past history in an impartial manner will be driven to the conclusion that religion has
caused more suffering than it has prevented.

What is the meaning of life to the agnostic?

If feel inclined to answer by another question: What is the meaning
of "the meaning of life"? I suppose what is intended is some general
purpose. I do not think that life in general has any purpose. It just
happened. But individual human beings have purposes, and there is
nothing in agnosticism to cause them to abandon these purposes.
They cannot, of course, be certain of achieving the results at which
they aim; but you would think ill of a soldier who refused to fight
unless victory was certain. The person who needs religion to bolster
up his own purposes is a timorous person, and I cannot think as
well of him as of the man who takes his chances, while admitting
that defeat is not impossible.

*Does not the denial of religion mean the denial
of marriage and chastity?*

Here again, one must reply by another question: Does the man who
asks this question believe that marriage and chastity contribute to
earthly happiness here below, or does he think that, while they
cause misery here below, they are to be advocated as means of
getting to heaven? The man who takes the latter view will no doubt
expect agnosticism to lead to a decay of what he calls virtue, but he
will have to admit that what he calls virtue is not what ministers to
the happiness of the human race while on earth. If, on the other
hand, he takes the former view, namely, that there are terrestrial
arguments in favor of marriage and chastity, he must also hold that
these arguments are such as should appeal to an agnostic. Agnostics, as such, have no distinctive views about sexual morality.
But most of them would admit that there are valid arguments
against the unbridled indulgence of sexual desires. They would derive these arguments, however, from terrestrial sources and not from
supposed divine commands.

*Is not faith in reason alone a dangerous creed?
Is not reason imperfect and inadequate without
spiritual and moral law?*

No sensible man, however agnostic, has "faith in reason alone."
Reason is concerned with matters of fact, some observed, some inferred. The question whether there is a future life and the question
whether there is a God concern matters of fact, and the agnostic
will hold that they should be investigated in the same way as the
question, "Will there be an eclipse of the moon tomorrow?" But
matters of fact alone are not sufficient to determine action, since
they do not tell us what ends we ought to pursue. In the realm of
ends, we need something other than reason. The agnostic will find
his ends in his own heart and not in an external command. Let us
take an illustration: Suppose you wish to travel by train from New
York to Chicago; you will use reason to discover when the trains
run, and a person who thought that there was some faculty of insight or intuition enabling him to dispense with the timetable would
be thought rather silly. But no timetable will tell him that it is wise
to travel to Chicago. No doubt, in deciding that it is wise, he will
have to take account of further matters of fact; but behind all the

matters of fact, there will be the ends that he thinks fitting to pursue, and these, for an agnostic as for other men, belong to a realm which is not that of reason, though it should be in no degree contrary to it. The realm I mean is that of emotion and feeling and desire.

Do you regard all religions as forms of supersitition or dogma? Which of the existing religions do you most respect, and why?

All the great organized religions that have dominated large populations have involved a greater or less amount of dogma, but "religion" is a word of which the meaning is not very definite. Confucianism, for instance, might be called a religion, although it involves no dogma. And in some forms of liberal Christianity, the element of dogma is reduced to a minimum.

Of the great religions of history, I prefer Buddhism, especially in its earliest forms, because it has had the smallest element of persecution.

Communism, like agnosticism, opposes religion. Are agnostics communists?

Communism does not oppose religion. It merely opposes the Christian religion, just as Mohammedanism does. Communism, at least in the form advocated by the Soviet government and the Communist party, is a new system of dogma of a peculiarly virulent and persecuting sort. Every genuine agnostic must therefore be opposed to it.

Do agnostics think that science and religion are impossible to reconcile?

The answer turns upon what is meant by "religion." If it means merely a system of ethics, it can be reconciled with science. If it means a system of dogma, regarded as unquestionably true, it is incompatible with the scientific spirit, which refuses to accept matters of fact without evidence, and also holds that complete certainty is hardly ever attainable.

What kind of evidence could convince
you that God exists?

I think that if I heard a voice from the sky predicting all that was
going to happen to me during the next twenty-four hours, including
events that would have seemed highly improbable, and if all these
events then proceeded to happen, I might perhaps be convinced at
least of the existence of some superhuman intelligence. I can imagine other evidence of the same sort which might convince me, but
so far as I know, no such evidence exists.

5

Am I an Atheist or an Agnostic?
A Plea for Tolerance in the
Face of New Dogmas

I speak as one who was intended by my father to be brought up as a Rationalist. He was quite as much of a Rationalist as I am, but he died when I was three years old, and the Court of Chancery decided that I was to have the benefits of a Christian education.

I think that perhaps the Court of Chancery may have regretted that since. It does not seem to have done as much good as they hoped. Perhaps you may say that it would be rather a pity if Christian education were to cease, because you would then get no more Rationalists.

They arise chiefly out of reaction to a system of education which considers it quite right that a father should decree that his son should be brought up as a Muggletonian, we will say, or brought up on any other kind of nonsense, but he must on no account be brought up to try to think rationally. When I was young that was considered to be illegal.

SIN AND THE BISHOPS

Since I became a Rationalist I have found that there is still considerable scope in the world for the practical importance of a Rationalist outlook, not only in matters of geology, but in all sorts of

Published by Haldeman-Julius (1949).

practical matters, such as divorce and birth control, and a question which has come up quite recently, artificial insemination, where bishops tell us that something is gravely sinful, but it is only gravely sinful because there is some text in the Bible about it. It is not gravely sinful because it does anybody harm, and that is not the argument. As long as you can say, and as long as you can persuade Parliament to go on saying, that a thing must not be done solely because there is a text in the Bible about it, so long obviously there is great need of Rationalism in practice.

As you may know, I got into considerable trouble in the United States solely because, on some practical issues, I considered that the ethical advice given in the Bible was not conclusive, and that on some points one should act differently from what the Bible says. On that ground it was decreed by a Law Court that I was not a fit person to teach in any university in the United States, so that I have some practical ground for preferring Rationalism to other outlooks.

DON'T BE TOO CERTAIN!

The question of how to define Rationalism is not altogether an easy one. I do not think that you could define it by rejection of this or that Christian dogma. It would be perfectly possible to be a complete and absolute Rationalist in the true sense of the term and yet accept this or that dogma.

The question is how to arrive at your opinions and not what your opinions are. The thing in which we believe is the supremacy of reason. If reason should lead you to orthodox conclusions, well and good; you are still a Rationalist. To my mind the essential thing is that one should base one's arguments upon the kind of grounds that are accepted in science, and that one should not regard anything that one accepts as quite certain, but only as probable in a greater or a less degree. Not to be absolutely certain is, I think, one of the essential things in rationality.

PROOF OF GOD

Here there comes in a practical question which has often troubled me. Whenever I go into a foreign country or a prison or any similar place they always ask me what is my religion.

I never quite know whether I should say "Agnostic" or whether I should say "Atheist." It is a very difficult question and I daresay that some of you have been troubled about it. As a philosopher, if I were speaking to a purely philosophic audience I should say that I ought to describe myself as an Agnostic, because I do not think that there is a conclusive argument by which one can prove that there is not a God.

On the other hand, if I am to convey the right impression to the ordinary man in the street I think that I ought to say that I am an Atheist, because when I say that I cannot prove that there is not a God, I ought to add equally that I cannot prove that there are not the Homeric gods.

None of us would seriously consider the possibility that all the gods of Homer really exist, and yet if you were to set to work to give a logical demonstration that Zeus, Hera, Poseidon, and the rest of them did not exist you would find it an awful job. You could not get such proof.

Therefore, in regard to the Olympic gods, speaking to a purely philosophic audience, I would say that I am an Agnostic. But speaking popularly, I think that all of us would say in regard to those gods that we were Atheists. In regard to the Christian God, I should, I think, take exactly the same line.

SKEPTICISM

There is exactly the same degree of possibility and likelihood of the existence of the Christian God as there is of the existence of the Homeric God. I cannot prove that either the Christian God or the Homeric gods do not exist, but I do not think that there existence is an alternative that is sufficiently probable to be worth serious consideration. Therefore, I suppose that on these documents that they submit to me on these occasions I ought to say "Atheist," although it has been a very difficult problem, and sometimes I have said one and sometimes the other without any clear principle by which to go.

When one admits that nothing is certain one must, I think, also add that some things are much more nearly certain than others. It is much more nearly certain that we are here assembled tonight than it is that this or that political party is in the right. Certainly there are degrees of certainty, and one should be very careful to emphasize that fact, because otherwise one is landed in an utter skepticism, and complete skepticism would, of course, be totally barren and totally useless.

PERSECUTION

One must remember that some things are very much more probable than others and may be so probable that it is not worth while to remember in practice that they are not wholly certain, except when it comes to questions of persecution.

If it comes to burning somebody at the stake for not believing it, then it is worth while to remember that after all he may be right, and it is not worth while to persecute him.

In general, if a man says, for instance, that the earth is flat, I am quite willing that he should propagate his opinion as hard as he likes. He may, of course, be right but I do not think that he is. In practice you will, I think, do better to assume that the earth is round, although, of course, you may be mistaken. Therefore, I do not think that we should go in for complete skepticism, but for a doctrine of degrees of probability.

I think that, on the whole, that is the kind of doctrine that the world needs. The world has become very full of new dogmas. The old dogmas have perhaps decayed, but new dogmas have arisen and, on the whole, I think that a dogma is harmful in proportion to its novelty. New dogmas are much worse than old ones.

6

The Faith of a Rationalist
No Supernatural Reasons
Needed to Make Men Kind

When I try to discover what are the original sources of my opinions, both practical and theoretical, I find that most of them spring ultimately from admiration for two qualities—kindly feeling and veracity. To begin with kindly feeling: most of the social and political evils of the world arise through absence of sympathy and presence of hatred, envy, or fear. Hostile feelings of this sort are common between nations; at many times they have existed between different classes or different creeds within one nation; in many professions envy is an obstacle to the recognition of Negroes; contempt for all who are not white has brought and is bringing great suffering to would-be oppressors as well as to those whom they have sought to oppress. Every kind of hostile action or feeling provokes a reaction by which it is increased and so generates a progeny of violence and injustice which has a terrible vitality. This can only be met by cultivating in ourselves and attempting to generate in the young feelings of friendliness rather than hostility, of well-wishing rather than malevolence, and of cooperation rather than competition.

If I am asked "Why do you believe this?" I should not appeal to any supernatural authority, but only to the general wish for happiness. A world full of hate is a world full of sorrow. Each party, where there is mutual hatred, hopes that only the other party will suffer, but this is seldom the case. And even the most successful oppressors are filled with fear—slave-owners, for example, have

From the *Listener* (May 29, 1947).

been obsessed with dread of a servile insurrection. From the point of view of worldly wisdom, hostile feeling and limitation of sympathy are folly. Their fruits are war, death, oppression, and torture, not only for their original victims but, in the long run, also for their perpetrators or their descendants. Whereas if we could all learn to love our neighbors the world would quickly become a paradise for us all.

Veracity, which I regard as second only to kindly feeling, consists broadly in believing according to evidence and not because a belief is comfortable or a source of pleasure. In the absence of veracity, kindly feeling will often be defeated by self-deception. It used to be common for the rich to maintain either that it is pleasant to be poor or that poverty is the result of shiftlessness. Some healthy people maintain that all illness is self-indulgence. I have heard fox hunters argue that the fox likes being hunted. It is easy for those who have exceptional power to persuade themselves that the system by which they profit gives more happiness to the underdog than he would enjoy under a more just system. And even where no obvious bias is involved, it is only by means of veracity that we can acquire the scientific knowledge required to bring out our common purposes. Consider how many cherished prejudices had to be abandoned in the development of modern medicine and hygiene. To take a different kind of illustration: how many wars would have been prevented if the side which was ultimately defeated had formed a just estimate of its prospects instead of one based on conceit and wishfulfilment!

Vercity, or love of truth, is defined by John Locke as "not entertaining any proposition with greater assurance than the proofs it is built upon will warrant." This definition is admirable in regard to all those matters as to which proof may reasonably be demanded. But since proofs need premise, it is impossible to prove anything unless some things are accepted without proof. We must therefore ask ourselves: What sort of thing is it reasonable to believe without proof? I should reply: The facts of sense experience and the principles mathematics and logic—including the inductive logic employed in science. These are things which we can hardly bring ourselves to doubt and as to which there is a large measure of agreement among mankind. But in matters as to which men disagree, or as to which our own convictions are wavering, we should look for proofs, or, if proofs cannot be found, we should be content to confess ignorance.

There are some who hold that veracity should have limitations. Some beliefs, they say, are both comforting and morally beneficial, although it cannot be said that there are valid scientific grounds for supposing them to be true; these beliefs, they say, should not be critically examined. I cannot myself admit any such doctrine. I cannot believe that mankind can be the better for shrinking from the examination of this or that question. No sound morality can need to be based upon evasion, and a happiness derived from beliefs not justified on any ground except their pleasantness is not a kind of happiness that can be unreservedly admired.

These considerations apply especially to religious beliefs. Most of us have been brought up to believe that the universe owes its existence to an all-wise and all-powerful creator, whose purposes are beneficent even in what to us may seem evil. I do not think it is right to refuse to apply to this belief the kind of tests that we should apply to one that touches our emotions less intimately and profoundly. Is there any evidence of the existence of such a being? Undoubtedly belief in him is comforting and sometimes has some good moral effects on character and behavior. But this is no evidence that the belief is true. For my part, I think the belief lost whatever rationality it once possessed when it was discovered that the earth is not the center of the universe. So long as it was thought that the sun and the planets and the stars revolved about the earth, it was natural to suppose that the universe had a purpose connected with the earth, and, since man was what man most admired on earth, this purpose was supposed to be embodied in man. But astronomy and geology have changed all this. The earth is a minor planet of a minor star which is one of many millions of stars in a galaxy which is one of many millions of galaxies. Even within the life of our own planet man is only a brief interlude. Nonhuman life existed for countless ages before man evolved. Man, even if he does not commit scientific suicide, will perish ultimately through failure of water or air or warmth. It is difficult to believe that omnipotence needed so vast a setting for so small and transitory a result.

Apart from the minuteness and brevity of human species, I cannot feel that it is a worthy climax to such an enormous prelude. There is a rather repulsive smugness and self-complacency in the argument that man is so splendid as to be evidence of infinite wisdom and infinite power in his creator. Those who use this kind of reasoning always try to concentrate our attention on the few saints and sages; they try to make us forget the Neros and Attilas and

Hitlers and the millions of mean poltroons to whom such men owed their power. And even what is best in us is apt to lead to disaster. Religions that teach brotherly love have been used as an excuse for persecution, and our profoundest scientific insight is made into a means of mass destruction. I can imagine a sardonic demon producing us for his amusement, but I cannot attribute to a being who is wise, beneficent, and omnipotent the terrible weight of cruelty, suffering, and ironic degradation of what is best that has marred the history of man in increasing measure as he has become more master of his fate.

There is a different and vaguer conception of cosmic purpose as not omnipotent but slowly working its way through a recalcitrant material. This is a more plausible conception than that of a god who, though omnipotent and loving, has deliberately produced beings so subject to suffering and cruelty as the majority of mankind. I do not pretent to know that there is no such purpose; my knowledge of the universe is too limited. But I do say, and I say with confidence, that the knowledge of other human beings is also limited, and that no one can adduce any good evidence that cosmic processes have any purpose whatever. Our inadequate evidence, so far as it goes, tends in the opposite direction. It seems to show that energy is being more and more evenly distributed, while everything to which it is possible to attribute value depends upon uneven distribution. In the end, therefore, we should expect a dull uniformity, in which the universe would continue forever and ever without the occurrence of anything in the slightest degree interesting. I do not say that this will happen; I say only that, on the basis of our present knowledge, it is the most plausible conjecture.

Immortality, if we could believe in it, would enable us to shake off this gloom about the physical world. We should say that although our souls, during their sojourn here on earth, are in bondage to matter and physical laws, they pass at death into an eternal world beyond the empire of decay which science seems to reveal in the sensible world. But it is impossible to believe this unless we think a human being consists of two parts—soul and body—which are separable and can continue independently of each other. Unfortunately all the evidence is against this. The mind grows like the body; like the body it inherits characteristics from both parents; it is affected by disease of the body and by drugs; it is intimately connected with the brain. There is no scientific reason to suppose that after death the mind or soul acquires an independence of the brain which it never had in life. I do not pretent that this argument is conclusive, but it is all that we have to go on except the slender evidence supplied by physical research.

Many people fear that, without the theoretical beliefs that I find myself compelled to reject, the ethical beliefs which I accept could not survive. They point to the growth of cruel systems opposed to Christianity. But these systems, which grew up in a Christian atmosphere, could never have grown up if either kindly feeling or veracity had been practiced; they are evil myths, inspired by hate and without scientific support. Men tend to have the beliefs that suit their passions. Cruel men believe in a cruel god and use their belief to excuse cruelty. Only kindly men believe in a kindly god, and they would be kindly in any case. The reasons for the ethic that, in common with many whose beliefs are more orthodox, I wish to see prevail are reasons derived from the course of events in this world. We have seen a great system of cruel falsehood, the Nazi system, lead a nation to disaster at immense cost to its opponents. It is not by such systems that happiness is to be achieved; even without the help of revelation it is not difficult to see that human welfare requires a less ferocious ethic. More and more people are becoming unable to accept traditional beliefs. If they think that, apart from these beliefs, there is no reason for kindly behavior the results may be needlessly unfortunate. This is why it is important to show no supernatural reasons are needed to make men kind and to prove that only through kindness can the human race achieve happiness.

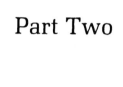

Part Two

7

The Essence of Religion

The decay of traditional religious beliefs, bitterly bewailed by up-
holders of the Churches, welcomed with joy by those who regard the
old creeds as mere superstition, is an undeniable fact. Yet when the
dogmas have been rejected, the question of the place of religion in
life is by no means decided. The dogmas have been valued, not so
much on their own account, as because they were believed to facilitate a certain attitude toward the world, an habitual direction of our
thoughts, a life in the whole, free from the finiteness of self and
providing an escape from the tyranny of desire and daily cares.
Such a life in the whole is possible without dogma, and ought not to
perish through the indifference of those to whom the beliefs of
former ages are no longer credible. Acts inspired by religion have
some quality of infinity in them: they seem done in obedience to a
command, and though they may achieve great ends, yet it is no
clear knowledge of these ends that makes them seem imperative.
The beliefs which underlie such acts are often so deep and so instinctive as to remain unknown to those whose lives are built upon
them. Indeed, it may be not belief but feeling that makes religion: a
feeling which, when brought into the sphere of belief, may involve
the conviction that this or that is good, but may, if it remains un-
touched by intellect, be only a feeling and yet be dominant in action.
It is the quality of infinity that makes religion, the selfless, un-
trammelled life in the whole which frees men from the prison house
of eager wishes and little thoughts. This liberation from the prison

From *Hilbert Journal* 2 (October 1912).

is given by religion, but only by a religion without fettering dogmas; and dogmas become fettering as soon as assent to them becomes unnatural.

The soul of man is a strange mixture of God and brute, a battle-ground of two natures, the one particular, finite, self-centered, the other universal, infinite, and impartial. The finite life, which man shares with the brutes, is tied to the body, and views the world from the standpoint of the *here* and *now*. All those loves and hatreds which are based upon some service to the self belong to the finite life. The love of man and woman, and the love of parents and children, when they do not go beyond the promptings of instinct, are still part of the animal nature: they do not pass into the infinite life until they overcome instinct and cease to be subservient only to the purposes of the finite self. The hatred of enemies and the love of allies in battle are part of what man shares with other gregarious animals: they view the universe as grouped about one point, the single struggling self. Thus the finite part of our life contains all that makes the individual man essentially separate from other men and from the rest of the universe, all those thoughts and desires that cannot, in their nature, be shared by the inhabitant of a different body, all the distortions that make error, and all the insistent claims that lead to strife.

The infinite part of our life does not see the world from one point of view: it shines impartially, like the diffused light on a cloudy sea. Distant ages and remote regions of space are as real to it as what is present and near. In thought, it rises above the life of the senses, seeking always what is general and open to all men. In desire and will, it aims simply at the good, without regarding the good as mine or yours. In feeling, it gives love to all, not only to those who further the purposes of self. Unlike the finite life, it is impartial: its im-partiality leads to truth in thought, justice in action, and universal love in feeling. Unlike the nature which man shares with the brutes, it has a life without barriers, embracing in its survey the whole universe of existence and essence; nothing in it is essentially priv-ate, but its thoughts and desires are such as all may share, since none depend upon the exclusiveness of *here* and *now* and *me*. Thus the infinite nature is the principle of union in the world, as the fin-ite nature is the principle of division. Between the infinite nature in one man and the infinite nature in another, there can be no es-sential conflict: if its embodiments are incomplete, they supplement each other; its division among different men is accidental to its character, and the infinite in all constitutes one universal nature. There is thus a union of all the infinite natures of different men in a sense in which there is no union of all the finite natures. In proportion as the infinite grows strong in us, we live more completely the life of that one universal nature which embraces what is infinite in each of us.

The finite self, impelled by the desire for self-preservation, builds prison walls round the infinite part of our nature, and endeavors to restrain it from that free life in the whole which constitutes its being. The finite self aims at dominion: it sees the world in concentric circles round the *here* and *now,* and itself as the God of that wished-for heaven. The universal soul mocks at this vision, but the finite self hopes always to make it true, and thus to quiet its troublesome critic. In many men, the finite self remains always the jailer of the universal soul; in others, there is a rare and momentary escape; in a few, the prison walls are demolished wholly, and the universal soul remains free through life. It is the escape from prison that gives to some moments and some thoughts a quality of infinity, like light breaking through from some greater world beyond. Sudden beauty in the midst of strife, uncalculating love, or the night wind in the trees, seem to suggest the possibility of a life free from the conflicts and pettinesses of our everyday world, a life where there is peace which no misfortune can disturb. The things which have this quality of infinity seem to give an insight deeper than the piecemeal knowledge of our daily life. A life dominated by this insight, we feel, would be a life free from struggle, a life in harmony with the whole, outside the prison walls built by the instinctive desires of the finite self.

It is this experience of sudden wisdom which is the source of what is essential in religion. Mysticism interprets this experience as a contact with a deeper, truer, more unified world than that of our common beliefs. Behind a thin veil, it sees the glory of God, dimly as a rule, sometimes with dazzling brightness. All the evils of our daily world it regards as merely shadows on the veil, illusions, nothings, which vanish from the sight of those who see the splendor beyond. But in this interpretation mysticism diminishes the value of the experience upon which it is based. The quality of infinity, which we feel, is not to be accounted for by the perception of new objects, other than those that at most times seem finite; it is to be accounted for, rather, by a different way of regarding the same objects, a contemplation more impersonal, more vast, more filled

with love, than the fragmentary, disquiet consideration we give to
things when we view them as means to help or hinder our own
purposes. It is not in some other world that that beauty and that
peace are to be found; it is in this actual everyday world, in the
midst of action and the business of life. But it is in the everyday
world as viewed by the universal soul, and in the midst of action
and business inspired by its vision. The evils and the smallnesses
are not illusions, but the universal soul finds within itself a love to
which imperfections are no barrier, and thus unifies the world by
the unity of its own contemplation.

The transition from the life of the finite self to the infinite life in
the whole requires a moment of absolute self-surrender, when all
personal will seems to cease, and the soul feels itself in passive
submission to the universe. After passionate struggle for some particular good, there comes some inward or outward necessity to
abandon the pursuit of the object which has absorbed all our desire,
and no other desire is ready to replace the one that has been re-
linquished. Hence arises a state of suspension of the will, when the
soul no longer seeks to impose itself upon the world, but is open to
every impression that comes to it from the world. It is at such a time
that the contemplative vision first comes into being, bringing with
it universal love and universal worship. From universal worship
comes joy, from universal love comes a new desire, and thence the
birth of that seeking after universal good which constitutes the will
of our infinite nature. Thus from the moment of self-surrender,
which to the finite self appears like death, a new life begins, with a
larger vision, a new happiness, and wider hopes.

The self-surrender in which the infinite life is born may be made
easier to some men by belief in an all-wise God to whom submission
is a duty. But it is not in its essence dependent upon this belief or
upon any other. The religions of the past, it is true, ahve all depended to a greater or less degree upon dogma, upon some theory as
to the nature and the purpose of the universe. But the decay of
traditional beliefs has made every religion that rests on dogma precarious, and even impossible, to many whose nature is strongly
religious. Hence those who cannot acept the creeds of the past, and
yet believe that a religious outlook requires dogma, lose what is
infinite in life, and become limited in their thoughts to everyday
matters; they lose consciousness of the life of the whole, they lose
that inexplicable sense of union which gives rise to compassion and
the unhesitating service of humanity. They do not see in beauty the

adumbration of a glory which a richer vision would see in every common thing, or in love a gateway to that transfigured world in which our union with the universe is fulfilled. Thus their outlook is impoverished, and their life is rendered smaller even in its finite parts. For right action they are thrown back upon bare morality; and bare morality is very inadequate as a motive for those who hunger and thirst after the infinite. Thus it has become a matter of the first importance to preserve religion without any dependence upon dogmas to which an intellectually honest assent grows daily more difficult.

There are in Christianity three elements which it is desirable to preserve if possible: worship, acquiescence, and love. Worship is given by Christianity to God; love is enjoined toward my neighbors, my enemies, and, in fact, toward all men. The love which Christianity enjoins, and indeed any love which is to be universal and yet strong, seems in some way dependent upon worship and acquiescence. Yet these, in the form in which they appear in Christianity, depend upon belief in God, and are therefore no longer possible to those who cannot entertain this belief. Something, in worship, must be lost when we lose belief in the existence of supreme goodness and power combined. But much can be preserved, and what can be preserved seems sufficient to constitute a very strong religious life. Acquiesence, also, is rendered more difficult by loss of belief in God, since it takes away the assurance that apparent evil in the constitution of the world is really good. But it is not rendered impossible; and in consequence of its greater difficulty it becomes, when achieved, nobler, deeper, more filled by self-surrender than any acquiesence which Christianity produces. In some ways, therefore, the religion which has no dogma is greater and more religious than one which rests upon the belief that in the end our ideals are fulfilled in the outer world.

WORSHIP

Worship is not easily defined, because it grows and changes as the worshipper grows. In crude religions it may be inspired by fear alone, and given to whatever is powerful. This element lingers in the worship of God, which may consist largely of fear and be given largely from respect for power. But the element of fear tends more and more to be banished by love, and in all the best worship fear is wholly absent. As soon as the worship inspired by fear has been surpassed, worship brings joy in the contemplation of what is worshipped. But joy alone does not constitute worship: there must be also some reverence and sense of mystery not easy to define. These three things, contemplation with joy, reverence, and sense of mystery, seem essential to constitute any of the higher forms of worship.

Within worship in this very wide sense there are varieties which it is important to distinguish. There is a selective worship, which demands that its object shall be good, and admits an opposite attitude toward a bad object; and there is an impartial worship, which can be given to whatever exists, regardless of its goodness or badness. Besides this division, there is another, equally important. There is a worship which can only be given to an actually existing object, and another worship which can be given to what merely has its place in the world of ideals; these two kinds may be distinguished as worship of the actual and worship of the ideal. The two are combined in worship of God, since God is conceived as both actual and the complete embodiment of the ideal.

Worship of God is selective, since it depends upon God's goodness. So is all worship of great men or great deeds, and of everything of which the worship depends upon some preeminent quality which calls forth our admiration. Worship of this sort, though it can be given to much of what exists in the actual world, cannot be given unreservedly and so as to produce a religious attitude toward the universe as a whole, except by those who believe in an omnipotent Creator or in a pantheistic all-pervading spiritual unity. For those in whom there is no such belief, the selective worship finds its full object only in the ideal good which creative contemplation imagines. The ideal good forms an essential part of the religious life, since it supplies the motive to action by giving content to the desire for universal good which forms a part of universal love. Without the knowledge and worship of the ideal good, the love of man is blind, not knowing in what direction to seek the welfare of those whom it loves. Every embodiment of good in the actual world is imperfect, if only by its brevity. Only the ideal good can satisfy fully our hunger for perfection. Only the ideal good demands no surrender to power, no sacrifice of aspiration to possibility, and no slavery of thought to fact. Only the vision of the ideal good gives infinity to our pursuit, in action, of those fragments of good which the world permits us to create, but the worship of the ideal good, though it brings with it the joy that springs from the contemplation of what is perfect, brings with it also the pain that results from the imperfection of the actual world. When this worship stands alone, it produces a sense of exile in a world of shadows, of infinite solitude amid alien forces. Thus this worship, though necessary to all religious action, does not alone suffice, since it does not produce that sense of union with the actual world which compels us to descend from the world of contemplation and seek, with however little success, to realize what is possible of the good here on earth.

For this purpose we need the kind of worship which is only given to what exists. Such worship, where there is belief in God, can be selective, since God exists and is completely good. Where there is not belief in God, such worship may be selective in regard to great men and great deeds, but toward such objects selective worship is always hampered by their imperfection and their limitation of duration and extent. The worship which can be given to whatever exists must not be selective, it must not involve any judgment as to the goodness of what is worshipped, but must be a direct impartial emotion. Such a worship is given by the contemplative vision, which finds mystery and joy in all that exists, and brings with it love to all that has life. This impartial worship has been thought, wrongly, to require belief in God, since it has been thought to involve the judgment that whatever exists is good. In fact, however, it involves no judgment whatever; hence it cannot be intellectually mistaken, and cannot be in any way dependent upon dogma. Thus the combination of this worship with the ideal good gives a faith wholly independent of beliefs as to the nature of the actual world, and therefore not assailable by the arguments which have destroyed the tenets of traditional religion.

Religion, therefore, results from the combination of two different kinds of worship—the selective, which is given to the good on account of its goodness, and the impartial, which is given to everything that exists. The former is the source of the belief in theism, the latter of the belief in pantheism, but in neither case is such a belief necessary for the worship which gives rise to it. The object of the selective worship is the ideal good, which belongs to the world of universals. Owing to oblivion of the world of universals, men have supposed that the ideal good could not have being or be worshipped unless it formed part of the actual world; hence they have believed that without God this worship could not survive. But the study of the world of universals shows that this was an error: the object of this worship need not exist, though it will be an essential part of the worship to wish it to exist as fully as possible. The object of the impartial worship, on the other hand, is whatever exists; in this case, though the object is known to exist, it is not known to be good, but it is an essential part of the worship to wish that it may be as good as possible. Pantheism, from the contemplative joy of impartial worship, and from the unity of its outlook on the universe, infers, mistakenly, that such worship involves the belief that the universe is good and is one. This belief is no more necessary to the impartial worship than the belief in God is to the selective worship. The two worships subsist side by side, without any dogma: the one involving the goodness but not the existence of its object, the other involving the existence but not the goodness of its object. Religious action is a continual endeavor to bridge the gulf between the objects of these two worships, by making more good exist and more of existence good. Only in the complete union of the two could the soul find permanent rest.

ACQUIESCENCE

Although, in a world where much evil exists and much good does not exist, no religion which is true can give permanent rest or free the soul from the need for action, yet religion can give acquiesence in evil which it is not within our power to cure. Christianity effects this by the belief that, since the apparent evil is in accordance with the will of God, it cannot really be evil. This view, however, demands a falsification of our standard of good and evil, since much that exists is evil to any unbiased consideration. Moreover, if pursued to a conclusion, it destroys all motive to action, since the reason given for acquiesence, namely, that whatever happens must be for the best, is a reason which renders our efforts after the best superfluous. If, to avoid this consequence, we limit either the omnipotence or the goodness of God, acquiesence can no longer be urged on the same ground, since what happens may be either not in accordance with the will of God, or not good in spite of being in accordance with His will. For these reasons, though Christianity is in fact often effective both in causing acquiesence and in providing a religious motive for action, yet this effectiveness is due to a confusion of thought, and tends to cease as men grow more clear-sighted.

The problem we have to deal with is more difficult than the Christian's problem. We have to learn to acquiesce in the inevitable without judging that the inevitable must be good, to keep the feeling which prompts Christians to say;, "Thy will be done," while yet admitting that what is done may be evil.

Acquiescence, whatever our religion may be, must always require a large element of moral discipline. But this discipline may be made easier, and more visibly worth the pain which it involves, by religious considerations. There are two different though closely related kinds of acquiescence, the one in our private griefs, the other in the fundamental evils of the world. Acquiescence in our private griefs comes in the moment of submission which brings about the birth of the impartial will. Our private life, when it absorbs our thoughts and wishes, becomes a prison, from which, in times of grief, there is no escape but by submission. By submission our thoughts are freed, and our will is led to new aims which, before, had been hidden by the personal goods which had been uselessly desired. A large contemplation, or the growth of universal love, will produce a certain shame of absorption in our own life; hence the will is led away from protest against the inevitable, toward the pursuit of more general goods which are not wholly unattainable. Thus acquiescence in private griefs is an essential element in the growth of universal love and the impartial will.

Acquiescence does not consist in judging that things are not bad when in fact they are so. It consists in freedom from anger and indignation and preoccupied regret. Anger and indignation against those who cause our griefs will not be felt if universal love is strong; preoccupied regret will be avoided where the desire of contemplative freedom exists. The man to whom a large contemplation has become habitual will not readily allow himself to be turned aside from the thoughts which give breadth to his life: in the absence of such thoughts he will feel something small and unworthy, a bondage of the infinite to the finite. In this way both contemplation and and universal love will promote acquiescence so far as our own sorrows are concerned.

It is possible, however, to emerge from private protest, not into complete acquiescence, but into a Promethean indignation against the universe. Contemplation may only universalize our griefs; it may show us all life as a tragedy, so full of pain as to make us wish that consciousness could vanish wholly from the world. The belief that this would be desirable if it were possible is one which cannot be refuted, though it also cannot be shown to be true. But even this belief is not incompatible with acquiescence. What is incompatible is indignation, and a preoccupation with evils which makes goods invisible or only partially visible. Indignation seems scarcely possible in regard to evils for which no one is responsible; those who feel indignation in regard to the fundamental evils of the universe feel it against God or the Devil or an imaginatively personified Fate. When it is realized that the fundamental evils are due to the blind empire of matter, and are the wholly necessary effects of forces which have no consciousness and are therefore neither good nor bad in themselves, indignation becomes absurd, the Xerxes chastising the Hellespont. Thus the realization of necessity is the liberation from indignation. This alone, however, will not prevent an undue preoccupation with evil. It is obvious that some things that exist are good, some bad, and we have no means of knowing whether the good or the bad preponderate. In action, it is essential to have knowledge of good and evil; thus in all the matters subject to our will, the question what is good and what bad must be borne in mind. But in matters which lie outside our power, the question of good or bad, though knowledge about it, like all knowledge, is worth acquiring, has not that fundamental religious importance which has been assigned to it in discussions of theism and optimism. The dualism of good and bad, when it is too strongly present to our minds, prevents impartial contemplation and interferes with universal love and worship. There is, in fact, something finite and unduly human about the practice of emphasizing good and bad in regard to matters with which action is not concerned. Thus acquiescence in fundamental evils, like acquiescence in personal griefs, is furthered by the impartiality of contemplation and universal love and worship, and must already exist to some extent before these become possible. Acquiescence is at once a cause and an effect of faith, in much the same way when faith dispenses with dogma as when it rests upon a belief in God. In so far as acquiescence is a cause of faith, it rests upon moral discipline, a suppression of self and its demands, which is necessary to any life in harmony with the universe, and to any emergence from the finite into the infinite. This discipline is more severe in the absence of all optimistic dogma, but in proportion as it is more severe its outcome is greater, more unshakable, more capable of so enlarging the bounds of self as to make it welcome with love whatever of good or evil may come before it.

LOVE

Love is of two kinds: the selective earthly love, which is given to what is delightful, beautiful, or good, and the impartial heavenly love, which is given to all indifferently. The earthly love is balanced by an opposing hatred: to friends are opposed foes; to saints, sinners; to God, the Devil. Thus this love introduces disunion into the world, with hostile camps and a doubtful warfare. But the heavenly love does not demand that its object shall be delightful, beautiful, or good; it can be given to everything that has life, to the best and the worst, to the greatest and to the least. It is not merely compassion, since it does not merely wish to relieve misfortune, but finds joy in what it loves, and is given to the fortunate as well as to the unfortunate. Though it includes benevolence, it is greater than benevolence: it is contemplative as well as active, and can be given where there is no possibility of benefiting the object. It is love, contemplative in origin, but becoming active wherever action is possible; and it is a kind of love to which there is no opposing hatred.

To the divine love, the division of the world into good and bad, though it remains true, seems lacking in depth; it seems finite and limited in comparison with the boundlessness of love. The division into two hostile camps seems unreal; what is felt to be real is the oneness of the world in love.

It is the birth of divine love that the life of feeling begins for the universal soul. What contemplation is to the intellect of the universal soul, divine love is to its emotions. More than anything else, divine love frees the soul from its prison and breaks down the walls of self that prevent its union with the world. Where it is strong, duties become easy, and all service is filled with joy. Sorrow, it is true, remains, perhaps deeper and wider than before, since the lives of most human beings are largely tragic. But the bitterness of personal defeat is avoided, and aims become so wide that no complete overthrow of all hope is possible. The loves of the natural life survive, but harmonized with universal love, and no longer setting up walls of division between the loved and the unloved. And above all, through the bond of universal love the soul escapes from the separate loneliness in which it is born, and from which no permanent deliverance is possible while it remains within the walls of its prison.

Christianity enjoins love of God and love of man as the two great commandments. Love of God differs, however, from love of man, since we cannot benefit God, while we cannot regard man as wholly good. Thus love of God is more contemplative and full of worship, while love of man is more active and full of service. In a religion which is not theistic, love of God is replaced by worship of the ideal good. As in Christianity, this worship is quite as necessary as love of man, since without it love of man is left without guidance in its wish to create the good in human lives. The worship of good is indeed the greater of the two commandments, since it leads us to know that love of man is good, and this knowledge helps us to feel the love of man. Moreover, it makes us conscious of what human life might be, and of the gulf between what it might be and what it is; hence springs an infinite compassion, which is a large part of love of man, and is apt to cause the whole. Acquiescence, also, greatly furthers love of man, since in its absence anger and indignation and strife come between the soul and the world, preventing the union in which love of man has its birth. The three elements of religion, namely worship, acquiescence, and love, are intimately interconnected; each helps to produce the others, and all three together form a unity in which it is impossible to say which comes first, which last. All three can exist without dogma, in a form which is capable of dominating life and of giving infinity to action and thought and feeling; and life in the infinite, which is the combination of the three, contains all that is essential to religion, in spite of its absence of dogmatic beliefs.

Religion derives its power from the sense of union with the universe which it is able to give. Formerly, union was achieved by assimiliating the universe to our own conception of the good; union with God was easy since God was love. But the decay of traditional belief has made this way of union no longer one which can be relied upon: we must find a mode of union which asks nothing of the world and depends only upon ourselves. Such a mode of union is possible through impartial worship and universal love, which ignore the difference of good and bad and are given to all alike. In order to free religion from all dependence upon dogma, it is necessary to abstain from any demand that the world shall conform to our standards. Every such demand is an endeavor to impose self upon the world. From this endeavor the religion which can survive the decay of dogma must be freed. And in being freed from this endeavor, religion is freed from an element extraneous to its spirit and not compatible with its unhampered development. Religion seeks union with the universe by subordination of the demands of self; but this subordination is not complete if it depends upon a belief that the universe satisfies some at least of the demands of self. Hence for the sake of religion itself, as well as because such a belief appears unfounded, it is important to discover a form of union with the universe which is independent of all beliefs as to the nature of the universe. By life in the infinite, such a form of union is rendered possible; and to those who achieve it, it gives nearly all, and in some ways more than all, that has been given by the religions of the past.

The essence of religion, then, lies in subordination of the finite part of our life to the infinite part. Of the two natures in man, the particular or animal being lives in instinct, and seeks the welfare of the body and its descendants, while the universal or divine being seeks union with the universe, and desires freedom from all that impedes its seeking. The animal being is neither good nor bad in itself; it is good or bad solely as it helps or hinders the divine being in its search for union with the world. In union with the world the soul finds its freedom. There are three kinds of union: union in thought, union in feeling, union in will. Union in thought is knowledge, union in feeling is love, union in will is service. There are three kinds of disunion: error, hatred, and strife. What promotes disunion is insistent instinct, which is of the animal part of man: what promotes union is the combination of knowledge, love, and consequent service which is wisdom, the supreme good of man.

The life of instinct views the world as a means for the ends of instinct; thus it makes the world of less account than self. It confines knowledge to what is useful, love to allies in conflict of rival instinct, service to those with whom there is some instinctive tie. The world in which it finds a home is a narrow world, surrounded by alien and probably hostile forces; it is prisoned in a beleaguered fortress, knowing that ultimate surrender is inevitable.

The life of wisdom seeks an impartial end, in which there is no rivalry, no essential enmity. The union which it seeks has no boundaries: it wishes to know all, to love all, and to serve all. Thus it finds its home everywhere: no lines of circumvallation bar its progress. In knowledge it makes no division of useful and useless, in love it makes no division of friend and foe, in service it makes no division of deserving and undeserving.

The animal part of man, knowing that the individual life is brief and impotent, is appalled by the fact of death, and, unwilling to admit the hopelessness of the struggle, it postulates a prolongation in which its failures shall be turned into triumphs. The divine part of man, feeling the individual to be but of small account, thinks little of death, and finds its hopes independent of personal continuance.

The animal part of man, being filled with the importance of its own desires, finds it intolerable to suppose that the universe is less aware of this importance; a blank indifference to its hopes and fears is too painful to contemplate, and is therefore not regarded as admissible. The divine part of man does not demand that the world shall conform to a pattern: it accepts the world, and finds in wisdom a union which demands nothing of the world. Its energy is not checked by what seems hostile, but interpenetrates it and becomes one with it. It is not the strength of our ideals, but their weakness, that makes us dread the admission that they are ours, not the world's. We with our ideals must stand alone, and conquer, inwardly, the world's indifference. It is instinct, not wisdom, that finds this difficult and shivers at the solitude it seems to entail. Wisdom does not feel this solitude, because it can achieve union even with what seems most alien. The insistent demand that our ideals shall be readily realized in the world is the last prison from which wisdom must be freed. Every demand is a prison, and wisdom is only free when it asks nothing.

8

Religion and the Churches

Almost all the changes which the world has undergone since the end of the Middle Ages are due to the discovery and diffusion of new knowledge. This was the primary cause of the Renaissance, the Reformation, and the Industrial Revolution. It was also, very directly, the cause of the decay of dogmatic religion. The study of classical texts and early Church history, Copernican astronomy and physics, Darwinian biology and comparative anthropology have each in turn battered down some part of the edifice of Catholic dogma, until, for almost all thinking and instructed people, the most that seems defensible is some inner spirit, some vague hope, and some not very definite feeling of moral obligation. The result might perhaps have remained limited to the educated minority, but for the fact that the Churches have almost everywhere opposed political progress with the same bitterness with which they have opposed progress in thought. Political conservatism has brought the Churches into conflict with whatever was vigorous in the working classes, and has spread free thought in wide circles which might otherwise have remained orthodox for centuries. The decay of dogmatic religion is, for good or evil, one of the most important facts in the modern world. Its effects have hardly yet begun to show themselves: what they will be it is impossible to say, but they will certainly be profound and far-reaching.

Religion is partly personal, partly social: to the Protestant primarily personal, to the Catholic primarily social. It is only when

From *Unpopular Review* 5 (April 1916): 392-409.

the two elements are intimately blended that religion becomes a powerful force in molding society. The Catholic Church, as it existed from the time of Constantine to the time of the Reformation, represented a blending which would have seemed incredible if it had not been actually achieved, the blending of Christ and Caesar, of the morality of humble submission with the pride of Imperial Rome. Those who loved the one could find it in the Thebaid; those who loved the other could admire it in the pomp of metropolitan archbishops. In St. Francis and Innocent III the same two sides of the Church are still represented. But since the Reformation personal religion has been increasingly outside the Catholic Church, while the religion which has remained Catholic has been increasingly a matter of institutions and politics and historic continuity. This division has weakened the force of religion: religious bodies have not been strengthened by the enthusiasm and single-mindedness of the men in whom personal religion is strong, and these men have not found their teaching diffused and made permanent by the power of ecclesiastical institutions.

The Catholic Church achieved, during the Middle Ages, the most organic society and the most harmonious inner synthesis of instinct, mind, and spirit, that the Western world has ever known. St. Francis, Thomas Aquinas, and Dante represent its summit as regards individual development. The cathedrals, the mendicant orders, and the triumph of the papacy over the empire represent its supreme political success. But the perfection which had been achieved was a narrow perfection: instinct, mind, and spirit all suffered from curtailment in order to fit into the pattern; laymen found themselves subject to the Church in ways which they resented, and the Church used its power for rapacity and oppression. The perfect synthesis was an enemy to new growth, and after the time of Dante all that was living in the world had first to fight for its right to live against the representatives of the old order. This fight is even now not ended. Only when it is quite ended, both in the external world of politics and in the internal world of men's own thoughts will it be possible for a new organic society and a new inner synthesis to take the place which the Church held for a thousand years.

The clerical profession suffers from two causes, one of which it shares with some other professions, while the other is peculiar to itself. The cause peculiar to it is the convention that clergymen are more virtuous than other men. Any average selection of mankind, set apart and told that it excels the rest in virtue, must tend to sink below the average. This is an ancient commonplace in regard to princes and those who used to be called "the great." But it is no less true as regards those of the clergy who are not genuinely and by nature as much better than the average as they are conventionally supposed to be. The other source of harm to the clerical profession is endowments. Property which is only available for those who will support an established institution has a tendency to warp men's judgments as to the excellence of the institution. The tendency is aggravated when the property is associated with social consideration and opportunities for petty power. It is at its worst when the institution is tied by law to an ancient creed, almost impossible to change, and yet quite out of touch with the unfettered thought of the present day. All these causes combine to damage the moral force of the Church.

It is not so much that the creed of the Church is the wrong one. What is amiss is the mere existence of a creed. As soon as income, position, and power are dependent upon acceptance of no matter what creed, intellectual honesty is imperilled. Men will tell themselves that a formal assent is justified by the good which it will enable them to do. They fail to realize that, in those whose mental life has any vigor, loss of complete intellectual integrity puts an end to the power of doing good, by producing gradually in all directions an inability to see truth simply. The strictness of party discipline has introduced the same evil in politics; there, because the evil is comparatively new, it is visible to many who think it unimportant as regards the Church. But the evil is greater as regards the Church, because religion is of more importance than politics, and because it is more necessary that the exponents of religion should be wholly free from taint.

The evils we have been considering seem inseparable from the existence of a professional priesthood. If religion is not to be harmful in a world of rapid change, it must, like the Society of Friends, be carried on by men who have other occupations during the week, who do their religious work from enthusiasm, without receiving any payment. And such men, because they know the everyday world, are not likely to fall into a remote morality which no one regards as applicable to common life. Being free, they will not be bound to reach certain conclusions decided in advance, but will be able to consider moral and religious questions genuinely, without bias. Except in a quite stationary society, no religious life can be living or a real support to the spirit unless it is freed from the incubus of a professional priesthood.

It is largely for these reasons that so little of what is valuable in morals and religion comes nowadays from the men who are eminent in the religious world. It is true that among professed believers there are many who are wholly sincere, who feel still the inspiration which Christianity brought before it had been weakened by the progress of knowledge. These sincere believers are valuable to the world because they keep alive the conviction that the life of the spirit is what is of most importance to men and women. Some of them, in all the countries now at war, have had the courage to preach peace and love in the name of Christ, and have done what lay in their power to mitigate the bitterness of hatred. All praise is due to these men, and without them the world would be even worse than it is.

But it is not through even the most sincere and courageous believers in the traditional religion that a new spirit can come into the world. It is not through them that religion can be brought back to those who have lost it because their minds were active, not because their spirit was dead. Believers in the traditional religion necessarily look to the past for inspiration rather than to the future. They seek wisdom in the teaching of Christ, which, admirable as it is, remains quite inadequate for many of the social and spiritual issues of modern life. Art and intellect and all the problems of government are ignored in the Gospels. Those who, like Tolstoy, endeavor seriously to take the Gospels as a guide to life are compelled to regard the ignorant peasant as the best type of man, and to brush aside political questions by an extreme and impracticable anarchism.

If a religious view of life and the world is ever to reconquer the thoughts and feelings of free-minded men and women, much that we are accustomed to associate with religion will have to be discarded. The first and greatest change that is required to establish a morality of initiative, not a morality of submission, a morality of hope rather than fear, of things to be done rather than of things to be left undone. It is not the whole duty of man to slip through the world so as to escape the wrath of God. The world is *our* world, and it rests with us to make it a heaven or a hell. The power is ours, and the kingdom and the glory would be ours also if we had courage and insight to create them. The religious life that we must seek will not be one of occasional solemnity and superstitious prohibitions, it will not be sad or ascetic, it will concern itself little with rules of conduct. It will be inspired by a vision of what human life may be, and will be happy with the joy of creation, living in a large free world of initiative and hope. It will love mankind, not for what they are to the outward eye, but for what imagination shows that they have it in them to become. It will not readily condemn, but it will give praise to positive achievement rather than negative sinlessness, to the joy of life, the quick affection, the creative insight, by which the world may grow young and beautiful and filled with vigor.

"Religion" is a word which has many meanings and a long history. In origin, it was concerned with certain rites, inherited from a remote past, performed originally for some reason long since forgotten, and associated from time to time with various myths to account for their supposed importance. Much of this lingers still. A religious man is one who goes to church, a communicant, one who "practices," as Catholics say. How he behaves otherwise, or how he feels concerning life and man's place in the world, does not bear upon the question whether he is "religious" in this simple but historically correct sense. Many men and women are religious in this sense without having in their natures anything that deserves to be called religion in the sense in which I mean the word. The mere familiarity of the Church service has made them impervious to it; they are unconscious of all the history and human experience by which the liturgy has been enriched, and unmoved by the glibly repeated words of the Gospel, which condemn almost all the activities of those who fancy themselves disciples of Christ. This fate must overtake any habitual rite: it is impossible that it should continue to produce much effect after it has been performed so often as to grow mechanical.

The activities of men may be roughly derived from three sources, not in actual fact sharply separate one from another, but sufficiently distinguishable to deserve different names. The three sources I mean are instinct, mind, and spirit, and of these three it is the life of the spirit that makes religion.

The life of instinct includes all that man shares with the lower animals, all that is concerned with self-preservation and reproduction and the desires and impulses derivative from these. It includes vanity and love of possessions, love of family, and even much of what makes love of country. It includes all the impulses that are essentially concerned with the biological success of oneself or one's group—for among gregarious animals the life of instinct includes the group. The impulses which it includes may not in fact make for success, and may often in fact militate against it but are nevertheless those of which success is the *raison d'être,* those which express the animal nature of man and his position among a world of competitors.

The life of the mind is the life of pursuit of knowledge, from mere childish curiosity up to the greatest efforts of thought. Curiosity exists in animals, and serves an obvious biological purpose; but it is only in men that it passes beyond the investigation of particular objects which may be edible or poisonous, friendly or hostile. Curiosity is the primary impulse out of which the whole edifice of scientific knowledge has grown. Knowledge has been found so useful that most actual acquisition of it is no longer prompted by curiosity; innumerable other motives now contribute to foster the intellectual life. Nevertheless, direct love of knowledge and dislike of error still play a very large part, especially with those who are most successful in learning. No man acquires much knowledge unless the acquisition is in itself delightful to him, apart from any consciousness of the use to which the knowledge may be put. The impulse to acquire knowledge and the activities which center round it constitute what I mean by the life of the mind. The life of the mind consists of thought which is wholly or partially impersonal, in the sense that it concerns itself with objects on their own account, and not merely on account of their bearing upon our instinctive life.

The life of the spirit centers round impersonal feeling, as the life of the mind centers round impersonal thought. In this sense, all art belongs to the life of the spirit, though its greatness is derived from its being also intimately bound up with the life of instinct. Art starts from instinct and rises into the region of the spirit; religion starts from the spirit and endeavors to dominate and inform the life of instinct. It is possible to feel the same interest in the joys and sorrows of others as in our own, to love and hate independently of all relation to ourselves, to care about the destiny of man and the development of the universe without a thought that we are personally involved. Reverence and worship, the sense of an obligation to mankind, the feeling of imperativeness and acting under orders which traditional religion has interpreted as Divine inspiration, all belong to the life of the spirit. And deeper than all these lies the sense of a mystery half revealed, of a hidden wisdom and glory, of a transfiguring vision in which common things lose their solid importance and become a thin veil behind which the ultimate truth of the world is dimly seen. It is such feelings that are the source of religion, and if they were to die most of what is best would vanish out of life.

Instinct, mind, and spirit are all essential to a full life; each has its own excellence and its own corruption. Each can attain a spurious excellence at the expense of the others; each has a tendency to encroach upon the others; but in the life which is to be sought all three will be developed in coordination, and intimately blended in a single harmonious whole. Among uncivilized men instinct is supreme, and mind and spirit hardly exist. Among educated men at the present day mind is developed, as a rule, at the expense of both instinct and spirit, producing a curious inhumanity and lifelessness, a paucity of both personal and impersonal desires, which leads to cynicism and intellectual destructiveness. Among ascetics and most of those who would be called saints, the life of the spirit has been developed at the expense of instinct and mind, producing an outlook which is impossible to those who have a healthy animal life and to those who have a love of active thought. It is not in any case of these one-sided developments that we can find wisdom or a philosophy which will bring new life to the civilized world.

Among civilized men and women at the present day it is rare to find instinct, mind, and spirit in harmony. Very few have achieved a practical philosophy which gives its due place to each; as a rule, instinct is at war with either mind or spirit, and mind and spirit are at war with each other. This strife compels men and women to direct much of their energy inwards, instead of being able to expend it all in objective activities. When a man achieves a precarious inward peace by the defeat of a part of his nature, his vital force is impaired, and his growth is no longer quite healthy. If men are to remain whole, it is very necessary that they should achieve a reconciliation of instinct, mind, and spirit.

Instinct is the source of vitality, the bond that unites the life of the individual with the life of the race, the basis of all profound sense of union with others, and the means by which the collective life nourishes the life of the separate units. But instinct by itself leaves us powerless to control the forces of Nature, either in ourselves or in our physical environment, and keeps us in bondage to the same unthinking impulse by which the trees grow. Mind can liberate us from this bondage, by the power of impersonal thought, which enables us to judge critically the purely biological purposes toward which instinct more or less blindly tends. But mind, in its dealings with instinct, is *merely* critical: so far as instinct is concerned, the unchecked activity of the mind is apt to be destructive and to generate cynicism. Spirit is an antidote to the cynicism of mind: it universalizes the emotions that spring from instinct, and by universalizing them makes them impervious to mental criticism. And when thought is informed by spirit it loses its cruel, destructive quality; it no longer promotes the death of instinct, but only its purification from insistence and ruthlessness and its emancipation from the prison walls of accidental circumstance. It is instinct that gives force, mind that gives the means of directing force to desired ends, and spirit that suggests impersonal uses for force of a kind that thought cannot discredit by criticism. This is an outline of the parts that instinct, mind, and spirit would play in a harmonius life.

Instinct, mind, and spirit are each a help to the others when their development is free and unvitiated; but when corruption comes into any one of the three, not only does that one fail, but the others also become poisoned. All three must grow together. And if they are to grow to their full stature in any one man or woman, that man or woman must not be isolated, but must be one of a society where growth is not thwarted and made crooked.

The life of instinct, when it is unchecked by mind or spirit, consists of instinctive cycles, which begin with impulses to more or less definite acts, and pass on to satisfaction of needs through the consequences of these impulsive acts. Impulse and desire are not directed towards the whole cycle, but only towards its initiation: the rest is left to natural causes. We desire to eat, but we do not desire to be nourished unless we are valetudinarians. Yet without the nourishment eating is a mere momentary pleasure, not part of the general impulse to life. Men desire sexual intercourse, but they do not as a rule desire children strongly or often. Yet without the hope of children and its occasional realization, sexual intercourse remains for most people an isolated and separate pleasure, not uniting their personal life with the life of mankind, not continuous with the central purposes by which they live, and not capable of bringing that profound sense of fulfilment which comes from completion by children. Most men, unless the impulse is atrophied through disuse, feel a desire to create something, great or small according to their capacities. Some few are able to satisfy this desire: some happy men can create an empire, a science, a poem, or a picture. The men of science, who have less difficulty than any others in finding an outlet for creativeness, are the happiest of intelligent men in the modern world, since their creative activity affords full satisfaction to mind and spirit as well as to the instinct of creation.[1] In them a beginning is to be seen of the new way of life which is to be sought; in their happiness we may perhaps find the germ of a future happiness for all mankind. The rest, with few exceptions, are thwarted in their creative impulses. They cannot build their own house or make their own garden, or direct their own labor to producing what their free choice would lead them to produce. In this way the instinct of creation, which should lead on to the life of mind and spirit, is checked and turned aside. Too often it is turned to destruction, as the only effective action which remains possible. Out of its defeat grows envy, and out of envy grows the impulse to destroy the creativeness of more fortunate men. This is one of the greatest sources of corruption in the life of instinct.

The life of instinct is important, not only on its own account, or because of the direct usefulness of the actions which it inspires, but also because, if it is unsatisfactory, the individual life becomes detached and separated from the general life of man. All really profound sense of unity with others depends upon instinct, upon cooperation or agreement in some instinctive purpose. This is most obvious in the relations of men and women and parents and children. But it is true also in wider relations. It is true of large assemblies swayed by a strong common emotion, and even of a whole nation in times of stress. It is part of what makes the value of religion as a social institution. Where this feeling is wholly absent, other human beings seem distant and aloof. Where it is actively thwarted, other human beings become objects of instinctive hostility. The aloofness or the instinctive hostility may be masked by religious love, which can be given to all men regardless of their relation to ourselves. But religious love does not bridge the gulf that parts man from man: it looks across the gulf, it views others with compassion or impersonal symapthy, but it does not live with the same life with which they live. Instinct alone can do this, but only when it is fruitful and sane and direct. To this end it is necessary that instinctive cycles should be fairly often completed, not interrupted in the middle of their course. At present they are constantly interrupted, partly by purposes which conflict with them for economic or other reasons, partly by the pursuit of pleasure, which picks out the most agreeable part of the cycle and avoids the rest. In this way instinct is robbed of its importance and seriousness; it becomes incapable of bringing any real fulfilment, its demands grow more and more excessive, and life becomes no longer a whole with a single movement, but a series of detached moments, some of them pleasurable, most of them full of weariness and discouragement.

The life of the mind, although supremely excellent in itself, cannot bring health into the life of instinct, except when it results in a not too difficult outlet for the instinct of creation. In other cases it is, as a rule, too widely separated from instinct, too detached, too destitute of inward growth, to afford either a vehicle for instinct or a means of subtilizing and refining it. Thought is in its essence impersonal and detached, instinct is in its essence personal and tied to particular circumstances: between the two, unless both reach a high level, there is a war which is not easily appeased. This is the fundamental reason for vitalism, futurism, pragmatism, and the various other philosophies which advertise themselves as vigorous and virile. All these represent the attempt to find a mode of thought which shall not be hostile to instinct. The attempt, in itself, is deserving of praise, but the solution offered is far too facile. What is proposed amounts to a subordination of thought to instinct, a refusal to allow thought to achieve its own ideal. Thought which does not rise above what is personal is not thought in any true sense: it is merely a more or less intelligent use of instinct. It is thought and spirit that raise man above the level of the brutes. By discarding them we may lose the proper excellence of men, but cannot acquire the excellence of animals. Thought must achieve its full growth before a reconciliation with instinct is attempted.

When refined thought and unrefined instinct coexist, as they do in many intellectual men, the result is a complete disbelief in any important good to be achieved by the help of instinct. According to their disposition, some such men will as far as possible discard instinct and become ascetic, while others will accept it as a necessity, leaving it degraded and separated from all that is really important in their lives. Either of these courses prevents instinct from remaining vital, or from being a bond with others; either produces a sense of physical solitude, a gulf across which the minds and spirits of others may speak, but not their instincts. To very many men, the instinct of patriotism, when the war broke out, was the first instinct that had bridged the gulf, the first that had made them feel a really profound unity with others. This instinct, just because, in its intense form, it was new and unfamiliar, had remained uninfected by thought, not paralyzed or devitalized by doubt and cold detachment. The sense of unity which it brought is capable of being brought by the instinctive life of more normal times, if thought and spirit are not hostile to it. And so long as this sense of unity is absent, instinct and spirit cannot be in harmony, nor can the life of the community have vigor and the seeds of new growth.

The life of the mind, because of its detachment, tends to separate a man inwardly from other men, so long as it is not balanced by the life of the spirit. For this reason, mind without spirit can render instinct corrupt or atrophied, but cannot add any excellence to the life of instinct. On this ground, some men are hostile to thought. But no good purpose is served by trying to prevent the growth of thought, which has its own insistence, and if checked in the directions in which it tends naturally, will turn into other directions where it is more harmful. And thought is in itself God-like: if the opposition between thought and instinct were irreconcilable, it would be thought that ought to conquer. But the opposition is not irreconcilable: all that is necessary is that both thought and instinct should be informed by the life of the spirit.

In order that human life should have vigor, it is necessary for the instinctive impulses to be strong and direct; but in order that human life should be good, these impulses must be dominated and controlled by desires less personal and ruthless, less liable to lead to conflict than those that are inspired by instinct alone. Something impersonal and universal is needed over and above what springs out of the principle of individual growth. It is this that is given by the life of the spirit.

Patriotism affords an example of the kind of control which is needed. Patriotism is compounded out of a number of instinctive feelings and impulses: love of home, love of those whose ways and outlook resemble our own, the impulse to cooperation in a group, the sense of pride in the achievements of one's group. All these impulses and desires, like everything belonging to the life of instinct, are personal, in the sense that the feelings and actions which they inspire towards others are determined by the relation of those others to ourselves, not by what those others are intrinsically. All these impulses and desires unite to produce a love of a man's own country which is more deeply implanted in the fibre of his being, and more closely united to his vital force, than any love not rooted in instinct. But if spirit does not enter in to generalize love of country, the exclusiveness of instinctive love makes it a source of hatred of other countries. What spirit can effect is to make us realize that other countries equally are worthy of love, that the vital warmth which makes us love our own country reveals to us that it deserves to be loved, and that only the poverty of our nature prevents us from loving all countries as we love our own. In this way instinctive love can be extended in imagination, and a sense of the value of all mankind can grow up, which is more living and intense than any that is possible to those whose instinctive love is weak. Mind can only show us that it is irrational to love our own country best; it can weaken patriotism, but cannot strengthen the love of all mankind. Spirit alone can do this, by extending and universalizing the love that is born of instinct. And in doing this it checks and purifies whatever is insistent or ruthless or oppressively personal in the life of instinct.

The same extension through spirit is necessary with other instinctive loves, if they are not to be enfeebled or corrupted by thought. The love of husband and wife is capable of being a very good thing, and when men and women are sufficiently primitive, nothing but instinct and good fortune is needed to make it reach a certain limited perfection. But as thought begins to assert its right to criticize instinct the old simplicity becomes impossible. The love of husband and wife, as unchecked instinct leaves it, is too narrow and personal to stand against the shafts of satire, until it is enriched by the life of the spirit. The romantic view of marriage, which our fathers and mothers professed to believe, will not survive an imaginative peregrination down a street of suburban villas, each containing its couple, each couple having congratulated themselves as they first crossed the threshold, that here they could love in peace, without interruption from others, without contact with the cold outside world. The separateness and stuffiness, the fine names for cowardices and timid vanities, that are shut within the four walls of thousands upon thousands of little villas, present themselves coldly and mercilessly to those in whom mind is dominant at the expense of spirit.

Nothing is good in the life of a human being except the very best that his nature can achieve. As men advance, things which have been good cease to be good, merely because something better is possible. So it is with the life of instinct: for those whose mental life is strong, much that was really good while mind remained less developed has now become bad merely through the greater degree of truth in their outlook on the world. The instinctive man in love feels that his emotion is unique, that the lady of his heart has perfections such as no other woman ever equalled. The man who has acquired the power of impersonal thought realizes, when he is in love, that he is one of so many millions of men who are in love at this moment, that not more than one of all the millions can be right in thinking his love supreme, and that it is not likely that that one is oneself. He perceives that the state of being in love in those whose instinct is unaffected by thought or spirit, is a state of illusion, serving the ends of Nature and making a man a slave to the life of the species, not a willing minister to the impersonal ends which he sees to be good. Thought rejects this slavery; for no end that Nature may have in view will thought abdicate, or forgo its right to think truly. "Better the world should perish than that I or any other human being should believe a lie"—this is the religion of thought, in whose scorching flames the dross of the world is being burnt away. It is a good religion, and its work of destruction must be completed. But it is not all that man has need of. New growth must come after the destruction, and new growth can come only through the spirit.

Both patriotism and the love of man and woman, when they are merely instinctive, have the same defects: their exclusions, their enclosing walls, their indifference or hostility to the outside world. It is through this that thought is led to satire, that comedy has infected what men used to consider their holiest feelings. The satire and the comedy are justified, but not the death of instinct which they may produce if they remain in supreme command. They are justified, not as the last word of wisdom, but as the gateway of pain through which men pass to a new life, where instinct is purified and yet nourished by the deeper desires and insight of spirit.

The man who has the life of the spirit within him views the love of man and woman, both in himself and in others, quite differently from the man who is exclusively dominated by mind. He sees, in his moments of insight, that in all human beings there is something deserving of love, something mysterious, something appealing, a cry out of the night, a groping journey, and a possible victory. When his instinct loves, he welcomes its help in seeing and feeling the value of the human being whom he loves. Instinct becomes a reinforcement to spiritual insight. What instinct tells him spiritual insight confirms, however much the mind may be aware of littlenesses, limitations, and enclosing walls that prevent the spirit from shining forth. His spirit divines in all men what his instinct shows him in the object of his love.

The love of parents for children has need of the same transformation. The purely instinctive love, unchecked by thought, uninformed by spirit, is exclusive, ruthless, and unjust. No benefit to others is felt, by the purely instinctive parent, to be worth an injury to one's own children. Honor and conventional morality place certain important practical limitations on the vicarious selfishness of parents, since a civilized community exacts a certain minimum before it will give respect. But within the limits allowed by public opinion, parental affection, when it is merely instinctive, will seek the advantage of children without regard to others. Mind can weaken the impulse to injustice, and diminish the force of instinctive love, but it cannot keep the whole force of instinctive love and turn it to more universal ends. Spirit can do this. It can leave the instinctive love of children undimmed, and extend the poignant devotion of a parent, in imagination, to the whole world. And parental love itself will prompt the parent who has the life of the spirit to give to his children the sense of justice, the readiness for service, the reverence, the will that controls self-seeking, which he feels to be a greater good than any personal success.

The life of the spirit has suffered in recent times by its association with traditional religion, by its apparent hostility to the life of the mind, and by the fact that it has seemed to center in renunciation. The life of the spirit demands readiness for renunciation when the occasion arises, but is in its essence as positive and as capable of enriching individual existence as mind and instinct are. It brings with it the joy of vision, of the mystery and profundity of the world, of the contemplation of life, and above all the joy of universal love. It liberates those who have it from the prison-house of insistent personal passion and mundane cares. It gives freedom and breadth and beauty to men's thoughts and feelings, and to all their relations with others. It brings the solution of doubts, the end of the feeling that all is vanity. It restores harmony between mind and instinct, and leads the separated unit back into his place in the life of mankind. For those who have once entered the world of thought, it is only through spirit that happiness and peace can return.

NOTE

1. I should add artists, but for the fact that most modern artists seem to find much greater difficulty in creation than men of science usually find.

9

A Debate on the Existence of God
Bertrand Russell and F. C. Copleston

COPLESTON: As we are going to discuss the existence of God, it might perhaps be as well to come to some provisional agreement as to what we understand by the term "God." I presume that we mean a supreme personal being—distinct from the world and creator of the world. Would you agree—provisionally at least—to accept this statement as the meaning of the term "God"?

RUSSELL: Yes, I accept this definition.

COPLESTON: Well, my position is the affirmative position that such a being actually exists, and that His existence can be proved philosophically. Perhaps you would tell me if your position is that of agnosticism or of atheism. I mean, would you say that the non-existence of God can proved?

RUSSELL: No, I should not say that: my position is agnostic.

COPLESTON: Would you agree with me that the problem of God is a problem of great importance? For example, would you agree that if God does not exist, human beings and human history can have no other purpose than the purpose they choose to give themselves, which—in practice—is likely to mean the purpose which those impose who have the power to impose it?

This debate was a Third Programme broadcast of the British Broadcasting Corporation in 1948. Reprinted by permission of Father Copleston and the legal heirs of Lord Russell.

RUSSELL: Roughly speaking, yes, though I should have to place some limitation on your last clause.

COPLESTON: Would you agree that if there is no God—no absolute Being—there can no absolute values? I mean, would you agree that if there is no absolute good that the relativity of values results?

RUSSELL: No, I think these questions are logically distinct. Take, for instance, G. E. Moore's *Principia Ethica,* where he maintains that there is a distinction of good and evil, that both of these are definite concepts. But he does not bring in the idea of God to support that contention.

COPLESTON: Well, suppose we leave the question of good till later, till we come to the moral argument, and I give first a metaphysical argument. I'd like to put the main weight on the metaphysical argument based on Leibniz's argument from "Contingency" and then later we might discuss the moral argument. Suppose I give a brief statement on the metaphysical argument and that then we go on to discuss it?

RUSSELL: That seems to me to be a very good plan.

THE ARGUMENT FROM CONTINGENCY

COPLESTON: Well, for clarity's sake, I'll divide the argument into distinct stages. First of all, I should say, we know that there are at least some beings in the world which do not contain in themselves the reason for their existence. For example, I depend on my parents, and now on the air, and on food, and so on. Now, secondly, the world is simply the real or imagined totality or aggregate of individual objects, none of which contain in themselves alone the reason for their existence. There isn't any world distinct from the objects which form it, any more than the human race is something apart from the members. Therefore, I should say, since objects or events exist, and since no object of experience contains within itself the reason of its existence, this reason, the totality of objects, must have a reason external to itself. That reason must be an existent being. Well, this being is either itself the reason for its own existence, or it is not. If it is, well and good. If it is not, then we must proceed farther. But if we proceed to infinity in that sense, then there's no explanation of existence at all. So, I should say, in order to explain existence, we must come to a being which contains within itself the reason for its own existence, that is to say, which cannot not-exist.

RUSSELL: This raises a great many points and it is not altogether easy to know where to begin, but I think that, perhaps, in answering your argument, the best point at which to begin is the question of necessary being. The word "necessary" I should maintain, can only be applied significantly to propositions. And, in fact, only to such as are analytic—that is to say—such as it is self-contradictory to deny. I could only admit a necessary being if there were a being whose existence it is self-contradictory to deny. I should like to know whether you would accept Leibniz's division of propositions into truths of reason and truths of fact. The former—the truths of reason—being necessary.

COPLESTON: Well, I certainly should not subscribe to what seems to be Leibniz's idea of truths of reason and truths of fact, since it would appear that, for him, there are in the long run only analytic propositions. It would seem that for Leibniz truths of fact are ultimately reducible to truths of reason. That is to say, to analytic propositions, at least for an omniscient mind. Well, I couldn't agree with that. For one thing, it would fail to meet the requirements of the experience of freedom. I don't want to uphold the whole philosophy of Leibniz. I have made use of his argument from contingent to necessary being, basing the argument on the principle of sufficient reason, simply because it seems to me a brief and clear formulation of what is, in my opinion, the fundamental metaphysical argument for God's existence.

RUSSELL: But, to my mind, "a necessary proposition" has got to be analytic. I don't see what else it can mean. And analytic propositions are always complex and logically somewhat late. "Irrational animals are animals" is an analyic proposition; but a proposition such as "This is an animal" can never by analytic. In fact, all the propositions that can be analytic are somewhat late in the build-up of propositions.

COPLESTON: Take the proposition "If there is a contingent being then there is a necessary being." I consider that that proposition hypothetically expressed is a necessary proposition. If you are going to call every necessary propositon an analytic proposition, then—in order to avoid a dispute in terminology—I would agree to call it analytic, though I don't consider it a tautological proposition. But the proposition is a necessary proposition only on the supposition that there is a contingent being. That there is a contingent being actually existing has to be discovered by experience, and the proposition that there is a contingent being is certainly not an analytic proposition, though once you know, I should maintain, that there is a contingent being, it follows of necessity that there is a necessary being.

RUSSELL: The difficulty of this argument is that I don't admit the idea of a necessary being and I don't admit that there is any particular meaning in calling other beings "contingent." These phrases don't for me have a significance except within a logic that I reject.

COPLESTON: Do you mean that you reject these terms because they won't fit in with what is called "modern logic"?

RUSSELL: Well, I can't find anything that they could mean. The word "necessary," it seems to me, is a useless word, except as applied to analytic propositions, not to things.

COPLESTON: In the first place, what do you mean by "modern logic"? As far as I know, there are somewhat differing systems. In the second place, not all modern logicians surely would admit the meaninglessness of metaphysics. We both know, at any rate, one very eminent modern thinker whose knowledge of modern logic was profound, but who certainly did not think that metaphysics are meaningless or, in particular, that the problem of God is meaningless. Again, even if all modern logicians held that metaphysical terms are meaningless, it would not follow that they were right. The proposition that metaphysical terms are meaningless seems to me to be a proposition based on an assumed philosophy. The dogmatic position behind it seems to be this: What will not go into my machine is nonexistent, or it is meaningless; it is the expression of emotion. I am simply trying to point out that anybody who says that a particular system of modern logic is the sole criterion of meaning is saying something that is over dogmatic; he is dogmatically insisting that a part of philosophy is the whole of philosophy. After all, a "contingent" being is a being which has not in itself the complete reason for its existence, that's what I mean by a contingent being. You know, as well as I do, that the existence of neither of us can be explained without reference to something or somebody outside us, our parents, for example. A "necessary" being, on the other hand, means a being that must and cannot not-exist. You may say that there is no such being, but you will find it hard to convince me that you do not understand the terms I am using. If you do not understand them, then how can you be entitled to say that such a being does not exist, if that is what you do say?

RUSSELL: Well, there are points here that I don't propose to go into at length. I don't maintain the meaninglessness of metaphysics in general at all. I maintain the meaninglessness of certain particular terms—not on any general ground, but simply because I've not been able to see an interpretation of those particular terms. It's not a general dogma—it's a particular thing. But those points I will leave out for the moment. And I will say that what you have been saying brings us back, it seems to me, to the ontological argument that there is a being whose essence involves existence, so that his existence is analytic. That seems to me to be impossible, and it raises, of course, the question what one means by existence, and as to this, I think a subject named can never be significantly said to exist but only a subject described. And that existence, in fact, quite definitely is not a predicate.

COPLESTON: Well, you say, I believe, that is bad grammar, or rather bad syntax to say, for example, "T. S. Eliot exists"; one ought to say, for example, "He, the author of *Murder in the Cathedral*, exists." Are you going to say that the proposition, "The cause of the world exists," is without meaning? You may say that the world has no cause; but I fail to see how you can say that the proposition that "the cause of the world exists" is meaningless. Put it in the form of a question: "Has the world a cause?" or "Does a cause of the world exist?" Most people surely would understand the question, even if they don't agree about the answer.

RUSSELL: Well, certainly the question "Does the cause of the world exist?" is a question that has meaning. But if you say "Yes, God is the cause of the world" you're using God as a proper name; then "God exists" will not be a statement that has meaning; that is the position that I'm maintaining. Because, therefore, it will follow that it cannot be an analytic proposition ever to say that this or that exists. For example, suppose you take as your subject "the existent round-square," it would look like an analytic proposition that "the existent round-square exists," but it doesn't exist.

COPLESTON: No, it doesn't, then surely you can't say it doesn't exist unless you have a conception of what existence is. As to the phrase "existent round-square," I should say that it has no meaning at all.

RUSSELL: I quite agree, Then I should say the same thing in another context in reference to a "necessary being."

COPLESTON: Well, we seem to have arrived at an impasse. To say that a necessary being is a being that must exist and cannot not-exist has for me a definite meaning. For you it has no meaning.

RUSSELL: Well, we can press the point a little, I think. A being that must exist and cannot not-exist, would surely, according to you, be a being whose essence involves existence.

COPLESTON: Yes, a being the essence of which is to exist. But I should not be willing to argue the existence of God simply from the idea of His essence because I don't think we have any clear intuition of God's essence as yet. I think we have to argue from the world of experience to God.

RUSSELL: Yes, I quite see the distinction. But, at the same time, for a being with sufficient knowledge it would be true to say "Here is this being whose essence involves existence!"

COPLESTON: Yes, certainly if anybody saw God, he would see that God must exist.

RUSSELL: So that I mean there is a being whose essence involves existence although we don't know that essence. We only know there is such a being.

COPLESTON: Yes; I should add we don't know the essence *a priori*. It is only *a posteriori* through our experience of the world that we come to a knowledge of the existence of that being. And then one argues, the essence and existence must be identical. Because if God's essence and God's existence were not identical, then some sufficient reason for this existence would have to be found beyond God.

RUSSELL: So it all turns on this question of sufficient reason, and I must say you haven't defined "sufficient reason" in a way that I can understand—what do you mean by sufficient reason? You don't mean cause?

COPLESTON: Not necessarily. Cause is a kind of sufficient reason. Only contingent being can have a cause. God is His own sufficient reason; and He is not cause of Himself. By sufficient reason in the full sense I mean an explanation adequate for the existence of some particular being.

RUSSELL: But when is an explanation adequate? Suppose I am about to make a flame with a match. You may say that the adequate explanation of that is that I rub it on the box.

COPLESTON: Well, for practical purposes—but theoretically, that is only a partial explanation. An adequate explanation must ultimately be a total explanation, to which nothing further can be added.

RUSSELL: Then I can only say that you're looking for something which can't be got, and which one ought not to expect to get.

COPLESTON: To say that one has not found it is one thing; to say that one should not look for it seems to me rather dogmatic.

RUSSELL: Well, I don't know. I mean, the explanation of one thing is another thing which makes the other thing dependent on yet another, and you have to grasp this sorry scheme of things entire to do what you want, and that we can't do.

COPLESTON: But are you going to say that we can't, or we shouldn't even raise the question of the existence of the whole of this sorry scheme of things—of the whole universe?

RUSSELL: Yes. I don't think there's any meaning in it at all. I think the word "universe" is a handy word in some connections, but I don't think it stands for anything that has a meaning.

COPLESTON: If the word is meaningless, it can't be so very handy. In any case, I don't say that the universe is something different from the objects which compose it (I indicated that in my brief summary of the proof), what I'm doing is to look for the reason, in this case the cause of the objects—the real or imagined totality of which constitute what we call the universe. You say, I think, that the universe—or my existence if you prefer, or any other existence—is unintelligible?

RUSSELL: First may I take up the point that if a word is meaningless it can't be handy. That sounds well but isn't in fact correct. Take, say, such a word as "the" or "than." You can't point to any object that those words mean, but they are very useful words; I should say the same of "universe." But leaving that point, you ask whether I consider that the universe is unintelligible. I shouldn't say unintelligible—I think it is without explanation. Intelligible, to my mind, is a different thing. Intelligible has to do with the thing itself intrinsically and not with its relations.

COPLESTON: Well, my point is that what we call the world is intrinsically unintelligible, apart from the existence of God. You see, I don't believe that the infinity of the series of events—I mean a horizontal series, so to speak—if such an infinity could be proved, would be in the slightest degree relevant to the situation. If you add up chocolates you get chocolates after all and not a sheep. If you add up chocolates to infinity, you presumably get an infinite number of chocolates. So if you add up contingent beings to infinity, you still get contingent beings, not a necessary being. An infinite series of contingent beings will be, to my way of thinking, as unable to cause itself as one contingent being. However, you say, I think, that it is illegitimate to raise the question of what will explain the existence of any particular object?

RUSSELL: It's quite all right if you mean by explaining it, simply finding a cause for it.

COPLESTON: Well, why stop at one particular object? Why shouldn't one raise the question of the cause of the existence of all particular objects?

RUSSELL: Because I see no reason to think there is any. The whole concept of cause is one we derive from our observation of particular things; I see no reason whatsoever to suppose that the total has any cause whatsoever.

COPLESTON: Well, to say that there isn't any cause is not the same thing as saying that we shouldn't look for a cause. The statement that there isn't any cause should come, if it comes at all, at the end of the enquiry, not the beginning. In any case, if the total has no cause, then to my way of thinking it must be its own cause, which seems to me impossible. Moreover, the statement that the world is simply there if in answer to a question, presupposes that the question has meaning.

RUSSELL: No, it doesn't need to be its own cause, what I'm saying is that the concept of cause is not applicable to the total.

COPLESTON: Then you would agree with Sartre that the universe is what he calls "gratuitous"?

RUSSELL: Well, the word "gratuitous" suggests that it might be something else; I should say that the universe is just there, and that's all.

COPLESTON: Well, I can't see how you can rule out the legitimacy of asking the question how the total, or anything at all comes to be there. Why something rather than nothing, that is the question? The fact that we gain our knowledge of causality empirically, from particular causes, does not rule out the possibility of asking what the cause of the series is. If the word "cause" were meaningless or if it could be shown that Kant's view of the matter were correct, the question would be illegitimate I agree; but you don't seem to hold that the word "cause" is meaningless, and I do not suppose you are a Kantian.

RUSSELL: I can illustrate what seems to me your fallacy. Every man who exists has a mother, and it seems to me your argument is that therefore the human race must have a mother, but obviously the human race hasn't a mother—that's a different logical sphere.

COPLESTON: Well, I can't really see any parity. If I were saying "every object has a phenomenal cause, therefore, the whole series has a phenomenal cause," there would be a parity; but I'm not saying that; I'm saying, every object has a phenomenal cause if you insist on the infinity of the series—but the series of phenomenal causes is an insufficient explanation of the series. Therefore, the series has not a phenomenal cause but a transcendent cause.

RUSSELL: That's always assuming that not only every particular thing in the world, but the world as a whole must have a cause. For that assumption I see no ground whatever. If you'll give me a ground I'll listen to it.

COPLESTON: Well, the series of events is either caused or it's not caused. If it is caused, there must obviously be a cause outside the series. If it's not caused then its sufficient to itself, and if it's sufficient to itself it is what I call necessary. But it can't be necessary since each member is contingent, and we've agreed that the total is no reality apart from its members, therefore, it can't be necessary. Therefore, it can't be (caused)—uncaused—therefore it must have a cause. And I should like to observe in passing that the statement "the world is simply there and is inexplicable" can't be got out of logical analysis.

RUSSELL: I don't want to seem arrogant, but it does seem to me that I can conceive things that you say the human mind can't conceive. As for things not having a cause, the physicists assure us that individual quantum transition in atoms have no cause.

COPLESTON: Well, I wonder now whether that isn't simply a temporary inference.

RUSSELL: It may be, but it does show that physicists' minds can conceive it.

COPLESTON: Yes, I agree, some scientists—physicists—are willing to allow for indetermination within a restricted field. But very many scientists are not so willing. I think that Professor Dingle, of London University, maintains that the Heisenberg uncertainty principle tells us something about the success (or the lack of it) of the present atomic theory in correlating observations, but not about nature in itself, and many physicists would accept this view. In any case, I don't see how physicists can fail to accept the theory in practice, even if they don't do so in theory. I cannot see how science could be conducted on any other assumption than that of order and intelligibility in nature. The physicist presupposes, at least tacitly, that there is some sense in investigating nature and looking for the causes of events, just as the detective presupposes that there is some sense in looking for the cause of a murder. The metaphysician assumes that there is sense in looking for the reason or cause of phenomena, and, not being a Kantian, I consider that the metaphysician is as justified in his assumption as the physicist. When Sartre, for example, says that the world is gratuitous, I think that he has not sufficiently considered what is implied by "gratuitous."

RUSSELL: I think—there seems to me a certain unwarrantable extension here; a physicist looks for causes; that does not necessarily imply that there are causes everywhere. A man may look for gold without assuming that there is gold everywhere; if he finds gold, well and good, if he doesn't he's had bad luck. The same is true when the physicists look for causes. As for Sartre, I don't profess to know what he means, and I shouldn't like to be thought to interpret him, but for my part, I do think the notion of the world having an explanation is a mistake. I don't see why one should expect it to have, and I think what you say about what the scientist assumes is an over-statement.

COPLESTON: Well, it seems to me that the scientist does make some such assumption. When he experiments to find out some particular truth, behind that experiment lies the assumption that the universe is not simply discontinuous. There is the possibility of finding out a truth by experiment. The experiment may be a bad one, it may lead to no result, or not to the result that he wants, but that at any rate there is the possibility, through experiment, of finding out the truth that he assumes. And that seems to me to assume an ordered and intelligible universe.

RUSSELL: I think you're generalizing more than is necessary. Undoubtedly the scientist assumes that this sort of thing is likely to be found and will often be found. He does not assume that it will be found, and that's a very important matter in modern physics.

COPLESTON: Well, I think he does assume or is bound to assume it tacitly in practice. It may be that, to quote Professor Haldane, "when I light the gas under the kettle, some of the water molecules will fly off as vapor, and there is no way of finding out which will do so," but it doesn't follow necessarily that the idea of chance must be introduced except in relation to our knowledge.

RUSSELL: No it doesn't—at least if I may believe what he says. He's finding out quite a lot of things—the scientist is finding out quite a lot of things that are happening in the world, which are, at first, beginnings of causal chains—first causes which haven't in themselves got causes. He does not assume that everything has a cause.

COPLESTON: Surely that's a first cause within a certain selected field. It's a relatively first cause.

RUSSELL: I don't think he'd say so. If there's a world in which most events, but not all, have causes, he will then be able to depict the probabilities and uncertainties by assuming that this particular event you're interested in probably has a cause. And since in any case you won't get more than probability that's good enough.

COPLESTON: It may be that the scientist doesn't hope to obtain more than probability, but in raising the question he assumes that the question of explanation has a meaning. But your general point then,

Lord Russell, is that it's illegitimate even to ask the question of the cause of the world?

RUSSELL: Yes, that's my position.

COPLESTON: If it's a question that for you has no meaning, it's of course very difficult to discuss it, isn't it?

RUSSELL: Yes, it is very difficult. What do you say—shall we pass on to some other issue?

RELIGIOUS EXPERIENCE

COPLESTON: Let's. Well, perhaps I might say a word about religious experience, and then we can go on to moral experience. I don't regard religious experience as a strict proof of the existence of God, so the character of the discussion changes somewhat, but I think it's true to say that the best explanation of it is the existence of God. By religious experience I don't mean simply feeling good. I mean a loving, but unclear, awareness of some object which irresistibly seems to the experiencer as something transcending the self, something transcending all the normal objects of experience, something which cannot be pictured or conceptualized, but of the reality of which doubt is impossible—at least during the experience. I should claim that cannot be explained adequately and without residue, simply subjectively. The actual basic experience at any rate is most easily explained on the hypotheses that there is actually some objective cause of that experience.

RUSSELL: I should reply to that line of argument that the whole argument from our own mental states to something outside us, is a very tricky affair. Even where we all admit its validity, we only feel justified in doing so, I think, because of the consensus of mankind. If there's a crowd in a room and there's a clock in a room, they can all see the clock. The fact that they can all see it tends to make them think that it's not an hallucination: whereas these religious experiences do tend to be very private.

COPLESTON: Yes, they do. I'm speaking strictly of mystical experience proper, and I certainly don't include, by the way, what are called visions. I mean simply the experience, and I quite admit it's indefinable, of the transcendent object or of what seems to be a transcendent object. I remember Julian Huxley in some lecture say-ing that religious experience, or mystical experience, is as much a real experience as falling in love or appreciating poetry and art. Well, I believe that when we appreciate poetry and art we appreciate definite poems or a definite work or art. If we fall in love, well, we fall in love with somebody and not with nobody.

RUSSELL: May I interrupt for a moment here. That is by no means always the case. Japanese novelists never consider that they have achieved a success unless large numbers of real people commit suicide for love of the imaginary heroine.

COPLESTON: Well, I must take your word for these goings on in Japan. I haven't committed suicide, I'm glad to say, but I have been strongly influenced in the taking of two important steps in my life by two biographies. However, I must say I see little resemblance between the real influence of those books on me and the mystic experience proper, so far, that is, as an outsider can obtain an idea of that experience.

RUSSELL: Well, I mean we wouldn't regard God as being on the same level as the characters in a work of fiction. You'll admit there's a distinction here?

COPLESTON: I certainly should. But what I'd say is that the best explanation seems to be the not purely subjectivist explanation. Of course, a subjectivist explanation is possible in the case of certain people in whom there is little relation between the experience and life, in the case of deluded people and hallucinated people, and so on. But when you get what one might call the pure type, say St. Francis of Assisi, when you get an experience that results in an overflow of dynamic and creative love, the best explanation of that it seems to me is the actual existence of an objective cause of the experience.

RUSSELL: Well, I'm not contending in a dogmatic way that there is not a God. What I'm contending is that we don't know that there is. I can only take what is recorded as I should take other records and I do find that a very great many things are reported, and I am sure you would not accept things about demons and devils and what not—and they're reported in exactly the same tone of voice and with exactly the same conviction. And the mystic, if his vision is ver-idical, may be said to know that there are devils. But I don't know that there are.

COPLESTON: But surely in the case of the devils there have been people speaking mainly of visions, appearances, angels or demons and so on. I should rule out the visual appearances, because I think they can be explained apart from the existence of the object which is supposed to be seen.

RUSSELL: But don't you think there are abundant recorded cases of people who believe that they've heard Satan speaking to them in their hearts, in just the same way as the mystics assert God—and I'm not talking now of an external vision, I'm talking of a purely mental experience. That seems to be an experience of the same sort as mystics' experience of God, and I don't seek that from what mystics tell us you can get any argument for God which is not equally an argument for Satan.

COPLESTON: I quite agree, of course, that people have imagined or thought they have heard or seen Satan. And I have no wish in passing to deny the existence of Satan. But I do not think that people have claimed to have experienced Satan in the precise way in which mystics claim to have experienced God. Take the case of a non-Christian, Plotinus. He admits the experience is something inexpressible, the object is an object of love, and therefore, not an object that causes horror and disgust. And the effect of that experience is, I should say, borne out, or I mean the validity of the experience is borne out in the records of the life of Plotinus. At any rate it is more reasonable to suppose that he had that experience if we're willing to accept Porphyry's account of Plotinus's general kindness and benevolence.

RUSSELL: The fact that a belief has a good moral effect upon a man is no evidence whatsoever in favor of its truth.

COPLESTON: No, but if it could actually be proved that the belief was actually responsible for a good effect on a man's life, I should consider it a presumption in favor of some truth, at any rate of the positive part of the belief not of its entire validity. But in any case I am using the character of the life as evidence in favor of the mystic's veracity and sanity rather than as a proof of the truth of his beliefs.

RUSSELL: But even that I don't think is any evidence. I've had experiences myself that have altered my character profoundly. And I thought at the time at any rate that it was altered for the good.

Those experiences were important, but they did not involve the existence of something outside me, and I don't think that if I'd thought they did, the fact that they had a wholesome effect would have been any evidence that I was right.

COPLESTON: No, but I think that the good effect would attest your veracity in describing your experience. Please remember that I'm not saying that a mystic's mediation or interpretation of his experience should be immune from discussion or criticism.

RUSSELL: Obviously the character of a young man may be—and often is—immensely affected for good by reading about some great man in history, and it may happen that the great man is a myth and doesn't exist, but the boy is just as much affected for good as if he did. There have been such people. Plutarch's *Lives* take Lycurgus as an example, who certainly did not exist, but you might be very much influenced by reading Lycurgus under the impression that he had previously existed. You would then be influenced by an object that you'd loved, but it wouldn't be an existing object.

COPLESTON: I agree with you on that, of course, that a man may be influenced by a character in fiction. Without going into the question of what it is precisely that influences him (I should say a real value) I think that the situation of that man and of the mystic are different. After all the man who is influenced by Lycurgus hasn't got the irresistible impression that he's experienced in some way the ultimate reality.

RUSSELL: I don't think you've quite got my point about these historical characters—these unhistorical characters in history. I'm not assuming what you call an effect on the reason. I'm assuming that the young man reading about this person and believing him to be real loves him—which is quite easy to happen, and yet he's loving a phantom.

COPLESTON: In one sense he's loving a phantom that's perfectly true, in the sense, I mean, that he's loving X or Y who doesn't exist. But at the same time, it is not, I think, the phantom as such that the young man loves; he perceives a real value, an idea which he recognizes as objectively valid, and that's what excites his love.

RUSSELL: Well, in the same sense we had before about the characters in fiction.

COPLESTON: Yes, in one sense the man's loving a phantom—perfectly true. But in another sense he's loving what he perceives to be a value.

THE MORAL ARGUMENT

RUSSELL: But aren't you now saying in effect, I mean by God whatever is good or the sum total of what is good—the system of what is good, and, therefore, when a young man loves anything that is good he is loving God. Is that what you're saying, because if so, it wants a bit of arguing.

COPLESTON: I don't say, of course, that God is the sum-total or system of what is good in the pantheistic sense; I'm not a pantheist, but I do think that all goodness reflects God in some way and proceeds from Him, so that in a sense the man who loves what is truly good, loves God even if he doesn't advert to God. But still I agree that the validity of such an interpretation of a man's conduct depends on the recognition of God's existence, obviously.

RUSSELL: Yes, but that's a point to be proved.

COPLESTON: Quite so, but I regard the metaphysical argument as probative, but there we differ.

RUSSELL: You see, I feel that some things are good and that other things are bad. I love the things that are good, that I think are good, and I hate the things that I think are bad. I don't say that these things are good because they participate in the Divine goodness.

COPLESTON: Yes, but what's your justification for distinguishing between good and bad or how do you view the distinction between them?

RUSSELL: I don't have any justification any more than I have when I distinguish between blue and yellow. What is my justification for distinguishing between blue and yellow? I can see they are different.

COPLESTON: Well, that is an excellent justification, I agree. You distinguish blue and yellow by seeing them, so you distinguish good and bad by what faculty?

RUSSELL: By my feelings.

COPLESTON: By your feelings. Well, that's what I was asking. You think that good and evil have reference simply to feeling?

RUSSELL: Well, why does one type of object look yellow and another look blue? I can more or less give an answer to that thanks to the physicists, and as to why I think one sort of thing good and another **evil, probably there is an answer of the same sort, but it hasn't been** gone into in the same way and I couldn't give it you.

COPLESTON: Well, let's take the behavior of the Commandant of Belsen. That appears to you as undesirable and evil and to me too. To Adolf Hitler we suppose it appeared as something good and desirable. I suppose you'd have to admit that for Hitler it was good and for you it is evil.

RUSSELL: No, I shouldn't quite go so far as that. I mean, I think people can make mistakes in that as they can in other things. If you have jaundice you see things yellow that are not yellow. You're making a mistake.

COPLESTON: Yes, one can make mistakes, but can you make a mistake if it's simply a question of reference to a feeling or emotion? Surely Hitler would be the only possible judge of what appealed to his emotions.

RUSSELL: It would be quite right to say that it appealed to his emotions, but you can say various things about that among others, that if that sort of thing makes that sort of appeal to Hitler's emotions, then Hitler makes quite a different appeal to my emotions.

COPLESTON: Granted. But there's no objective criterion outside feeling then for condemning the conduct of the Commandant of Belsen, in your view?

RUSSELL: No more than there is for the color-blind person who's in exactly the same state. Why do we intellectually condemn the color-blind man? Isn't it because he's in the minority?

COPLESTON: I would say because he is lacking in a thing which normally belongs to human nature.

RUSSELL: Yes, but if he were in the majority, we shouldn't say that.

COPLESTON: Then you'd say that there's no criterion outside feeling that will enable one to distinguish between the behavior of the Commandant of Belsen and the behavior, say, of Sir Stafford Cripps or the Archbishop of Canterbury.

RUSSELL: The feeling is a little too simplified. You've got to take account of the effects of actions and your feelings toward those effects. You see, you can have an argument about it if you say that certain sorts of occurrences are the sort you like and certain others the sort you don't like. Then you have to take account of the effects of actions. You can very well say that the effects of the actions of the Commandant of Belsen were painful and unpleasant.

COPLESTON: They certainly were, I agree, very painful and unpleasant to all the people in the camp.

RUSSELL: Yes, but not only to the people in the camp, but to outsiders contemplating them also.

COPLESTON: Yes, quite true in imagination. But that's my point. I don't approve of them, and I know you don't approve of them, but I don't see what ground you have for not approving of them, because after all, to the Commandant of Belsen himself, they're pleasant, those actions.

RUSSELL: Yes, but you see I don't need any more ground in that case than I do in the case of color perception. There are some people who think everything is yellow, there are people suffering from jaundice, and I don't agree with these people. I can't prove that the things are not yellow, there isn't any proof, but most people agree with me that they're not yellow, and most people agree with me that the Commandant of Belsen was making mistakes.

COPLESTON: Well, do you accept any moral obligation?

RUSSELL: Well, I should have to answer at considerable length to answer that. Practically speaking—yes. Theoretically speaking I should have to define moral obligation rather carefully.

COPLESTON: Well, do you think that the word "ought" simply has an emotional connotation?

RUSSELL: No, I don't think that, because you see, as I was saying a moment ago, one has to take account of the effects, and I think right conduct is that which would probably produce the greatest possible balance in intrinsic value of all the acts possible in the circumstances, and you've got to take account of the probable effects of your action in considering what is right.

COPLESTON: Well, I brought in moral obligation because I think that one can approach the question of God's existence in that way. The vast majority of the human race will make, and always have made, some distinction between right and wrong. The vast majority I think has some consciousness of an obligation in the moral sphere. It's my opinion that the perception of values and the consciousness of moral law and obligation are best explained through the hypothesis of a transcendent ground of value and of an author of the moral law. I do mean by "author of the moral law" an arbitrary author of the moral law. I think, in fact, that those modern atheists who have argued in the converse way "there is no God; therefore, there are no absolute values and no absolute law," are quite logical.

RUSSELL: I don't like the word "absolute." I don't think there is anything absolute whatever. The moral law, for example, is always changing. At one period in the development of the human race, almost everybody thought cannibalism was a duty.

COPLESTON: Well, I don't see that differences in particular moral judgments are any conclusive argument against the universality of the moral law. Let's assume for the moment that there are absolute moral values, even on that hypothesis it's only to be expected that different individuals and different groups should enjoy varying degrees of insight into those values.

RUSSELL: I'm inclined to think that "ought," the feeling that one has about "ought" is an echo of what has been told one by one's parents or one's nurses.

COPLESTON: Well, I wonder if you can explain away the idea of the "ought" merely in terms of nurses and parents. I really don't see how it can be conveyed to anybody in other terms than itself. It seems to me that if there is a moral order bearing upon the human conscience, that that moral order is unintelligible apart from the existence of God.

RUSSELL: Then you have to say one or other of two things. Either God only speaks to a very small percentage of mankind—which happens to include yourself—or He deliberately says things are not true in talking to the consciences of savages.

COPLESTON: Well, you see, I'm not suggesting that God actually dictates moral precepts to the conscience. The human being's ideas of the content of the moral law depends certainly to a large extent on education and environment, and a man has to use his reason in assessing the validity of the actual moral ideas of his social group. But the possibility of criticizing the accepted moral code presupposes that there is an objective standard, that there is an ideal moral order, which imposes itself (I mean the obligatory character of which can be recognized). I think that the recognition of this ideal moral order is part of the recognition of contingency. It implies the existence of a real foundation of God.

RUSSELL: But the law-giver has always been, it seems to me, one's parents or someone like. There are plenty of terrestrial law-givers to account for it, and that would explain why people's consciences are so amazingly different in different times and places.

COPLESTON: It helps to explain differences in the perception of particular moral values, which otherwise are inexplicable. It will help to explain changes in the matter of the moral law in the content of the precepts as accepted by this or that nation, or this or that individual. But the form of it, what Kant calls the categorical imperative, the "ought," I really don't see how that can possibly be conveyed to anybody by nurse or parent because there aren't any possible terms, so far as I can see, with which it can be explained. It can't be defined in other terms than itself, because once you've defined it in other terms than itself you've explained it away. It's no longer a moral "ought." It's something else.

RUSSELL: Well, I think the sense of "ought" is the effect of somebody's imagined disapproval, it may be God's imagined disapproval, but it's somebody's imagined disapproval. And I think that is what is meant by "ought."

COPLESTON: It seems to me to be external customs and taboos and things of that sort which can most easily be explained simply through environment and education, but all that seems to me to belong to what I call the matter of the law, the content. The idea of the "ought" as such can never be conveyed to a man by the tribal chief or by anybody else, because there are no other terms in which it could be conveyed. It seems to me entirely—[Russell breaks in].

RUSSELL: But I don't see any reason to say that—I mean we all know about conditioned reflexes. We know that an animal, if punished habitually for a certain sort of act, after a time will refrain. I don't think the animal refrains from arguing within himself, "Master will be angry if I do this." He has a feeling that that's not the thing to do. That's what we can do with ourselves and nothing more.

COPLESTON: I see no reason to suppose that an animal has a consciousness of moral obligation; and we certainly don't regard an animal as morally responsible for his acts of disobedience. But a man has a consciousnes of obligation and of moral values. I see no reason to suppose that one could conditon all men as one can "condition" an animal, and I don't suppose you'd really want to do so even if one could. If "behaviorism" were true, there would be no objective moral distinction between the emperor Nero and St. Francis of Assisi. I can't help feeling, Lord Russell, you know, that you regard the conduct of the Commandant at Belsen as morally reprehensible, and that you yourself would never under any circumstances act in that way, even if you thought, or had reason to think, that possibly the balance of the happiness of the human race might be increased through some people being treated in that abominable manner.

RUSSELL: No. I wouldn't imitate the conduct of a mad dog. The fact that I wouldn't do it doesn't really bear on this question we're discussing.

COPLESTON: No, but if you were making a utilitarian explanation of right and wrong in terms of of consequences, it might be held, and I suppose some of the Nazis of the better type would have held that although it's lamentable to have to act in this way, yet the balance in the long run leads to greater happiness. I don't think you'd say that, would you? I think you'd say that that sort of action is wrong—and in itself, quite apart from whether the general balance of happiness is increased or not. Then, if you're prepared to say that, then I think you must have some criterion of right and wrong, that is outside the criterion of feeling, at any rate. To me, that admission would ultimately result in the admission of an ultimate ground of value in God.

RUSSELL: I think we are perhaps getting into confusion. It is not direct feeling about the act by which I should judge, but rather a feeling as to the effects. And I can't admit any circumstances in which certain kinds of behavior, such as you have been discussing, would do good. I can't imagine circumstances in which they would have a beneficial effect. I think the persons who think they do are deceiving themselves. But if there were circumstances in which they would have a beneficial effect, then I might be obliged, however reluctantly, to say—"Well, I don't like these things, but I will acquiesce in them," just as I acquiesce in the Criminal Law, although I profoundly dislike punishment.

COPLESTON: Well, perhaps it's time I summed up my position. I've argued two things. First, that the existence of God can be philosophically proved by a metaphysical argument; secondly, that it is only the existence of God that will make sense of man's moral experience and of religious experience. Personally, I think that your way of accounting for man's moral judgments leads inevitably to a contradiction between what your theory demands and your own spontaneous judgments. Moreover, your theory explains moral obligation away, and explaining away is not explanation. As regards the metaphysical argument, we are apparently in agreement that what we call the world consists simply of contingent beings. That is, of beings no one of which can account for its own existence. You say that the series of events needs no explanation: I say that if there were no necessary being, no being which must exist and cannot not-exist, nothing would exist. The infinity of the series of contingent beings, even if proved, would be irrelevant. Something does exist; therefore, there must be something which accounts for this fact, a being which is outside the series of contingent beings. If you had admitted this, we could then have discussed whether that being is personal, good, and so on. On the actual point discussed, whether there is or is not a necessary being, I find myself, I think, in agreement with the great majority of classical philosophers.

You maintain, I think, that existing beings are simply there, and that I have no justification for raising the question of the explanation of their existence. But I would like to point out that this position cannot be substantiated by logical analysis; it expresses a philosophy which itself stands in need of proof. I think we have reached an impasse because our ideas of philosophy are radically different; it seems to me that what I call a part of philosophy, that you call the whole, insofar at least as philosophy is rational. It seems to me, if you will pardon my saying so, that besides your own logical system—which you call "modern" in opposition to antiquated logic (a tendentious adjective)—you maintain a philosophy which cannot be substantiated by logical analysis. After all, the problem of God's existence is an existential problem whereas logical analysis does not deal directly with problems of existence. So it seems to me, to declare that the terms involved in one set of problems are meaningless because they are not required in dealing with another set of problems, is to settle from the beginning the nature and extent of philosophy, and that is itself a philosophical act which stands in need of justification.

RUSSELL: Well, I should like to say just a few words by way of summary on my side. First, as to the metaphysical argument: I don't admit the connotations of such a term as "contingent" or the possibility of explanation in Father Copleston's sense. I think the word "contingent" inevitably suggests the possibility of something that wouldn't have this what you might call accidental character of just being there, and I don't think is true except in the purely causal sense. You can sometimes give a causal explanation of one thing as being the effect of something else, but that is merely referring one thing to another thing and there's no—to my mind—explanation in Father Copleston's sense of anything at all, nor is there any meaning in calling things "contingent" because there isn't anything else they could be. That's what I should say about that, but I should like to say a few words about Father Copleston's accusation that I regard logic as all philosophy—that is by no means the case. I don't by any means regard logic as all philosophy. I think logic is an essential part of philosophy and logic has to be used in philosophy, and in that I think he and I are at one. When the logic that he uses was new—namely, in the time of Aristotle, there had to be a great deal of fuss made about it; Aristotle made a lot of fuss about that logic. Nowadays it's become old and respectable, and you don't have to make so much fuss about it. The logic that I believe in is comparatively new, and therefore I have to imitate Aristotle in making a fuss about it; but it's not that I think it's all philosophy by any means—I don't think so. I think it's an important part of philosophy, and when I say that, I don't find a meaning for this or that word, that is a position of detail based upon what I've found out about that particular word, from thinking about it. It's not a general position that all words that are used in metaphysics are nonsense, or anything like that which I don't really hold.

As regards the moral argument, I do find that when one studies anthropology or history, there are people who think it their duty to perform acts which I think abominable, and I certainly can't, therefore, attribute Divine origin to the matter of moral obligation, which Father Copleston doesn't ask me to; but I think even the form of moral obligation, when it takes the form of enjoining you to eat your father or what not, doesn't seem to me to be such a very beautiful and noble thing; and, therefore, I cannot attribute a Divine origin to this sense of moral obligation, which I think is quite easily accounted for in quite other ways.

10

What Is the Soul?

One of the most painful circumstances of recent advances in science is that each one of them makes us know less than we thought we did. When I was young we all knew, or thought we knew, that a man consists of a soul and a body; that the body is in time and space, but the soul is in time only. Whether the soul survives death was a matter as to which opinions might differ, but that there is a soul was thought to be indubitable. As for the body, the plain man of course considered its existence self-evident, and so did the man of science, but the philosopher was apt to analyze it away after one fashion or another, reducing it usually to ideas in the mind of the man who had the body and anybody else who happened to notice him. The philosopher, however, was not taken seriously, and science remained comfortably materialistic, even in the hands of quite orthodox scientists.

Nowadays these fine old simplicities are lost: physicists assure us that there is no such thing as matter, and psychologists assure us that there is no such thing as mind. This is an unprecedented occurrence. Who ever heard of a cobbler saying that there was no such thing as boots, or a tailor maintaining that all men are really naked? Yet that would have been no odder than what physicists and certain psychologists have been doing. To begin with the latter, some of them attempt to reduce everything that seems to be mental activity to an activity of the body. There are, however, various difficulties in the way of reducing mental activity to physical

From *In Praise of Idleness* by Bertrand Russell, pp. 226-231. Copyright © 1935 by George and Allen Unwin. Reprinted by permission of the publisher.

activity. I do not think we can yet say with any assurance whether these difficulties are or are not insuperable. What we can say, on the basis of physics itself, is that what we have hitherto called our body is really an elaborate scientific construction not corresponding to any physical reality. The modern would-be materialist thus finds himself in a curious position, for, while he may with a certain degree of success reduce the activities of the mind to those of the body, he cannot explain away the fact that the body itself is merely a convenient concept invented by the mind. We find ourselves thus going round and round in a circle: mind is an emanation of body, and body is an invention of mind. Evidently this cannot be quite right, and we have to look for something that is neither mind nor body, out of which both can spring.

Let us begin with the body. The plain man thinks that material objects must certainly exist, since they are evident to the senses. Whatever else may be doubted, it is certain that anything you can bump into must be real; this is the plain man's metaphysic. This is all very well, but the physicist comes along and shows that you never bump into anything; even when you run your head against a stone wall, you do not really touch it. When you think you touch a thing, there are certain electrons and protons, forming part of your body, which are attracted and repelled by certain electrons and protons in the thing you think you are touching, but there is no actual contact. The electrons and protons in your body, becoming agitated by nearness to the other electrons and protons, are disturbed, and transmit a disturbance along your nerves to the brain; the effect in the brain is what is necessary to your sensation of contact, and by suitable experiments this sensation can be made quite deceptive. The electrons and protons themselves, however, are only a crude first approximation, a way of collecting into a bundle either trains of waves or the statistical probabilites of various different kinds of events. Thus matter has become altogether too ghostly to be used as an adequate stick with which to beat the mind. Matter in motion, which used to seem so unquestionable, turns out to be a concept quite inadequate for the needs of physics.

Nevertheless modern science gives no indication whatever of the existence of the soul or mind as an entity; indeed the reasons for disbelieving in it are of very much the same kind as the reasons for disbelieving in matter. Mind and matter were something like the lion and the unicorn fighting for the crown; the end of the battle is not the victory of one or the other, but the discovery that both are only heraldic inventions. The world consists of events, not of things that endure for a long time and have changing properties. Events can be collected into groups by their causal relations. If the causal relations are of one sort, the resulting group of events may be called a physical object, and if the causal relations are of another sort, the resulting group may be called a mind. Any event that occurs inside a man's head will belong to groups of both kinds; considered as belonging to a group of one kind, it is a constituent of his brain, and considered as belonging to a group of the other kind, it is a constituent of his mind.

Thus both mind and matter are merely convenient ways of organizing events. There can be no reason for supposing that either a piece of mind or a piece of matter is immortal. The sun is supposed to be losing matter at the rate of millions of tons a minute. The most essential characteristic of mind is memory, and there is no reason whatever to suppose that the memory associated with a given person survives that person's death. Indeed there is every reason to think the opposite, for memory is clearly connected with a certain kind of brain structure, and since this structure decays at death, there is every reason to suppose that memory also must cease. Although metaphysical materialism cannot be considered true, yet emotionally the world is pretty much the same as it would be if the materialists were in the right. I think the opponents of materialism have always been actuated by two main desires: the first to prove that the mind is immortal, and the second to prove that the ultimate power in the universe is mental rather than physical. In both these respects, I think the materialists were in the right. Our desires, it is true, have considerable power on the earth's surface; the greater part of the land on this planet has a quite different aspect from that which it would have if men had not utilized it to extract food and wealth. But our power is very strictly limited. We cannot at present do anything whatever to the sun or moon or even to the interior of the earth, and there is not the faintest reason to suppose that what happens in regions to which our power does not extend has any mental causes. That is to say, to put the matter in a nutshell, there is no reason to think that except on the earth's surface anything happens because somebody wishes it to happen. And since our power on the earth's surface is entirely dependent upon the supply of energy which the earth derives from the sun, we are necessarily dependent upon the sun, and could hardly realize any of our wishes if the sun grew cold. It is of course rash to dogmatize as to what science may achieve in the future. We may learn to prolong human existence longer than now seems possible, but if there is any truth in modern physics, more particularly in the second law of thermodynamics, we cannot hope that the human race will continue forever. Some people may find this conclusion gloomy, but if we are honest with ourselves, we shall have to admit that what is going to happen many millions of years hence has no very great emotional interest for us here and now. And science, while it diminishes our cosmic pretensions, enormously increases our terrestrial comfort. That is why, in spite of the horror of the theologians, science has on the whole been tolerated.

11

Mind and Matter in Modern Science

MENTALISM VS. MATERIALISM

Ever since Greek times there has been a controversy between those who regarded matter and those who regarded mind as the dominant power in the universe. Religious orthodoxy, whether pagan or Christian, has always tended to be associated with the Mentalist party. The Materialist party, on the other hand, has tended to ally itself with scientific orthodoxy. This alliance has sometimes been too intimate for prudence, for when new discoveries required a change in scientific doctrine, the older formulations of Materialism were apt to become untenable, thus enabling the Mentalists to claim that the latest results of science favored their case. This familiar process has been repeated in recent years; quantum theory, in particular, has been interpreted by theologically orthodox commentators as involving the bankruptcy of Materialism. For my part, I think this interpretation, in the main, mistaken. It is true that it would be better to substitute the word "physicalism" for the word "materialism": I should define "physicalism" as the doctrine that events are governed by the laws of physics. But this change has no theological implications whatever. It does not make it any more probable that the world has a purpose, or that it is evolving toward better things, or that it has any other property that would be agreeable to our cosmic hopes.

First published in *The Rationalist Annual* (1946) by Watts & Company for the Rationalist Press Association, and reprinted by permission of the Rationalist Press Association.

THE MEANING OF MATTER

"Matter," as formerly understood, was a straightforward common-sense concept, derived from the concept "thing"; it meant whatever occupied space, and displayed its existence by the qualities of hardness, resistance, and impenetrability. The atomists, in particular, thought of the world as composed of tiny billiard balls perpetually bumping into each other. This was a picture that anybody could imaginatively understand, and if it had been scientifically adequate physics would have been a very easy science. But a number of discoveries, mostly made within the last half-century, have shown that this simple picture will not do.

THE NATURE OF "MASS"

"Mass" used to be defined as "quantity of matter," but it was found that the mass of a body in rapid motion is greater than that of the same body at rest; if a body could move with the velocity of light its mass would become infinite. Since motion is relative the mass of a body will be differently estimated by different observers, according to their motion relative to the body. Thus mass is not an intrinsic property of a body, but is dependent on its relation to the observer who measures the mass. The result has been that mass has come to be viewed as a form of energy; the mass of a body is diminished when it emits energy, and increased when it absorbs energy.

This is not a mere theory, or a question of trivial correction; it is held that the sun, which is continually radiating energy in the form of light and heat, is losing mass at the rate of four million tons per second. All the other stars are doing likewise, at varying rates, according to their size and temperature. This mass is transformed into other kinds of energy, but these, for the most part, are not associated with what common sense would call "things." The stars, like a morning mist, are gradually dissolving into invisibility; in the end there will be only heat. On this ground alone we can no longer attribute to matter the comfortable solidity that it used to enjoy.

UPS AND DOWNS OF THE ATOMIC THEORY

The ups and downs of the atomic theory have been interesting. For a long time there were supposed to be 92 "elements," each having its own sort of atom. Then the picture was simplified: it appeared that each atom could be regarded as a system composed of only two kinds of constituents, electrons and protons. The electron had a negative charge of electricity, the proton an equal positive charge; the proton had about 1,850 times the mass of an electron. An atom consisted of a nucleus (composed of a number of protons and a small number of electrons) and a number of planetary electrons just sufficient to make the total number of electrons equal to the total number of protons. This was called, after its inventors, the Rutherford-Bohr atom.

This atom had for a while a great success, as it explained many observed facts almost perfectly. But after a reign of twelve years (1913-1925) it was deposed in favor of the Heisenberg-Schrodinger atom, which was a much more abstract and less imaginable affair. It is still permissible to talk about electrons and protons, just as we talk of sunrises and sunsets in spite of Copernicus; but the ultimate truth is supposed to be something different. Even on the level on which we can still retain electrons and protons two new kinds of units have to be added, called neutrons and positrons. The neutron is like the proton, except that it is not electrified; the positron is like the electron, except that its electricity is positive instead of negative. Perhaps the proton consists of a neutron and a positron, but this is uncertain. If this view proves tenable matter may be regarded, for most practical purposes, as composed of three kinds of fundamental units, neutrons, positrons, and electrons. But this is to be taken as no more than an approximation, permitted as a concession to our desire for an imaginative picture of physical processes.

QUANTUM THEORY

What really happens, according to quantum theory, can only be expressed in mathematical symbols, and even then not accurately; there is a theoretical limit to the accuracy with which the state of a material system can be ascertained. It is impossible to make modern quantum theory simple, but I will try to state, in general terms, what is relevant to our topic.

An atom, according to this theory, is a small region within which there is a certain amount of energy—an amount which is not constant, but changes discontinuously from one to another of certain possible values that are separated from each other by finite amounts. The amount of energy in the atom is increased when energy is absorbed from without and diminished when energy is emitted in the form of radiation. It is only when atoms emit energy that they have the kind of effects by which our senses are affected; a collection of atoms that all retained their energy would emit no light, and therefore be invisible. It is therefore only *changes* of energy that afford material for observation; what goes on in the atom while the energy within it remains unchanged is a matter of guesswork, as to which, from the very nature of the case, evidence is impossible.

THE BEHAVIOR OF MATTER IN BULK

There are rules governing the changes that atoms undergo from one energy-level to another, but these rules are not sufficient to determine which of several possible things an individual atom will do. They do, however, suffice to determine the average behavior of a large number of atoms. The case is analogous to throwing dice: with two dice there are thirty-six possibilities, and if the dice are "true" each of the thirty-six possibilities will be realized about equally often in a very large number of throws. So it is with atoms: given a very great many atoms, all capable of a certain definite set of transitions, we can tell, almost exactly, what proportion will choose each possibility, though we cannot tell which will be chosen by any one particular atom. Consequently the behavior of matter in bulk is statistically deterministic, although each separate atom may make any one of a certain definite set of transitions.

It will be seen that in this theory "matter" has been completely absorbed into "energy." An atom is merely a small region in which is concentrated a certain amount of energy, which is not constant, but undergoes variations which are subject to certain rules. There is nothing that can be called "substantial identity" between an atom at one time and what at another time we choose to regard as the "same" atom.

PHYSICS IS STILL DETERMINISTIC

The failure of determinism, where atomic occurrences are concerned, has much less importance than is sometimes attributed to it. Except in a well-equipped physical laboratory nothing can be discovered about the behavior of an individual atom or electron; all the occurrences of which we are aware in ordinary life involve many millions of atoms, and are therefore just as predictable as they used to be. It is true that the prediction is now only probable, but the probability is so near to certainty that the element of doubt due to this cause is very much less than that which will always be present owing to other causes. Dependence upon statistical regularity occurs also within classical physics. It might happen, for example, that all the air in a room would collect itself in one half of the room, leaving a vacuum in the other half. We cannot say that this is impossible, but it is so improbable that a rational man would disbelieve the statement that it had happened on a certain occasion, even if the statement were made by all the Fellows of the Royal Society together with the Archbishops of Canterbury and York. For practical purposes, therefore, physics is still deterministic; the only change is that the deterministic laws are all statistical.

What, assuming the truth of modern physics, can we know about the physical world? There is no longer reason to believe that there is such a thing as "matter" consisting of atoms that persist and move. There is a collection of events ordered in the four-dimensional manifold of space-time. There is something called "energy," of which the total amount is constant, but of which the distribution is continually changing; moreover, energy has many different forms. Some of these forms characterize regions in which, for common sense, there is matter; others, like light, do not. We know something of the rules governing the changes in the distribution of energy, and its transitions from one form into another. It seems that these rules are sufficient to determine large-scale phenomena with a degree of accuracy and certainty which suffices for practical purposes, but the small-scale occurrences within the region that we call a single atom are not determined except to this extent, that in given circumstances what will happen must be one of certain enumerable possibilities, and the probability of each of these possibilities is determined by physical laws.

PSYCHOLOGY ALSO HAS CHANGED

Let us now turn to psychology, which, though a much less developed science than physics, has nevertheless gone through some not wholly dissimilar changes. In medieval and Cartesian orthodoxy there were two kinds of substance, mental and material; the business of material substance was to occupy space, and the business of mental substance was to "think." In modern physics, "substance" has disappeared: instead of persistent "things" that occupy space we have brief events that occupy space-time. In psychology, similarly, "substance" has disappeared. Descartes, after arguing "I think, therefore I am," goes on to say: "I am a thing that thinks." In the modern view "I" is a merely grammatical term; all that we know about thoughts can, if we choose, be expressed without the use of this word. Personal identity, like the identity of a piece of matter, is not the persistence of a "thing," but a certain kind of a causal connection between a series of events. In psychology the causal connection of most importance in defining personal identity is memory.

LIFE AS IT APPEARS IN BIOLOGY

Ignoring for the moment the question of "thought," let us first view life as it appears in biology. There is increasing reason to think that the whole of the difference between living and dead matter is chemical: living matter has the capacity of transforming suitable other matter into something of the same chemical composition as itself. Plants can do this with inorganic matter, animals (broadly speaking) only with organic matter. The whole process of the transformation of soil into grain and grain into human bodies, though very complicated, is essentially of the same nature as the transformation of hydrogen and oxygen into water. There is no reason why it should not be possible, before very long, to generate living organisms in the laboratory. And it is clear that a chemical compound having the above characteristic of assimilation is bound, given opportunity, to spread in the kind of way in which living matter has spread.

From the standpoint of psychology the most important property of living matter is habit-formation. This property is not *wholly* absent in dead matter: paper which has been in a roll will roll itself up again if you flatten it out. But examples of habit in inorganic matter are few and unimportant. In living matter they are still rare among the lowest forms of life; they are more noteworthy among mammals than among other animals, and much more noteworthy among human beings than among the highest apes. A great deal of what we call "intelligence" consists in aptitude for the formation of useful habits; it includes, for example, skill in games, quickness in learning the multiplication table, and facility in acquiring languages. I do not contend that the acquisition of habits covers the *whole* of what we mean by intellectual or artistic ability; I say only that it covers much of the ground, and that it covers a good deal more than might appear at first sight. It certainly covers at least nine-tenths of what is tested in examinations.

WHAT WE MEAN BY HABIT

What, exactly, do we mean by habit? Let us take the matter first as it appears to external observation, in the behavior of animal bodies. An animal has certain ways of responding to stimuli that are independent of its experience—withdrawal from what is painful, approach to food that looks or smells good, and also certain specific reflexes such as sneezing, yawning, and making the noises characteristic of the species. Sucking in infancy and sexual behavior in adult life come under the same head. Now it is found that, if a kind of event *A* often happens to an animal at the same time as another kind of event *B*, and if *B* produces a reaction *C*, then in time *A* without *B* will produce the reaction *C*. When my puppy infringes the moral law I chastise it, and at the same time say "bad dog" in a tone of reprobation. The puppy slinks away to escape the chastisement, but in time it learns to slink away when I utter a reproof. A dog that enjoys a walk learns to jump and bark excitedly as soon as his master puts on a great-coat. All training of domestic animals proceeds on this principle.

Knowing a language, whether one's own or another, is entirely a matter of habit-formation. If someone shouts "Fire!" you feel the same kind of emotion as if you saw the fire, and behave in a similar way. Obscene literature is forbidden because it arouses, though more faintly, the passions that would be aroused by what it describes. The words "William the Conqueror, 1066," become a verbal habit during early years at school; a sufficient number of such habits will make you a learned historian. Memory is one kind of habit. All learning by experience consists in the formation of habits, in accordance with the proverb "once bit, twice shy."

HABIT PRIMARILY PHYSICAL

From our point of view, the important thing about habit is that it is primarily physiological rather than psychological. Consequently the psychological area covered by it is brought into subjection to a kind of causation that is physical rather than mental, and the greater the region of habit the wider is the range of mental phenomena deprived of causal autonomy. The causal framework of the laws of human behavior seems to be, at any rate in the main, a matter, not for psychology, but for physics, chemistry, and physiology. I say "in the main" because the question is one to be decided by surveying the field in detail, not by any general principle assumed in advance of investigations.

It remains to examine a concept which is held to be peculiar to mental occurrences, namely, "introspection."

The traditional view is that there are two kinds of senses, the "outer senses" and the "inner sense." The outer senses are supposed to tell us what goes on in the physical world, while the inner sense tells us what goes on in our own mind. The outer senses tell me that my friend So-and-so is coming along the street, while the inner sense tells me that I am glad to see him. "Introspection" consists of knowing occurrences by means of the inner sense; it is supposed to show us that there are in the world thoughts and feelings as well as events in space.

This way of looking at things seems to me radically mistaken; I do not believe there is any such duality of inner and outer senses. I hold that everything directly known by the senses happens in me, not in the outer world. I might say, roughly, that I believe only in the inner sense, but this would be somewhat misleading. What I can say is that the senses directly reveal thoughts and feelings and sensations, while events in the outer world have to be inferred.

As regards what would traditionally be called the outer senses, this point of view is forced on us by the physical causation of our sensations. When I have the experience which we call "seeing the sun" the immediate causal antecedents of my experience are in the eye, the optic nerve, and the brain. If my eye were subjected to the same physical stimulus as it normally receives from the light of the sun (which is obviously possible, at least in theory), I should have exactly the experience which is called "seeing the sun." Consequently it cannot be said that in this experience I am aware of the sun itself, since I can have the experience without the sun being present. We can go farther: if a surgeon could directly stimulate the optic nerve as it is usually stimulated by sunlight falling on the eye, I should still have an experience indistinguishable from "seeing the sun"; and so I should if it were the appropriate center in the brain that was stimulated, not the optic nerve. Therefore all that is certainly involved when I think I see the sun is my own sensation and an occurrence in my brain. And the occurrence in the brain is known only by a long and difficult process of scientific inference; what I know directly is only my own sensation.

PHYSICAL CAUSES OF INTROSPECTION

According to this view, the outer senses, such as those of sight and hearing and touch, are much more akin to what is commonly called introspection than is usually supposed. Does there, then, remain any valid distinction more or less corresponding to the old distinction of inner and outer senses? I think there does. When I see the sun other people can see it too; when I listen to a politician making a speech other people in the same hall can also hear him. This leads us to infer a common outside cause for the similar visual or auditory sensations of different people in the same environment. But when I feel a toothache others in the same room with me usually feel nothing similar. We conclude that the toothache is private, while the sun and the speech are public. The toothache, like seeing the sun and hearing the speech, has a physical cause, but the cause is in my body and therefore does not affect other people as it affects me. I think accordingly, that "introspection" may be defined as consisting of sensations whose physical causes are in my body and under my skin.

"But," you may object, "introspection is not concerned with such things as toothaches; it is concerned with thoughts and feelings. I may think that not all continuous functions can be differentiated, and I may be aware of thinking this; I may feel sorrow that Roosevelt is dead, and be aware of feeling this. It is knowledge of this sort that introspection reveals." I do not for a moment deny that there is knowledge of this sort; what I do deny is that it is fundamentally different from the knowledge directly obtained through the outer senses. As soon as we realize that the sun itself has only a remote causal connection with the experience called "seeing the sun," it becomes clear that this experience is not nearly so different as it seemed from thoughts and feelings. Whether we are aware of a sensation or whether we are aware; we are never aware without interference of anything except events happening to ourselves. I refrain from attempting to define the word "aware," which I have been using. I have discussed the definition of this word elsewhere (cf. *Inquiry Into Meaning and Truth*), and as it is complicated and not very relevant I shall leave this question on one side.

THE PHYSICAL AND MENTAL OVERLAP

Discussions of mind and matter and their relations seldom trouble to give definitions of the terms involved; it seems to be thought that we all know by the light of nature that every person has a mind and a body, which are separate things. This point of view is not primitive, but was originally adopted for religious reasons. From Orphism it got into philosophy through Plato; Christian theology gave it the definiteness and sharpness of distinction which has now come to seem a matter of course to most people. I hold, on the contrary, that the distinction is by no means sharp, and that there are events which are both mental and physical. Let us try to obtain definitions of the adjectives "mental" and "physical," which, in our view of rejection of "substance," we must substitute for the substantives "mind" and "matter." If, as I have been contending, the world consists of events, we have to inquire whether there are characteristics by which some events can be classed as "physical" and some as "mental," and whether, if so, the two classes overlap.

DEFINITION OF "PHYSICAL"

Let us begin with the adjective "physical." My own definition of this adjective is one which may, at first sight, seem an odd one: I should define an event as "physical" when it is the sort of event that is dealt with by physics. Now the character of these events is only determined in certain very abstract respects: they have spatio-temporal positions, and they consist of changes in the distribution of something called "energy." True, there is one other characteristic of "physical" events which is essential, and that is their relation to sensations. Physics is an empirical science—that is to say, its laws are accepted because they are confirmed by observation. But here we meet with a difficulty: the physical world, as it appears in quantum theory, is quite unlike the world of our everyday perceptions, and it is not obvious how it can predict what our perceptions will be. The truth is that the empirical verification of physical laws depends upon something which is not properly a part of physics—namely, upon the correlation of physical events with sensations. When radiant energy of a certain frequency reaches the eye we see a certain color; if theory has predicted that frequency, our seeing of the corresponding color is held to be an empirical confirmation of the theory, but it only is a confirmation if the correlation of physical events with sensations is included, along with pure physics, as part of the total of theory to be verified.

Now sensations and perceptions are part of the subject-matter of psychology, and are commonly classed as "mental." Thus physics derives its empirical justification entirely from its connection with events belonging to the domain of psychology, which alone are capable of being data. "Data," as I intend the word, are to be defined as events known otherwise than by inference. All such events belong to psychology. I should define a "mental" event as one that can be known to some one otherwise than by inference—*i.e.*, as one that is or may be a "datum." By means of certain postulates— causality, induction, and spatio-temporal continuity—we can, from data, infer events which are not data. If you put an egg in boiling water and leave it, and when you return you find that it is boiled, you assume that it existed meanwhile. The egg that existed meanwhile was not something oval and whitish, such as you can see, but was a system of many billions of transitions of an unknown something from one energy-level to another; this is the egg of physics, whereas the egg that you see is the egg of psychology. It is because of your experience of the egg of psychology, which you can see and taste, that you believe in the effect of the boiling water of physics upon the egg of physics.

The egg of psychology cannot be supposed to exist in the absence of a percipient, since it is caused by the effect of our sense-organs upon energy that travels into their neighborhood. But although it exists only when it is perceived, it supplies our only reason for believing in the physical egg which can exist unseen.

THE RELATIONS BETWEEN MENTAL
AND PHYSICAL EVENTS

The questions of the relations between mental and physical events is complicated by the fact that, while mental events come first in the order of knowledge, physical events seem to be supreme in the region of causal efficiency. I repeat that I mean by "mental" events the kind of events that someone can perceive, and by "physical" events the sort of events that are dealt with in physics.

The knowledge conferred by physics is abstract and mathematical; it does not tell us anything about the intrinsic character of physical events. Physics does not entitle us to say that physical events differ from thoughts and feelings, nor yet that they do not differ. The inference to physical events is entirely by means of causal laws, which only enable us to infer structure. Let us take an illustration. A gramophone record can (with certain adjuncts) cause a piece of music; it can do so because of a certain identity of structure between the record and the music. But this identity is abstract and logical; in other respects the record is quite unlike the music. The physical causes of our sensations, in like manner, must have a certain structural similarity to the pattern of sensations that they cause, but need not otherwise resemble our sensations. If you could never perceive the record, and knew nothing about it except that it could cause the music, you would be in the same position with regard to it as you are with regard to the world of physics.

What physics treats as one event may, for aught that physics has to say to the contrary, be really a group of events, all in one spatio-temporal region. If what is for physics a bit of my brain is really a group of events, my sensations and thoughts and feelings may be members of this group. If so, the difference between the physical and the mental will be one of logical level: the unit for physics will be an assemblage of the units for psychology.

THE QUESTION OF "MATERIALISM"

The question of "materialism," as understood in the past, depended upon the notion of "substance"; in this old sense no one who rejects "substance" can be a Materialist. Nor can we be Materialists in the sense of believing that there are no mental events; mental events are more certain than physical events, since the physical is inferred from the mental by inferences; which confer only probability upon their conclusions.

But there is still a sense in which something closely akin to Materialism *may* be true, though it would be rash to say that it *is*. This sense has to do with the causal supremacy of physics. There is no reason whatever to suppose that living matter obeys laws different from those obeyed by dead matter. Although atomic physics is no longer deterministic, the physics of bodies of appreciable size remains as deterministic as it used to be. If there is a correlation between the state of the brain and the state of the mind, as it is plausible to suppose, then the laws of physics, together with the laws of this correlation, suffice to determine states of mind, unless (what seems improbable) the correlation is with a few atoms, not with larger portions of the brain. There is therefore some reason—though by no means conclusive reason—for regarding the laws of physics as, in a sense, controlling our mental life. This is a large part of what Materialists have contended, and this part of their contention *may* be true.

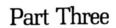

Part Three

12

Science and Religion

In recent times, the bulk of eminent physicists and a number of eminent biologists have made pronouncements stating that recent advances in science have disproved the older materialism, and have tended to reestablish the truths of religion. The statements of the scientists have as a rule been somewhat tentative and indefinite, but the theologians have seized upon them and extended them, while the newspapers in turn have reported the more sensational accounts of the theologians, so that the general public has derived the impression that physics confirms practically the whole of the Book of Genesis. I do not myself think that the moral to be drawn from modern science is at all what the general public has thus been led to suppose. In the first place, the men of science have not said nearly as much as they are thought to have said, and in the second place what they have said in the way of support for traditional religious beliefs has been said by them not in their cautious, scientific capacity, but rather in their capacity of good citizens, anxious to defend virtue and property. The [First World] War, and the Russian Revolution, have made all timid men conservative, and professors are usually temperamentally timid. Such considerations, however, are beside the point. Let us examine what science really has to say.

From *The Scientific Outlook* by Bertrand Russell, pp. 101-133. Copyright © 1931 by George and Allen Unwin. Reprinted by permission of the publisher.

FREE WILL

Until very recent times theology, while in its Catholic form it admitted free will in human beings, showed an affection for natural law in the universe, tempered only by belief in occasional miracles. In the eighteenth century, under the influence of Newton, the alliance between theology and natural law became very close. It was held that God had created the world in accordance with a Plan, and that natural laws were the embodiment of this Plan. Until the nineteenth century theology remained hard and intellectual and definite. In order to meet the assaults of atheistic reason, however, it has, during the last hundred years, aimed more and more at appealing to sentiment. It has tried to catch men in their intellectually relaxed moods; and from having been a strait-jacket it has become a dressing-gown. In our day, only the fundamentalists and a few of the more learned Catholic theologians maintain the old respectable intellectual tradition. All the other religious apologists are engaged in blunting the edge of logic, appealing to the heart instead of the head, maintaining that our feelings can demonstrate the falsity of a conclusion to which our reason has been driven. As Lord [Alfred] Tennyson nobly says:

> And like a man in wrath the heart
> Stood up and answered "I have felt."

In our day the heart has feelings about atoms, about the respiratory system, about the growth of sea-urchins and other such topics, concerning which, but for science, it would remain indifferent.

One of the most remarkable developments in religious apologetics in recent times is the attempt to rescue free will in man by means of ignorance as to the behavior of atoms. The older laws of mechanics which governed the movements of bodies large enough to be seen remain true to a very close approximation as regards such bodies, but are found to be not applicable to single atoms, still less to single electrons and protons. It is not yet known with any certainty whether there are laws governing the behavior of single atoms in all respects, or whether the behavior of such atoms is in part random. It is thought possible that the laws governing the behavior of large bodies may be merely statistical laws, expressing the average result of a large number of random motions. Some, such as the second law of thermodynamics, are known to be statistical laws, and it is possible that others may be. In the atom there are various possible states which do not merge continuously into each other, but are separated by small finite gaps. An atom may hop from one of these states to another, and there are various different hops that it may make. At present no laws are known to decide which of the possible hops will take place on any given occasion, and it is suggested that the atom is not subject to laws at all in this respect, but has what might be called, by analogy, "free will." [Sir Arthur] Eddington, in his book on the *Nature of the Physical World*, has made great play with this possibility (p. 311 ff.). He thinks, apparently, that the mind can decide the atoms in the brain to make one or another of the possible transitions at a given moment, and thus, by means of some kind of trigger action, produce large-scale results in accordance with its volition. The volition itself, he thinks, is uncaused. If he is right, the course of the physical world, even where fairly large masses are concerned, is not completely predetermined by physical laws, but is liable to be altered by the uncaused volitions of human beings.

Before examining this position I should like to say a few words about what is called "the Principle of Indeterminacy." This principle was introduced into physics in 1927, by [Werner] Heisenberg, and has been seized on by clergymen—chiefly, I think, on account of its name—as something capable of giving them an escape from thraldom to mathematical laws. It is, to my mind, somewhat surprising that Eddington should countenance this use of the principle (see page 306). The Principle of Indeterminacy states that it is impossible to determine with precision both the position and the momentum of a particle; there will be a margin of error in each, and the product of the two errors is constant. That is to say, the more accurately we determine the one, the less accurately we shall be determining the other, and *vice versa*. The margin of error involved is, of course, very small. I am surprised, I repeat, that Eddington should have appealed to this principle in connection with the question of free will, for the principle does nothing whatever to show that the course of nature is not determined. It shows merely that the old space-time apparatus is not quite adequate to the needs of modern physics, which, in any case, is known on other grounds. Space and time were invented by the Greeks, and served their purpose admirably until the present century. [Albert] Einstein replaced them by a kind of centaur which he called "space-time," and this did well enough for a couple of decades, but modern quantum mechanics has made it evident that a more fundamental reconstruction is necessary. The Principle of Indeterminacy is merely an illustration of this necessity, not of the failure of physical laws to determine the course of nature.

As J. E. Turner has pointed out (*Nature*, December 27, 1930), "The use to which the Principle of Indeterminacy has been put is largely due to an ambiguity in the word 'determined.'" In one sense a quantity is determined when it is measured, in the other sense an event is determined when it is caused. The Principle of Indeterminacy has to do with measurement, not with causation. The velocity and position of a particle are declared by the Principle to be undetermined in the sense that they cannot be accurately measured. This is a physical fact causally connected with the fact that the measuring is a physical process which has a physical effect upon what is measured. There is nothing whatever in the Principle of Indeterminacy to show that any physical event is uncaused. As Turner says: "Every argument that, since some change cannot be 'determined' in the sense of 'ascertained,' it is therefore not 'determined' in the absolutely different sense of 'caused,' is a fallacy of equivocation."

Returning now to the atom and its supposed free will, it should be observed that it is not known that the behavior of the atom is capricious. It is false to say the behavior of the atom is known to be capricious, and it is also false to say the behavior is known to be not capricious. Science has quite recently discovered that the atom is not subject to the laws of the older physics, and some physicists have somewhat rashly jumped to the conclusion that the atom is not subject to laws at all. Eddington's argument about the effect of the mind on the brain inevitably reminds one of [René] Descartes's argument on the same subject. Descartes knew of the conservation of *vis viva*, but not of the conservation of momentum. He therefore thought that the mind could alter the direction of the motion of the animal spirits, though not its amount. When, shortly after the publication of his theory, the conservation of momentum was discovered, Descartes's view had to be abandoned. Eddington's view, similarly, is at the mercy of the experimental physicists, who may at any moment discover laws regulating the behavior of individual atoms. It is very rash to erect a theological superstructure upon a piece of ignorance which may be only momentary. And the effects of this procedure, so far as it has any, are necessarily bad, since they make men hope that new discoveries will not be made.

There is, moreover, a purely empirical objection to the belief in free will. Wherever it has been possible to subject the behavior of animals or of human beings to careful scientific observation, it has been found, as in Pavlov's experiments, that scientific laws are just as discoverable as in any other sphere. It is true that we cannot predict human actions with any completeness, but this is quite sufficiently accounted for by the complication of the mechanism, and by no means demands the hypothesis of complete lawlessness, which is found to be false wherever it can be carefully tested.

Those who desire caprice in the physical world seem to me to have failed to realize what this would involve. All inference in regard to the course of nature is causal, and if nature is not subject to causal laws all such inference must fail. We cannot, in that case, know anything outside of our personal experience; indeed, strictly speaking, we can only know our experience in the present moment, since all memory depends upon causal laws. If we cannot infer the existence of other people, or even of our own past, how much less can we infer God, or anything else that the theologians desire. The principle of causality may be true or may be false, but the person who finds the hypothesis of its falsity cheering is failing to realize the implications of his own theory. He usually retains unchallenged all those causal laws which he finds convenient, as, for example, that his food will nourish him and that his bank will honor his checks so long as his account is in funds, while rejecting all those that he finds inconvenient. This, however, is altogether to *naïve* a procedure.

There is, in fact, no good reason whatever for supposing that the behavior of atoms is not subject to law. It is only quite recently that experimental methods have been able to throw any light on the behavior of individual atoms, and it is no wonder if the laws of this behavior have not yet been discovered. The prove that a given set of phenomena is not subject to laws is essentially and theoretically impossible. All that can be affirmed is that the laws, if any, have not yet been discovered. We may say, if we choose, that the men who have been investigating the atom are so clever that they must have discovered the laws if there were any. I do not think, however, that this is a sufficiently solid premise upon which to base a theory of the universe.

GOD AS MATHEMATICIAN

Eddington deduces religion from the fact that atoms do not obey the laws of mathematics. [Sir James H.] Jeans deduces it from the fact that they do. Both these arguments have been accepted with equal enthusiasm by the theologians, who hold, apparently, that the demand for consistency belongs to the cold reason and must not interfere with our deeper religious feelings.

We have examined Eddington's argument from the way that atoms jump. Let us now examine Jeans's argument from the way that stars cool. Jeans's God is Platonic. He is not, we are told, a biologist or an engineer, but a pure mathematician (*The Mysterious Universe*, p. 134). I confess to a preference for this type of God rather than the one that is conceived after the analogy of big business; but that, no doubt, is because I prefer thinking to doing. This suggests a treatise dealing with the influence of muscular tone upon theology. The man whose muscles are taut believes in a God of action, while the man whose muscles are relaxed believes in a God of thought and contemplation. Jeans, confident no doubt in his own theistic arguments, is not very complimentary to those of the evolutionists. His book on the Mysterious Universe begins with a biography of the sun, one might almost say an epitaph. It seems that not more than one star in about one hundred thousand has planets, but that some two thousand million years ago the sun had the good fortune to have a fruitful meeting with another star, which led to the existing planetary offspring. The stars that do not have planets cannot give rise to life, so that life must be a very rare phenomenon in the universe. "It seems incredible," says Jeans, "that the universe can have been designed primarily to produce life like our own: had it been so, surely we might have expected to find a better proportion between the magnitude of the mechanism and the amount of the product." And even in this rare corner of the universe the possibility of life exists only during an interlude between weather that is too hot and weather that is too cold. "It is a tragedy of our race that it is probably destined to die of cold, while the greater part of the substance of the universe still remains too hot for life to obtain a footing." Theologians who argue as if human life were the purpose of creation seem to be as faulty in their astronomy as they are excessive in their estimation of themselves and their fellow-creatures. I shall not attempt to summarize Jeans's admirable chapters on modern physics, matter and radiation, and relativity and the ether;

they are already as brief as possible, and no summary can do them justice. I will, however, quote Jeans's own summary in order to whet the reader's appetite. "To sum up, a soap-bubble with irregularities and corrugations on its surface is perhaps the best representation, in terms of simple and familiar materials, of the new universe revealed to us by the theory of relativity. The universe is not the interior of the soap-bubble but its surface, and we must always remember that, while the surface of the soap-bubble, has only two dimensions, the universe-bubble has four—three dimensions of space and one of time. And the substance out of which this bubble is blown, the soap-film, is empty space welded on to empty time."

The last chapter of the book is concerned to argue that this soap-bubble has been blown by a mathematical Deity because of His interest in its mathematical properties. This part has pleased the theologians. Theologians have grown grateful for small mercies, and they do not much care what sort of God the man of science gives them so long as he gives them one at all. Jeans's God, like Plato's, is one who has a passion for doing sums, but being a pure mathematician, is quite indifferent as to what the sums are about. By prefacing his argument by a lot of difficult and recent physics, the eminent author manages to give it an air of profundity which it would not otherwise possess. In essence the argument is as follows: since two apples and two apples together make four apples, it follows that the Creator must have known that two and two are four. It might be objected that, since one man and one woman together sometimes make three, the Creator was not yet quite as well versed in sums as one could wish. To speak seriously: Jeans reverts explicitly to the theory of Bishop Berkeley, according to which the only things that exist are thoughts, and the quasi-permanence which we observe in the external world is due to the fact that God keeps on thinking about things for quite a long time. Material objects, for example, do not cease to exist when no human being is looking at them, because God is looking at them all the time, or rather because they are thoughts in His mind at all times. The universe, he says, "can best be pictured, although still very imperfectly and inadequately, as consisting of pure thought, the thought of what, for want of a wider word, we must describe as a mathematical thinker." A little later we are told that the laws governing God's thoughts are those which govern the phenomena of our waking hours, but not apparently of our dreams.

The argument is, of course, not set out with the formal precision which Jeans would demand in a subject not involving his emotions. Apart from all detail, he has been guilty of a fundamental fallacy in confusing the realms of pure and applied mathematics. Pure mathematics at no point depends upon observation; it is concerned with symbols, and with proving that different collections of symbols have the same meaning. It is because of this symbolic character that it can be studied without the help of experiment. Physics, on the contrary, however mathematical it may become, depends throughout on observation and experiment, that is to say, ultimately upon sense perception. The mathematician provides all kinds of mathematics, but only some of what he provides is useful to the physicist. And what the physicist asserts when he uses mathematics is something totally different from what the pure mathematician asserts. The physicist asserts that the mathematical symbols which he is employing can be used for the interpretation, colligation, and prediction of sense impressions. However abstract his work may become, it never loses its relation to experience. It is found that mathematical formulas can express certain laws governing the world that we observe. Jeans argues that the world must have been created by a mathematician for the pleasure of seeing these laws in operation. If he had ever attempted to set out this argument formally, I cannot doubt that he would have seen how fallacious it is. To begin with, it seems probably that any world, no matter what, could be brought by a mathematician of sufficient skill within the scope of general laws. If this be so, the mathematical character of modern physics is not a fact about the world, but merely a tribute to the skill of the physicist. In the second place, if God were as pure a pure mathematician as His knightly champion supposes, He would have no wish to give a gross external existence to His thoughts. The desire to trace curves and make geometrical models belongs to the schoolboy stage, and would be considered *infra dig* by a professor. Nevertheless it is this desire that Jeans imputes to his Maker. The world, he tells us, consists of thoughts; of these there are, it would seem, three grades: the thoughts of God, the thoughts of men when they are awake, and the thoughts of men when they are asleep and have bad dreams. One does not quite see what the two latter kinds of thought add to the perfection of the universe, since clearly God's thoughts are the best, and one does not quite see what can have been gained by creating so much muddle-headedness. I once knew an extremely learned and orthodox theologian who told me that as the result of long study he had come to understand everything except why God created the world. I commend this puzzle to the attention of Jeans, and I hope that he will comfort the theologians by dealing with it at no distant date.

GOD AS CREATOR

One of the most serious difficulties confronting science at the present time is the difficulty derived from the fact that the universe appears to be running down. There are, for example, radioactive elements in the world. These are perpetually disintegrating into less complex elements, and no process by which they can be built up is known. This, however, is not the most important or difficult respect in which the world is running down. Although we do not know of any natural process by which complex elements are built up out of simpler ones, we can imagine such processes, and it is possible that they are taking place somewhere. But when we come to the second law of thermodynamics we encounter a more fundamental difficulty.

The second law of thermodynamics states, roughly speaking, that things left to themselves tend to get into a muddle and do not tidy themselves up again. It seems that once upon a time the universe was all tidy, with everything in its proper place, and that ever since then it has been growing more and more disorderly, until nothing but a drastic spring cleaning can restore it to its pristine order. In its original form the second law of thermodynamics asserted something much less general: namely, that when there was a difference of temperature between two neighboring bodies, the hotter one would cool and the colder one would get warmer until they reached an equal temperature. In this form the law states a fact familiar to everyone: if you hold up a red-hot poker, it will get cool while the surrounding air gets warm. But the law was soon seen to have a much more general meaning. The particles of very hot bodies are in very rapid motion, while those of cold bodies move more slowly. In the long run, when a number of swiftly moving particles and a number of slowly moving particles find themselves in the same region, the swift ones will bump into the slow ones until both sets acquire on the average equal velocities. A similar truth applies to all forms of energy. Whenever there is a great deal of energy in one region and very little in a neighboring region, energy tends to travel from the one region to the other, until equality is established. This whole process may be described as a tendency toward democracy. It will be seen that this is an irreversible process, and that in the past energy must have been more unevenly distributed than it is now. In view of the fact that the material universe is now considered to be finite, and to consist of some definite though unknown number of electrons and protons, there is a theoretical limit to the possible heaping-up of energy in some places as opposed to others. As we trace the course of the world backwards in time, we arrive after some finite number of years (rather more than four thousand and four, however), at a state of the world which could not have been preceded by any other, if the second law of thermodynamics was then valid. This initial state of the world would be that in which energy was distributed as unevenly as possible. As Eddington says:

> The difficulty of an infinite past is appalling. It is inconceivable that we are the heirs of an infinite time of preparation; it is not less inconceivable that there was once a moment with no moment preceding it.
>
> This dilemma of the beginning of time would worry us more were it not shut out by another overwhelming difficulty lying between us and the infinite past. We have been studying the running-down of the universe; if our views are right, somewhere between the beginning of time and the present day we must place the winding up of the universe.
>
> Travelling backwards into the past we find a world with more and more organization. If there is no barrier to stop us earlier we must reach a moment when the energy of the world was wholly organized with none of the random element in it. It is impossible to go back any further under the present system of natural law. I do not think the phrase "wholly organized" begs the question. The organization we are concerned with is exactly definable, and there is a limit at which it becomes perfect. There is not an infinite series of states of higher and still higher organization; nor, I think, is the limit one which is ultimately approached more and more slowly. Complete organization does not tend to be more immune from loss than incomplete organization.
>
> There is no doubt that the scheme of physics as it has stood for the last three-quarters of a century postulates a date at which either the entities of the universe were created in a state of high organization, or pre-existing entities were endowed with that organization which they have been squandering ever since. Moreover, this organization is admittedly the antithesis of chance. It is something which could not occur fortuitously.
>
> This has long been used as an argument against a too aggressive materialism. I has been quoted as scientific proof of the intervention of the Creator at a time not infinitely remote from today. But I am not

advocating that we draw any hasty conclusions from it. Scientists and theologians alike must regard as somewhat crude the naïve theological doctrine which (suitably disguised) is at present to be found in every textbook of thermodynamics, namely, that some billions of years ago God wound up the material universe and has left it to chance ever since. This should be regarded as the working hypothesis of thermodynamics rather than its declaration of faith. It is one of those conclusions from which we can see no logical escape—only it suffers from the drawback that it is incredible. As a scientist I simply do not believe that the present order of things started off with a bang; unscientifically I feel equally unwilling to accept the implied discontinuity in the Divine nature. But I can make no suggestion to evade the deadlock.[1]

It will be seen that Eddington, in this passage, does not infer a definite act of creation by a Creator. His only reason for not doing so is that he does not like the idea. The scientific argument leading to the conclusion which he rejects is much stronger than the argument in favor of free will, since that is based upon ignorance, whereas the one we are now considering is based upon knowledge. This illustrates the fact that the theological conclusions drawn by scientists from their science are only such as please them, and not such as their appetite for orthodoxy is insufficient to swallow, although the argument would warrant them. We must, I think, admit that there is far more to be said for the view that the universe had a beginning in time at some not infinitely remote period, than there is for any of the other theological conclusions which scientists have recently been urging us to admit. The argument does not have demonstrative certainty. The second law of thermodynamics may not hold in all times and places, or we may be mistaken in thinking the universe spatially finite; but as arguments of this nature go, it is a good one, and I think we ought provisionally to accept the hypothesis that the world had a beginning at some definite, though unknown, date.

Are we to infer from this that the world was made by a Creator? Certainly not, if we are to adhere to the canons of valid scientific inference. There is no reason whatever why the universe should not have begun spontaneously, except that it seems odd that it should do so; but there is no law of nature to the effect that things which seem odd to us must not happen. To infer a Creator is to infer a cause, and causal inferences are only admissible in science when they proceed from observed causal laws. Creation out of nothing is an occurrence which has not been observed. There is, therefore, no better reason to suppose that the world was caused by a Creator than to suppose that it was uncaused; either equally contradicts the causal laws that we can observe.

Nor is there, so far as I can see, any particular comfort to be derived from the hypothesis that the world was made by a Creator. Whether it was, or whether it was not, it is what it is. If somebody tried to sell you a bottle of very nasty wine, you would not like it any better for being told that it had been made in a laboratory and not from the juice of the grape. In like manner, I see no comfort to be derived from the supposition that this very unpleasing universe was manufactured of set purpose.

Some people—among whom, however, Eddington is not included—drive comfort from the thought that if God made the world, He may wind it up again when it has completely run down. For my part, I do not see how an unpleasant process can be made less so by the reflection that it is to be indefinitely repeated. No doubt, however, that is because I am lacking in religious feeling.

The purely intellectual argument on this point may be put in a nutshell: is the Creator amenable to the laws of physics or is He not? If He is not, He cannot be inferred from physical phenomena, since no physical causal law can lead to Him; if He is, we shall have to apply the second law of thermodynamics to Him and suppose that He also had to be created at some remote period. But in that case He has lost His *raison d'être*. It is curious that not only the physicists, but even the theologians, seem to find something new in the arguments from modern physics. Physicists, perhaps, can scarcely be expected to know the history of theology, but the theologians ought to be aware that the modern arguments have all had their counterparts at earlier times. Eddington's argument about free will and the brain is, as we saw, closely parallel to Descartes's. Jeans's argument is a compound of Plato and Berkeley, and has no more warrant in physics than it had at the time of either of these philosophers. The argument that the world must have had a beginning in time is set forth with great clearness by [Immanuel] Kant, who, however, supplements it by an equally powerful argument to prove that the world had no beginning in time. Our age has been rendered conceited by the multitude of new discoveries and inventions, but in the realm of philosophy it is much less in advance of the past than it imagines itself to be.

We hear a great deal nowadays about the old-fashioned materialism, and its refutation by modern physics. As a matter of fact, there has been a change in the technique of physics. In old days, whatever philosophers might say, physics proceeded technically on the assumption that matter consisted of hard little lumps. Now it no longer does so. But few philosophers ever believed in the hard little lumps at any date later than that of Democritus. Berkeley and [David] Hume certainly did not; no more did [Gottfried] Leibniz, Kant, and [George W.] Hegel. [Ernst] Mach, himself a physicist, taught a completely different doctrine, and every scientist with even a tincture of philosophy was ready to admit that the hard little lumps were no more than a technical device. In that sense materialism is dead, but in another and more important sense it is more alive than it ever was. The important question is not whether matter consists of hard little lumps or of something else, but whether the course of nature is determined by the laws of physics. The progress of biology, physiology, and psychology has made it more probable than it ever was before that all natural phenomena are governed by the laws of physics; and this is the really important point. To prove this point, however, we must consider some of the dicta of those who deal with the sciences of life.

EVOLUTIONARY THEOLOGY

Evolution, when it was new, was regarded as hostile to religion, and is still so considered by fundamentalists. But a whole school of apologists has grown up who see in evolution evidence of a Divine Plan slowly unfolding through the ages. Some place this Plan in the mind of a Creator, while others regard it as immanent in the obscure strivings of living organisms. In the one view we fulfil God's purposes; in the other we fulfil our own, though these are better than we know. Like most controversial questions, the question of the purposiveness of evolution has become entangled in a mass of detail. When, long ago, [Thomas H.] Huxley and [William E.] Gladstone debated the truth of the Christian religion in the pages of the *Nineteenth Century,* this great issue was found to turn upon the question whether the Gadarene swine had belonged to a Jew or a Gentile, since in the latter case, but not in the former, their destruction involved an unwarrantable interference with private property. Similarly the question of purpose in evolution becomes entangled in the habits of the amophila, the behavior of sea-urchins when turned upside down, and the aquatic or terrestrial habits of the axolotl. But such questions, grave as they are, we may leave to specialists.

In passing from physics to biology one is conscious of a transition from the cosmic to the parochial. In physics and astronomy we are dealing with the universe at large, and not only with that corner of it in which we happen to live, nor with those aspects of it which we happen to exemplify. From a cosmic point of view, life is a very unimportant phenomenon: very few stars have planets; very few planets can support life. Life, even on the earth, belongs to only a very small proportion of the matter close to the earth's surface. During the greater part of the past existence of the earth, it was too hot to support life; during the greater part of its future existence, it will be too cold. It is by no means impossible that there is, at this moment, no life anywhere in the universe except on the earth; but even if, taking a very liberal estimate, we suppose that there are scattered through space some hundred thousand other planets on which life exists, it must still be admitted that living matter makes rather a poor show if considered as the purpose of the whole creation. There are some old gentlemen who are fond of prosy anecdotes leading at last to a "point"; imagine an anecdote longer than any you have ever heard, and the "point" shorter, and you will have a fair picture of the activities of the Creator according to the biologists. Moreover, the "point" of the anecdote, even when it is reached, appears hardly worthy of so long a preface. I am willing to admit that there is merit in the tail of the fox, the song of the thrush, or the horns of the ibex. But is not to these things that the evolutionary theologian points with pride: it is to the soul of man. Unfortunately, there is no impartial arbiter to decide on the merits of the human race; but for my part, when I consider their poison gases, their researches into bacteriological warfare, their meannesses, cruelties and oppressions, I find them, considered as the crowning gem of the creation, somewhat lacking in lustre. But let that pass.

Is there anything in the process of evolution that demands the hypothesis of a purpose, whether immanent or transcendent? This is the crucial question. For one who is not a biologist it is difficult to speak otherwise than with hesitation on this question. I am, however, entirely unconvinced by the arguments in favor of purpose that I have seen.

The behavior of animals and plants is on the whole such as to lead to certain results, which the observing biologist interprets as the purpose of the behavior. In the case of plants, at any rate, he is generally willing to concede that this purpose is not consciously entertained by the organism; but that is all the better if he wishes to prove that it is the purpose of a Creator. I am, however, quite unable to see why an intelligent Creator should have the purposes which we must attribute to Him if He has really designed all that happens in the world of organic life. Nor does the progress of scientific investigation afford any evidence that the behavior of living matter is governed by anything other than laws of physics and chemistry. Take, for example, the process of digestion. The first step in this process is the seizing of food. This has been carefully studied in many animals, more particularly in chickens. New-born chickens have a reflex which causes them to peck at any object having more or less the shape and size of edible grains. After some experience this unconditioned reflex becomes transformed into a conditioned reflex, exactly after the manner studied by Pavlov. The same thing may be observed in babies: they suck not only their mothers' breasts, but everything physically capable of being sucked; they endeavor to extract food out of shoulders and hands and arms. It is only after months of experience that they learn to confine their efforts after nourishment to the breast. Sucking in infants is at first an unconditioned reflex, and by no means an intelligent one. It depends for its success upon the intelligence of the mother. Chewing and swallowing are at first unconditioned reflexes, though through experience they become conditioned. The chemical processes which the food undergoes at various stages of digestion have been minutely studied, and none of them require the invocation of any peculiar vital principle.

Or take again reproduction, which, though not universal throughout the animal kingdom, is nevertheless one of its most interesting peculiarities. There is now nothing in this process that can rightly be called mysterious. I do not mean to say that it is all fully understood, but that mechanistic principles have explained enough of it to make it probable that, given time, they will explain the whole. Jacques Loeb, over twenty years ago, discovered means of fertilizing an ovum without the intervention of a spermatozoon. He sums up the results of his experiments and those of other investigators in the sentence: "We may, therefore, state that the complete imitation of the developmental effect of the spermatozoon by certain physico-chemical agencies has been accomplished."[2]

Take again the question of heredity, which is closely associated with that of reproduction. The present state of scientific knowledge in regard to this matter is set forth very ably by Professor [Lancelot] Hogben in his book on *The Nature of Living Matter,* more particularly in the chapter on the atomistic view of parenthood. In this chapter the reader can learn all that a layman needs to know about the Mendelian theory, chromosomes, mutants, etc. I do not see how anybody can, in view of what is now known on these subjects, maintain that there is anything in the theory of heredity requiring us to bow down before a mystery. The experimental stage of embryology is still recent, yet it has achieved remarkable results: it has shown that the conception of an organism which had dominated biology is not nearly so rigid as had been supposed.

> To graft the eye of one salamander tadpole on to the head of another individual is now a commonplace of experimental embryology. Five-legged and two-headed newts are now manufactured in the laboratory.[3]

But all this, the reader may say, is concerned only with the body; what are we to say concerning the mind? As to this, the question is not quite so simple. We may observe, to begin with, that the mental processes of animals are purely hypothetical, and that the scientific treatment of animals must confine itself to their behavior and to their physical processes, since these alone are observable. I do not mean that we should deny that animals have minds; I mean merely that in so far as we are scientific we should say nothing about their minds one way or the other. As a matter of fact, the behavior of their bodies appears to be causally self-contained, in the sense that its explanation does not, at any point, demand the intervention of some unobservable entity which we could call a mind. The theory of the conditioned reflex deals satisfactorily with all those cases in which it was formerly thought that a mental causation is essential for explaining the behavior of the animal. When we come to human beings, we seem still able to explain the behavior of human bodies on the assumption that there is no extraneous agent called mind acting upon them. But in the case of human beings this statement is much more questionable than in the case of other animals, both because the behavior of human beings is more complex, and because we know, or think we know, through introspection, that we have minds. There is no doubt that we do know something about ourselves which is commonly expressed by saying that we have minds; but, as often happens, although we know something it is very difficult to say what we know. More particularly it is difficult to show that the causes of our bodily behavior are not purely physical. It seems to introspection as though there were something called the will which causes those movements that we call voluntary. It is, however, quite possible that such movements have a complete chain of physical causes to which the will (whatever it may be) is a mere concomitant. Or perhaps, since the subject matter of physics is no longer matter in the old sense, it may be that what we call our thoughts are ingredients of the complexes with which physics has replaced the old conception of matter. The dualism of mind and matter is out-of-date: matter has become more like mind, and mind has become more like matter, than seemed possible at an earlier stage of science. One is led to suppose that what really exists is something intermediate between the billiard-balls of old-fashioned materialism and the soul of old-fashioned psychology.

There is here, however, an important distinction to be made. There is, on the one hand, the question as to the sort of stuff the world is made of, and on the other hand, the question as to its causal skeleton. Science has been from its inception, though at first not exclusively, a form of what may be called power-thought: that is to say, it has been concerned to understand what causes the processes we observe rather than to analyze the ingredients of which they are composed. The highly abstract scheme of physics gives, it would seem, the causal skeleton of the world, while leaving out all the color and variety and individuality of the things that compose the world. In suggesting that the causal skeleton supplied by physics is, in theory, adequate to give the causal laws governing the behavior of human bodies, we are not suggesting that this bare abstraction tells us anything about the contents of human minds, or for that matter about the actual constitution of what we regard as matter. The billiard-balls of old-fashioned materialism were far too concrete and sensible to be admitted into the framework of modern physics, but the same is true of our thoughts. The concrete variety of the actual world seems to be largely irrelevant when we are investigating these causal processes. Let us take an illustration. The principle of the lever is simple and easily understood. It depends only upon the relative positions of the fulcrum, force, and resistance. It may happen that the actual lever employed is covered with exquisite pictures by a painter of genius; although these may be of more importance from the emotional point of view than the mechanistic properties of the lever, they do not in any way affect those

properties, and may be wholly omitted in an account of what the
lever can do. So it is with the world. The world as we perceive it is
full of a rich variety: some of it is beautiful, some of it is ugly; parts
seem to us good, parts bad. But all this has nothing to do with the
purely causal properties of things, and it is these properties with
which science is concerned. I am not suggesting that if we knew
these properties completely we should have a complete knowledge of
the world, for its concrete variety is an equally legitimate object of
knowledge. What I am saying is that science is that sort of knowledge which gives causal understanding, and this sort of knowledge
can in all likelihood be completed, even where living bodies are
concerned, without taking account of anything but their physical
and chemical properties. In saying this we are, of course, going
beyond what can at present be said with any certainty, but the work
that has been done in recent times in physiology, biochemistry,
embryology, the mechanism of sensation,[4] and so on, irresistibly
suggests the truth of our conclusion.

One of the best statements of the point of view of a religiously-
minded biologist is to be found in Lloyd Morgan's *Emergent Evolution* (1923) and *Life, Mind and Spirit* (1926). Lloyd Morgan believes
that there is a Divine Purpose underlying the course of evolution,
more particularly of what he calls "emergent evolution." The definition of emergent evolution, if I understand it rightly, is as follows: it
sometimes happens that a collection of objects arranged in a suitable pattern will have a new property which does not belong to the
objects singly, and which cannot, so far as we can see, be deduced
from their several properties together with the way in which they
are arranged. He considers that there are examples of the same kind
of thing even in the inorganic realm. The atom, the molecule, and
the crystal will all have properties which, if I understand Lloyd
Morgan aright, he regards as not deducible from the properties of
their constituents. The same holds in a higher degree of living
organisms, and most of all with those higher organisms which
possess what are called minds. Our minds, he would say, are, it is
true, associated with the physical organism, but are not deducible
from the properties of that organism considered as an arrangement
of atoms in space. "Emergent evolution," he says, "is from first to
last a revelation and manifestation of that which I speak of as
Divine Purpose." Again he says: "Some of us, and I for one, end
with a concept of activity, under acknowledgment, as part and

parcel of Divine Purpose." Sin, however, is not contributory to the manifestation of the Divine Purpose (p. 288).

It would be easier to deal with this view if any reasons were advanced in its favor, but so far as I have been able to discover from Professor Lloyd Morgan's pages, he considers that the doctrine is its own recommendation and does not need to be demonstrated by appeals to the mere understanding. I do not pretend to know whether Professor Lloyd Morgan's opinion is false. For aught I know to the contrary, there may be a Being of infinite power who chooses that children should die of meningitis, and older people of cancer; these things occur, and occur as the result of evolution. If, therefore, evolution embodies a Divine Plan, these occurrences must also have been planned. I have been informed that suffering is sent as a purification for sin, but I find it difficult to think that a child of four or five years old can be sunk in such black depths of iniquity as to deserve the punishment that befalls not a few of the children whom our optimistic divines might see any day, if they chose, suffering torments in children's hospitals. Again, I am told that though the child himself may not have sinned very deeply, he deserves to suffer on account of his parents' wickedness. I can only repeat that if this is the Divine sense of justice it differs from mine, and that I think mine superior. If indeed the world in which we live has been produced in accordance with a Plan, we shall have to reckon Nero a saint in comparison with the Author of that Plan. Fortunately, however, the evidence of Divine Purpose is nonexistent; so at least one must infer from the fact that no evidence is adduced by those who believe in it. We are, therefore, spared the necessity for that attitude of impotent hatred which every brave and humane man would otherwise be called upon to adopt toward the Almighty Tyrant.

We have reviewed a number of different apologies for religion on the part of eminent men of science. We have seen that Eddington and Jeans contradict each other, and that both contradict the biological theologians, but all agree that in the last resort science should abdicate before what is called the religious consciousness. This attitude is regarded by themselves and by their admirers as more optimistic than that of the uncompromising rationalists. It is, in fact, quite the opposite: it is the outcome of discouragement and loss of faith. Time was when religion was believed with wholehearted fervor, when men went on crusades and burned each other at the stake because of the intensity of their convictions. After the wars of religion theology gradually lost this intense hold on men's minds. So far as anything has taken its place, its place has been taken by science. In the name of science we revolutionize industry, undermine family morals, enslave colored races, and skilfully exterminate each other with poison gases. Some men of science do not altogether like these uses to which science is being put. In terror and dismay they shrink from the uncompromising pursuit of knowledge and try to find refuge in the superstitions of an earlier day. As Professor Hogben says:

> The apologetic attitude so prevalent in science today is not a logical outcome of the introduction of new concepts. It is based upon the hope of reinstating traditional beliefs with which science was at one time in open conflict. This hope is not a by-product of scientific discovery. It has its roots in the social temper of the period. For half a decade the nations of Europe abandoned the exercise of reason in their relations with one another. Intellectual detachment was disloyalty. Criticism of traditional belief was treason. Philosophers and men of science bowed to the inexorable decree of herd suggestion. Compromise to traditional belief became the hallmark of good citizenship. Contemporary philosophy has yet to find a way out of the intellectual discouragement which is the heritage of a World War.[5]

It is not by going backward that we shall find an issue from our troubles. No slothful relapses into infantile fantasies will direct the new power which men have derived from science into the right channels; nor will philosophic skepticism as to the foundations arrest the course of scientific technique in the world of affairs. Men need a faith which is robust and real, not timid and half-hearted. Science is in its essence nothing but the systematic pursuit of knowledge, and knowledge, whatever ill-uses bad men make of it, is in its essence good. To lose faith in knowledge is to lose faith in the best of man's capacities; and therefore I repeat unhesitatingly that the unyielding rationalist has a better faith and a more unbending optimism than any of the timid seekers after the childish comforts of a less adult age.

NOTES

1. Eddington, *The Nature of the Physical World,* 1928, p. 83 ff.

2. *The Mechanistic Conception of Life,* 1912, p. 11.
3. Hogben, op. cit., p. 111.
4. See e.g. *The Basis of Sensation,* by E. D. Adrian, 1928.
5. Hogben, op. cit., p. 28.

13

Cosmic Purpose

Modern men of science, if they are not hostile or indifferent to religion, cling to one belief which, they think, can survive amid the wreck of former dogmas—the belief, namely, in Cosmic Purpose. Liberal theologians, equally, make this the central article of their creed. The doctrine has several forms, but all have in common the conception of evolution as having a direction toward something ethically valuable, which, in some sense, gives the reason for the whole long process. Sir J. Arthur Thomson, as we saw, maintained that science is incomplete because it cannot answer the question *Why?* Religion, he thought, can answer it. Why were stars formed? Why did the sun give birth to planets? Why did the earth cool, and at last give rise to life? Because, in the end, something admirable was going to result—I am not quite sure what, but I believe it was scientific theologians and religiously minded scientists.

The doctrine has three forms—theistic, pantheistic, and what may be called "emergent." The first, which is the simplest and most orthodox, holds that God created the world and decreed the laws of nature because He foresaw that in time some good would be evolved. In this view the purpose exists consciously in the mind of the Creator, who remains external to His creation.

In the pantheistic form, God is not external to the universe, but is merely the universe considered as a whole. There cannot therefore be an act of creation, but there is a kind of creative force *in* the universe, which causes it to develop according to a plan which this

From *Religion and Science* by Bertrand Russell, pp. 199-233. Copyright ⓒ 1935 by Oxford University Press. Reprinted by permission of the publisher.

creative force may be said to have had in mind throughout the process.

In the "emergent" form, the purpose is more blind. At an earlier stage, nothing in the universe foresees a later stage, but a kind of blind impulsion leads to those changes which bring more developed forms into existence, so that, in some rather obscure sense, the end is implicit in the beginning.

All these three forms are represented in the volume of B.B.C. [British Broadcasting Company] talks already mentioned. The Bishop of Birmingham advocates the theistic form, Professor J. S. Haldane the pantheistic form, and Professor Alexander the "emergent" form—though [Henri] Bergson and Professor Lloyd Morgan are perhaps more typical representatives of this last. The doctrines will perhaps become clearer by being stated in the words of those who hold them.

The Bishop of Birmingham maintains that "there is a rationality in the universe akin to the rational mind of man," and that "this makes us doubt whether the cosmic process is not directed by a mind." The doubt does not last long. We learn immediately that "there has obviously, in this vast panorama, been a progress which has culminated in the creation of civilized man. Is that progress the outcome of blind forces? It seems to me fantastic to say 'yes' in answer to this question. . . . In fact, the natural conclusion to draw from the modern knowledge won by scientific method is that the Universe is subject to the sway of thought—of thought directed by will towards definite ends. Man's creation was thus not a quite incomprehensible and wholly improbable consequence of the properties of electrons and protons, or, if you prefer so to say, of discontinuities in space-time: it was the result of some Cosmic Purpose. And the ends towards which that Purpose acted must be found in man's distinctive qualities and powers. In fact, man's moral and spiritual capacities, at their highest, show the nature of the Cosmic Purpose which is the source of his being."

The Bishop rejects pantheism, as we saw, because, if the world is God, the evil in the world is in God; and also because "we must hold that God is *not,* like his Universe, in the making." He candidly admits the evil in the world, adding: "We are puzzled that there should be so much evil, and this bewilderment is the chief argument against Christian theism." With admirable honesty, he makes no attempt to show that our bewilderment is irrational.

Dr. Barnes's exposition raises problems of two kinds—those concerned with Cosmic Purpose in general, and those specially concerned with its theistic form. The former I will leave to a later stage, but on the latter a few words must be said now.

The conception of purpose is a natural one to apply to a human artificer. A man who desires a house cannot, except in the Arabian Nights, have it rise before him as a result of his mere wish; time and labor must be expended before his wish can be gratified. But Omnipotence is subject to no such limitations. If God really thinks well of the human race—an unplausible hypothesis, as it seems to me—why not proceed, as in Genesis, to create man at once? What was the point of the ichthyosaurs, dinosaurs, diplodochi, mastodons, and so on? Dr. Barnes himself confesses, somewhere, that the purpose of the tapeworm is a mystery. What useful purpose is served by rabies and hydrophobia? It is no answer to say that the laws of nature inevitably produce evil as well as good, for God decreed the laws of nature. The evil which is due to sin may be explained as the result of our free will, but the problem of evil in the prehuman world remains. I hardly think Dr. Barnes will accept the solution offered by William Gillespie, that the bodies of beasts of prey were inhabited by devils, whose first sins antedated the brute creation; yet it is difficult to see what other logically satisfying answer can be suggested. The difficulty is old, but none the less real. An omnipotent Being who created a world containing evil not due to sin must Himself be at least partially evil.[1]

To this objection the pantheistic and emergent forms of the doctrine of Cosmic Purpose are less exposed.

Pantheistic evolution has varieties according to the particular brand of pantheism involved; that of Professor J. S. Haldane, which we are now to consider, is connected with Hegel, and, like everything Hegelian, is not very easy to understand. But the point of view is one which has had considerable influence throughout the past hundred years and more, so that it is necessary to examine it. Moreover, Professor Haldane is distinguished for his work in various special fields, and he has exemplified his general philosophy by detailed investigations, particularly in physiology, which appeared to him to demonstrate that the science of living bodies has need of other laws besides those of chemistry and physics. This fact adds weight to his general outlook.

According to this philosophy, there is not, strictly speaking, any such thing as "dead" matter, nor is there any living matter without something of the nature of consciousness; and, to go one step further, there is no consciousness which is not in some degree divine. The distinction between appearance and reality is involved in Professor Haldane's views, although he does not mention it; but now, as with Hegel, it has become a distinction of degree rather than of kind. Dead matter is least real, living matter a little more so, human consciousness still more, but the only complete reality is God, i.e., the Universe conceived as divine. Hegel professes to give logical proofs of these propositions, but we will pass these by, as they would require a volume. We will, however, illustrate Professor Haldane's views by some quotations from his B.B.C. talk.

"If we attempt," he says, "to make mechanistic interpretation the sole basis of our philosophy of life, we must abandon completely our traditional religious beliefs and many other ordinary beliefs." Fortunately, however, he thinks, there is no need to explain everything mechanistically, i.e., in terms of chemistry and physics, nor, indeed, is this possible, since biology needs the conception of *organism*. "From the physical standpoint life is nothing less than a standing miracle." "Hereditary transmission . . . itself implies the distinguishing feature of life as co-ordinated unity always tending to maintain and reproduce itself." "If we assume that life is not inherent in Nature, and that there must have been a time before life existed, this is an unwarranted assumption which would make the appearance of life totally unintelligible." "The fact that biology bars decisively the door against a final mechanistic or mathematical interpretation of our experience is at least very significant in connection with our ideas as to religion." "The relations of conscious behavior to life are analogous to those of life to mechanism." "For psychological interpretation the present is no mere fleeting moment: it holds within it both the past and the future." As biology needs the concept of *organism,* so (he maintains) psychology needs that of *personality;* it is a mistake to think of a person as made up of a soul *plus* a body, or to suppose that we know only sensations, not the external world, for in truth the environment is not *outside* us. "Space and time do not isolate personality: they express an order within it, so that the immensities of space and time are within it, as Kant saw." "Personalities do not exclude one another. It is simply a fundamental fact in our experience that an active ideal of truth, justice, charity and beauty is always present to us, and is our interest, but not our mere individual interest. The ideal is, moreover, one ideal, though it has different aspects."

From this point, we are ready to take the next step, from single personalities to God. "Personality is not merely individual. It is in this fact that we recognize the presence of God—God present not merely as a being outside us, but within and around us as Personality of personalities." "It is only within ourselves, in our active ideals of truth, right, charity and beauty, and consequent fellowship with others, that we find the revelation of God." Freedom and immortality, we are told, belong to God, not to human individuals, who, in any case, are not quite "real." "Were the whole human race to be blotted out, God would still, as from all eternity, be the only reality, and in His existence what is real in us would continue to live."

One last consoling reflection: from the sole reality of God, it follows that the poor ought not to mind being poor. It is foolish to grasp at "unreal shadows of the passing moment, such as useless luxury. . . . The real standard of the poor may be far more satisfying than that of the rich." For those who are starving, one gathers, it will be a comfort to remember that "the only ultimate reality is the spiritual or personal reality which we denote by the existence of God."

Many questions are raised by this theory. Let us begin with the most definite: In what sense, if any, is biology not reducible to physics and chemistry, or psychology to biology?

As regards the relation of biology to chemistry and physics, Professor Haldane's view is not that now held by most specialists. An admirable, though not recent, statement of the opposite point of view will be found in *The Mechanistic Conception of Life,* by Jacques Loeb (published in 1912), some of the most interesting chapters of which give the results of experiments on reproduction, which is regarded by Professor Haldane as obviously inexplicable on mechanical principles. The mechanistic point of view is sufficiently accepted to be that set forth in the last edition of the *Encyclopaedia Britannica,* where Mr. E. S. Goodrich, under the heading "Evolution," says:

> A living organism, then, from the point of view of the scientific observer, is a self-regulating, self-repairing, physico-chemical complex mechanism. What, from this point of view, we call "life" is the sum of its physico-chemical processes, forming a continuous interdependent series without break, and without the interference of any mysterious extraneous force.

You will look in vain through this article for any hint that in living matter there are processes not reducible to physics and chemistry. The author points out that there is no sharp line between living and dead matter: "No hard-and-fast line can be drawn between the living and the non-living. There is no special living chemical substance, no special vital element differing from dead matter, and no special vital force can be found at work. Every step in the process is determined by that which preceded it and determines that which follows." As to the origin of life, "it must be supposed that long ago, when conditions became favorable, relatively high compounds of various kinds were formed. Many of these would be quite unstable, breaking down almost as soon as formed; others might be stable and merely persist. But still others might tend to reform, to assimilate, as fast as they broke down. Once started on this track such a growing compound or mixture would inevitably tend to perpetuate itself, and might combine with or feed on others less complex than itself." This point of view, rather than that of Professor Haldane, may be taken as that which is prevalent among biologists at the present day. They agree that there is no sharp line between living and dead matter, but while Professor Haldane thinks that what we call dead matter is really living, the majority of biologists think that living matter is really a physico-chemical mechanism.

The question of the relation between physiology and psychology is more difficult. There are two distinct questions: Can our bodily behavior be supposed due to physiological causes alone? and, What is the relation of mental phenomena to concurrent actions of the body? It is only bodily behavior that is open to public observation; our thoughts may be *inferred* by others, but can be *perceived* only by ourselves. This, at least, is what common sense would say. In theoretical strictness, we cannot observe the actions of bodies, but only certain effects which they have on us; what others observe at the same time may be similar, but will always differ, in a greater or less degree, from what we observe. For this and other reasons, the gap between physics and psychology is not so wide as was formerly thought. Physics may be regarded as predicting what we shall see in certain circumstances, and in this sense it is a branch of psychology, since our seeing is a "mental" event. This point of view has come to the fore in modern physics through the desire to make only assertions that are empirically verifiable, combined with the fact that a verification is always an observation by some human being, and therefore an occurrence such as psychology considers. But all this belongs to the philosophy of the two sciences rather than to their practice: their technique remains distinct in spite of the *rapprochement* between their subject-matters.

To return to the two questions at the beginning of the preceding paragraph: as we saw in an earlier chapter, if our bodily actions all have physiological causes, our minds become causally unimportant. It is only by bodily acts that we can communicate with others, or have any effect upon the outer world; what we think matters only if it can affect what our bodies do. Since, however, the distinction between what is mental and what is physical is one of convenience only, our bodily acts may have causes lying wholly within physics, and yet mental events may be among their causes. The practical issue is not to be stated in terms of mind and body. It may, perhaps, be stated as follows: Are our bodily acts determined by physico-chemical laws? And, if they are, is there nevertheless an independent science of psychology, in which we study mental events directly, without the intervention of the artificially constructed concept of matter?

Neither of these questions can be answered with any confidence, though there is some evidence in favor of an affirmative answer to the first of them. The evidence is not direct; we cannot calculate a man's movements as we can those of the planet Jupiter. But no sharp line can be drawn between human bodies and the lowest forms of life; there is nowhere such a gap as would tempt us to say: Here physics and chemistry cease to be adequate. And as we have seen, there is also no sharp line between living and dead matter. It seems probable, therefore, that physics and chemistry are supreme throughout.

With regard to the possibility of an independent science of psychology, even less can be said at present. To some extent, psychoanalysis has attempted to create such a science, but the success of this attempt, in so far as it avoids physiological causation, may still be questioned. I incline—though with hesitation—to the view that there will ultimately be a science embracing both physics and psychology, though distinct from either as at present developed. The technique of physics was developed under the influence of a belief in the metaphysical reality of "matter" which now no longer exists, and the new quantum mechanics has a different technique which dispenses with false metaphysics. The technique of psychology, to some extent, was developed under a belief in the metaphysical reality of the "mind." It seems possible that, when physics and psychology have both been completely freed from these lingering errors, they will both develop into one science dealing neither with mind nor with matter, but with events, which will not be labelled either "physical" or "mental." In the meantime, the question of the scientific status of psychology must remain open.

Professor Haldane's views on psychology raise, however, a narrower issue, as to which much more definite things can be said. He maintains that the distinctive concept of psychology is "personality." He does not define the term, but we may take it as meaning some unifying principle which binds together the constituents of one mind, causing them all to modify each other. The idea is vague; it stands for the "soul," in so far as this is still thought to be defensible. It differs from the soul in not being a bare entity, but a kind of quality of wholeness. It is thought, by those who believe in it, that everything in the mind of John Smith has a John-Smithy quality which makes it impossible for anything quite similar to be in anyone else's mind. If you are trying to give a scientific account of John Smith's mind, you must not be content with general rules, such as can be given for all pieces of matter indiscriminately; you must remember that the events concerned are happening to that particular man, and are what they are because of his whole history and character.

There is something attractive about this view, but I see no reason to regard it as true. It is, of course, obvious that two men in the same situation may react differently because of differences in their past histories, but the same is true of two bits of iron of which one has been magnetized and the other not. Memories, one supposes, are engraved on the brain, and affect behavior through a difference of physical structure. Similar considerations apply to character. If one man is choleric and another phlegmatic, the difference is usually traceable to the glands, and could, in most cases, be obliterated by the use of suitable drugs. The belief that personality is mysterious and irreducible has no scientific warrant, and is accepted chiefly because it is flattering to our human self-esteem.

Take again the two statements: "For psychological interpretation the present is no mere fleeting moment: it holds within it both the past and the future"; and, "Space and time do not isolate personality: they express an order within it." As regards past and future, I think Professor Haldane has in mind such matters as our condition when we have just seen a flash of lightning, and are expecting the thunder. It may be said that the lightning, which is past, and the thunder, which is future, both enter into our present mental state. But this is to be misled by metaphor. The recollection of lightning is not lightning, and the expectation of thunder is not thunder. I am not thinking merely that recollection and expectation do not have physical effects; I am thinking of the actual quality of the subjective experience: seeing is one thing, recollecting is another; hearing is one thing, expecting is another. The relations of the present to the past and the future, in psychology as elsewhere, are causal relations, not relations of interpenetration. (I do not mean, of course, that my expectation causes the thunder, but that past experiences of lightning followed by thunder, together with present lightning, cause expectation of thunder.) Memory does not prolong the existence of the past; it is merely one way in which the past has effects.

With regard to space, the matter is similar but more complicated. There are two kinds of space, that in which one person's private experiences are situated, and that of physics, which contains other people's bodies, chairs and tables, the sun, moon and stars, not merely as reflected in our private sensations, but as we suppose them to be in themselves. This second sort is hypothetical, and can, with perfect logic, be denied by any man who is willing to suppose that the world contains nothing but his own experiences. Professor Haldane is not willing to say this, and must therefore admit the space which contains things other than his own experiences. As for the subjective kind of space, there is the visual space containing all my visual experiences; there is the space of touch; there is, as William James pointed out, the voluminousness of a stomachache; and so on. When I am considered as one thing among a world of things, every form of subjective space is inside me. The starry heavens that I see are not the remote starry heavens of astronomy, but an effect of the stars on me; what I see is in me, not outside of me. The stars of astronomy are in physical space, which is outside of me, but which I arrive at only by inference, not through analysis of my own experience. Professor Haldane's statement that space expresses an order within personality is true of my private space, not of physical space; his accompanying statement that space does not isolate personality would be correct only if physical space also were inside me. As soon as this confusion is cleared up, his position ceases to be plausible.

Professor Haldane, like all who follow Hegel, is anxious to show that nothing is really separate from anything else. He has now shown—if one could accept his arguments—that each man's past and future co-exist with his present, and that the space in which we all live is also inside each of us. But he has a further step to take in the proof that "personalities do not exclude one another." It appears that a man's personality is constituted by his ideals, and that our ideals are all much the same. I will quote his words once more: "An active ideal of truth, justice, charity and beauty is always present to us. . . . The ideal is, moreover, one ideal, though it has different aspects. It is these common ideals, and the fellowship they create, from which comes the revelation of God."

Statements of this kind, I must confess, leave me gasping, and I hardly know where to begin. I do not doubt Professor Haldane's word when he says that "an active ideal of truth, justice, charity, and beauty" is *always* present to *him;* I am sure it must be so, since he asserts it. But when it comes to attributing this extraordinary degree of virtue to mankind in general, I feel that I have as good a right to my opinion as he has to his. I find, for my part, untruth, injustice, uncharitableness and ugliness pursued, not only in fact, but as ideals. Does he really think that Hitler and Einstein have "one ideal, though it has different aspects"? It seems to me that each might bring a libel action for such a statement. Of course it may be said that one of them is a villain, and is not really pursuing the ideals in which, at heart, he believes. But this seems to me too facile a solution. Hitler's ideals come mainly from Nietzsche, in whom there is every evidence of complete sincerity. Until the issue has been fought out—by other methods than those of the Hegelian dialectic—I do not see how we are to know whether the God in whom *the* ideal is incarnate is Jehovah or Wotan.

As for the view that God's external blessedness should be a comfort to the poor, it has always been held by the rich, but the poor are beginning to grow weary of it. Perhaps, at this date, it is scarcely prudent to seem to associate the idea of God with the defense of economic injustice.

The pantheistic doctrine of Cosmic Purpose, like the theistic doctrine, suffers, though in a somewhat different way, from the difficulty of explaining the necessity of a temporal evolution. If time is not ultimately real—as practically all pantheists believe—why should the best things in the history of the world come late rather than early? Would not the reverse order have done just as well? If the idea that events have dates is an illusion, from which God is free, why should He choose to put the pleasant events at the end and the unplesant ones at the beginning? I agree with Dean Inge in thinking this question unanswerable.

The "emergent" doctrine, which we have next to consider, avoids this difficulty, and emphatically upholds the reality of time.

But we shall find that it incurs other difficulties at least as great.

The only representative of the "emergent" view, in the volume of B.B.C. talks from which I have been quoting, is Professor Alexander. He begins by saying that dead matter, living matter, and mind have appeared successively, and continues:

> Now this growth is one of what, since Mr. Lloyd Morgan introduced or reintroduced the idea and the term, is called emergence. Life emerges from matter and mind from life. A living being is also a material being, but one so fashioned as to exhibit a new quality which is life. . . . And the same thing may be said of the transition from life to mind. A "minded" being is also a living being, but one of such complexity of development, so finely organized in certain of its parts, and particularly in its nervous system, as to carry mind—or, if you please to use the word, consciousness.

He goes on to say that there is no reason why this process should cease with mind. On the contrary, it "suggests a further quality of existence beyond mind, which is related to mind as mind to life or life to matter. That quality I call deity, and the being which possesses it is God. It seems to me, therefore, that all things point to the emergence of this quality, and that is why I said that science itself, when it takes the wider view, requires deity." The world, he says, is "striving or tending to deity," but "deity has not in its distinctive nature as yet emerged at this stage of the world's existence." He adds that, for him, God "is not a creator as in historical religions, but created."

There is a close affinity between Professor Alexander's views and those of Bergson's *Creative Evolution*. Bergson holds that determinism is mistaken because, in the course of evolution, genuine novelties emerge, which could not have been predicted in advance, or even imagined. There is a mysterious force which urges everything to evolve. For example, an animal which cannot see has some mystic foreboding of sight, and proceeds to act in a way that leads to the development of eyes. At each moment something new emerges, but the past never dies, being preserved in memory—for forgetting is only apparent. Thus the world is continually growing richer in content, and will in time become quite a nice sort of place. The one essential is to avoid the intellect, which looks backward and is static; what we must use is intuition, which contains within itself the urge to creative novelty.

It must not be supposed that reasons are given for believing all this, beyond occasional bits of bad biology, reminiscent of Lamarck. Bergson is to be regarded as a poet, and on his own principles avoids everything that might appeal to the mere intellect.

I do not suggest that Professor Alexander accepts Bergson's philosophy in its entirety, but there is a similarity in their views, though they have developed them independently. In any case, their theories agree in emphasizing time, and in the belief that, in the course of evolution, unpredictable novelties emerge.

Various difficulties make the philosophy of emergent evolution unsatisfactory. Perhaps the chief of these is that, in order to escape from determinism, prediction is made impossible, and yet the adherents of this theory predict the future existence of God. They are exactly in the position of Bergson's shell-fish, which wants to see although it does not know what seeing is. Professor Alexander maintains that we have a vague awareness of "deity" in some experiences, which he describes as "numinous." The feeling which characterizes such experiences is, he says, "the sense of mystery, of something which may terrify us or may support us in our helplessness, but at any rate which is other than anything we know by our senses or our reflection." He gives no reason for attaching importance to this feeling, or for supposing that, as his theory demands, mental development makes it become a larger element in life. From anthropolgists one would infer the exact opposite. The sense of mystery, of a friendly or hostile non-human force, plays a far greater part in the life of savages than in that of civilized men. Indeed, if religion is to be identified with this feeling, every step in known human development has involved a diminution of religion. This hardly fits in with the supposed evolutionary argument for an emergent Deity.

The argument, in any case, is extraordinarily thin. There have been, it is urged, three stages in evolution: matter, life, and mind. We have no reason to suppose that the world has finished evolving, and there is therefore likely, at some later date, to be a fourth phase— and a fifth and a sixth and so on, one would have supposed. But no, with the fourth phase evolution is to be complete. Now matter could not have foreseen life, and life could not have foreseen mind, but mind can, dimly, foresee the next stage, particularly if it is the mind of a Papuan or a Bushman. It is obvious that all this is the merest guesswork. It may happen to be true, but there is no rational ground for supposing so. The philosophy of emergence is quite right in saying that the future is unpredictable, but, having said this, it at once proceeds to predict the future. People are more unwilling to give up the *word* "God" than to give up the idea for which the word has hitherto stood. Emergent evolutionists, having become persuaded that God did not create the world, are content to say that the world is creating God. But beyond the name, such a God has almost nothing in common with the object of traditional worship.

With regard to Cosmic Purpose in general, in whichever of its forms, there are two criticisms to be made. In the first place, those who believe in Cosmic Purpose always think that the world will go on evolving in the same direction as hitherto; in the second place, they hold that what has already happened is evidence of the good intentions of the universe. Both these propositions are open to question.

As to the direction of evolution, the argument is mainly derived from what has happened on this earth since life began. Now this earth is a very small corner of the universe, and there are reasons for supposing it by no means typical of the rest. Sir James Jeans considers it very doubtful whether, at the present time, there is life anywhere else. Before the Copernican revolution, it was natural to suppose that God's purposes were specially concerned with the earth, but now this has become an unplausible hypothesis. If it is the purpose of the Cosmos to evolve mind, we must regard it as rather incompetent in having produced so little in such a long time. It is, of course, *possible* that there will be more mind later on somewhere else, but of this we have no jot of scientific evidence. It may seem odd that life should occur by accident, but in such a large universe accidents will happen.

And even if we accept the rather curious view that the Cosmic Purpose is specially concerned with our little planet, we still find that there is reason to doubt whether it intends quite what the theologians say it does. The earth (unless we use enough poison gas to destroy all life) is likely to remain habitable for some considerable time, but not forever. Perhaps our atmosphere will gradually fly off into space; perhaps the tides will cause the earth to turn always the same face to the sun, so that one hemisphere will be too hot and the other too cold, perhaps (as in a moral tale by J. B. S. Haldane) the moon will tumble into the earth. If none of these things happen first, we shall in any case be all destroyed when the sun explodes and becomes a cold white dwarf, which, we are told by Jeans, is to happen in about a million million years, though the exact date is still somewhat uncertain.

A million million years gives us some time to prepare for the end, and we may hope that in the meantime both astronomy and gunnery will have made considerable progress. The astronomers may have discovered another star with habitable planets, and the gunners may be able to fire us off to it with a speed approaching that of light, in which case, if the passengers were all young to begin with, some might arrive before dying of old age. It is perhaps a slender hope, but let us make the best of it.

Cruising round the universe, however, even if it is done with the most perfect scientific skill, cannot prolong life forever. The second law of thermodynamics tells us that, on the whole, energy is always passing from more concentrated to less concentrated forms, and that, in the end, it will have all passed into a form in which further change is impossible. When that has happened, if not before, life must cease. To quote Jeans once more, "With universes as with mortals, the only possible life is progress to the grave." This leads him to certain reflections which are very relevant to our theme:

The three centuries which have elapsed since Giordano Bruno suffered martyrdom for believing in the plurality of worlds have changed our conception of the universe almost beyond description, but they have not brought us appreciably nearer to understanding the relation of life to the universe. We can still only guess as to the meaning of this life which, to all appearances, is so rare. Is it the final climax towards which the whole creation moves, for which the millions and millions of years of transformation of matter in uninhabited stars and nebulae, and of the waste of radiation in desert space, have been only an incredibly extravagant preparation? Or is it a mere accidental and possibly quite unimportant by-product of natural processes, which have some other and more stupendous end in view? Or, to glance at a still more modest line of thought, must we regard it as something of the nature of a disease, which affects matter in its old age when it has lost the high temperature and the capacity for generating high-frequency radiation with which younger and more vigorous matter would at once destroy life? Or, throwing humility aside, shall we venture to imagine that it is the only reality, which creates, instead of being created by, the colossal masses of the stars and nebulae and the almost inconceivably long vistas of astronomical time?

This, I think, states the alternatives, as presented by science, fairly and without bias. The last possibility, that mind is the only reality, and that the spaces and times of astronomy are created by it, is one for which, logically, there is much to be said. But those who adopt it, in the hope of escaping from depressing conclusions, do not quite realize what it entails. Everything that I know directly is part of my "mind," and the inferences by which I arrive at the existence of other things are by no means conclusive. It may be, therefore, that nothing exists except my mind. In that case, when I die the universe will go out. But if I am going to admit minds other than my own, I must admit the whole astronomical universe, since the evidence is exactly equally strong in both cases. Jeans's last alternative, therefore, is not the comfortable theory that other people's minds exist, though not their bodies; it is the theory that I am alone in an empty universe, inventing the human race, the geological ages of the earth, the sun and stars and nebulae, out of my own fertile imagination. Against this theory there is, so far as I know, no valid logical argument; but against any other form of the doctrine that mind is the only reality there is the fact that our evidence for other people's minds is derived by inference from our evidence for their bodies. Other people, therefore, if they have minds, have bodies; oneself alone may possibly be a disembodied mind, but only if oneself alone exists.

I come now to the last question in our discussion of Cosmic Purpose, namely: Is what has happened hitherto evidence of the good intentions of the universe? The alleged ground for believing this, as we have seen, is that the universe has produced US. I cannot deny it. But are we really so splendid as to justify such a long prologue? The philosophers lay stress on values: they say that we think certain things good, and that since these things are good, we must be very good to think them so. But this is a circular argument. A being with other values might think ours so atrocious as to be proof that we were inspired by Satan. Is there not something a trifle absurd in the spectacle of human beings holding a mirror before themselves, and thinking what they behold so excellent as to prove that a Cosmic Purpose must have been aiming at it all along? Why, in any case, this glorification of Man? How about lions and tigers? They destroy fewer animal or human lives than we do, and they are much more beautiful than we are. How about ants? They manage the Corporate State much better than any Fascist. Would not a world of nightingales and larks and deer be better than our human world of cruelty and injustice and war? The believers in Cosmic Purpose make much of our supposed intelligence, but their writings make one doubt it. If I were granted omnipotence, and millions of years to experiment in, I should not think Man much to boast of as the final result of all my efforts.

Man, as a curious accident in a backwater, is intelligible: his mixture of virtues and vices is such as much be expected to result from a fortuitous origin. But only abysmal self-complacency can see in Man a reason which Omniscience could consider adequate as a motive for the Creator. The Copernican revolution will not have done its work until it has taught men more modesty than is to be found among those who think Man sufficient evidence of Cosmic Purpose.

NOTES

1. As Dean Inge puts it: "We magnify the problem of evil by our narrow moralism, which we habitually impose upon the Creator. There is no evidence for the theory that God is a merely moral Being, and what we observe of His laws and operations here indicates strongly that He is not." *Outspoken Essays,* Vol. II, p. 24.

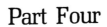

Part Four

14

An Outline of
Intellectual Rubbish

Man is a rational animal—so at least I have been told. Throughout a long life, I have looked diligently for evidence in favor of this statement, but so far I have not had the good fortune to come across it, though I have searched in many countries spread over three continents. On the contrary, I have seen the world plunging continually further into madness. I have seen great nations, formerly leaders of civilization, led astray by preachers of bombastic nonsense. I have seen cruelty, persecution, and superstition increasing by leaps and bounds, until we have almost reached the point where praise of rationality is held to mark a man as an old fogey regrettably surviving from a bygone age. All this is depressing, but gloom is a useless emotion. In order to escape from it, I have been driven to study the past with more attention than I had formerly given to it, and have found, as Erasmus found, that folly is perennial and yet the human race has survived. The follies of our own times are easier to bear when they are seen against the background of past follies. In what follows I shall mix the sillinesses of our day with those of former centuries. Perhaps the result may help in seeing our own times in perspective, and as not much worse than other ages that our ancestors lived through without ultimate disaster.

Aristotle, so far as I know, was the first man to proclaim explicitly that man is a rational animal. His reason for this view was

---

First published by Haldeman-Julius in 1943.

one which does not now seem very impressive; it was, that some people can do sums. He thought that there are three kinds of soul: the vegetable soul, possessed by all living things, both plants and animals, and concerned only with nourishment and growth; the animal soul, concerned with locomotion, and shared by man with the lower animals; and finally the rational soul, or intellect, which is the Divine mind, but in which men participate to a greater or less degree in proportion to their wisdom. It is in virtue of the intellect that man is a rational animal. The intellect is shown in various ways, but most emphatically by mastery of arithmetic. The Greek system of numerals was very bad, so that the multiplication table was quite difficult, and complicated calculations could only be made by very clever people. Now-a-days, however, calculating machines do sums better than even the cleverest people, yet no one contends that these useful instruments are immortal, or work by divine inspiration. As arithmetic has grown easier, it has come to be less respected. The consequence is that, though many philosophers continue to tell us what fine fellows we are, it is no longer on account of our arithmetical skill that they praise us.

Since the fashion of the age no longer allows us to point to calculating boys as evidence that man is rational and the soul, at least in part, immortal, let us look elsewhere. Where shall we look first? Shall we look among eminent statesmen, who have so triumphantly guided the world into its present condition? Or shall we choose the men of letters? Or the philosophers? All these have their claims, but I think we should begin with those whom all right-thinking people acknowledge to be the wisest as well as the best of men, namely the clergy. If *they* fail to be rational, what hope is there for us lesser mortals? And alas—though I say it with all due respect—there have been times when their wisdom has not been very obvious, and, strange to say, these were especially the times when the power of the clergy was greatest.

The Ages of Faith, which are praised by our neo-scholastics, were the time when the clergy had things all their own way. Daily life was full of miracles wrought by saints and wizardry perpetrated by devils and necromancers. Many thousands of witches were burnt at the stake. Men's sins were punished by pestilence and famine, by earthquake, flood, and fire. And yet, strange to say, they were even more sinful than they are now-a-days. Very little was known scientifically about the world. A few learned men remembered Greek proofs that the earth is round, but most people made fun of the notion that there are antipodes. To suppose that there are human beings at the antipodes was heresy. It was generally held (though modern Catholics take a milder view) that the immense majority of mankind are damned. Dangers were held to lurk at every turn. Devils would settle on the food that monks were about to eat, and would take possession of the bodies of incautious feeders who omitted to make the sign of the Cross before each mouthful. Old-fashioned people still say "bless you" when one sneezes, but they have forgotten the reason for the custom. The reason was that people were thought to sneeze out their souls, and before their souls could get back lurking demons were apt to enter the unsouled body; but if any one said "God bless you," the demons were frightened off.

Throughout the last 400 years, during which the growth of science had gradually shown men how to acquire knowledge of the ways of nature and mastery over natural forces, the clergy have fought a losing battle against science, in astronomy and geology, in anatomy and physiology, in biology and psychology and sociology. Ousted from one position, they have taken up another. After being worsted in astronomy, they did their best to prevent the rise of geology; they fought against Darwin in biology, and at the present time they fight against scientific theories of psychology and education. At each stage, they try to make the public forget their earlier obscurantism, in order that their present obscurantism may not be recognized for what it is. Let us note a few instances of irrationality among the clergy since the rise of science, and then inquire whether the rest of mankind are any better.

When Benjamin Franklin invented the lightning rod, the clergy, both in England and America, with the enthusiastic support of George III, condemned it as an impious attempt to defeat the will of God. For, as all right-thinking people were aware, lightning is sent by God to punish impiety or some other grave sin—the virtuous are never struck by lightning. Therefore if God wants to strike any one, Benjamin Franklin ought not to defeat His design; indeed, to do so is helping criminals to escape. But God was equal to the occasion, if we are to believe the eminent Dr. Price, one of the leading divines of Boston. Lightning having been rendered ineffectual by the "iron points invented by the sagacious Dr. Franklin," Massachusetts was shaken by earthquakes, which Dr. Price perceived to be due to God's wrath at the "iron points." In a sermon on the subject he said, "In Boston are more erected than elsewhere in New England, and Boston seems to be more dreadfully shaken. Oh! there is no getting out of the mighty hand of God." Apparently, however, Providence gave up all hope of curing Boston of its wickedness, for, though lightning rods became more and more common, earthquakes in Massachusetts have remained rare. Nevertheless, Dr. Price's point of view, or something very like it, is still held by one of the most influential of living men. When, at one time, there were several bad earthquakes in India, Mahatma Gandhi solemnly warned his compatriots that these disasters had been sent as a punishment for their sins.

Even in my own native island this point of view still exists. During the last war, the British Government did much to stimulate the production of food at home. In 1916, when things were not going well, a Scottish clergyman wrote to the newspapers to say that military failure was due to the fact that, with government sanction, potatoes had been planted on the Sabbath. However, disaster was averted, owing to the fact that the Germans disobeyed *all* the Ten Commandments, and not only one of them.

Sometimes, if pious men are to be believed, God's mercies are curiously selective. Toplady, the author of "Rock of Ages," moved from one vicarage to another; a week after the move, the vicarage he had formerly occupied burnt down, with great loss to the new vicar. Thereupon Toplady thanked God; but what the new vicar did is not known. Borrow, in his "Bible in Spain," records how without mishap he crossed a mountain pass infested by bandits. The next party to cross, however, were set upon, robbed, and some of them murdered; when Borrow heard of this, he, like Toplady, thanked God.

Although we are taught the Copernican astronomy in our textbooks, it has not yet penetrated to our religion or our morals, and has not even succeeded in destroying belief in astrology. People still think that the Divine Plan has special reference to human beings, and that a special Providence not only looks after the good, but also punishes the wicked. I am sometimes shocked by the blasphemies of those who think themselves pious—for instance, the nuns who never take a bath without wearing a bathrobe all the time. When asked why, since no man can see them, they reply: "Oh, but you forget the good God." Apparently they conceive of the Deity as a Peeping Tom, whose omnipotence enables Him to see through bathroom walls, but who is foiled by bathrobes. This view strikes me as curious.

The whole conception of "Sin" is one which I find very puzzling, doubtless owing to my sinful nature. If "Sin" consisted in causing needless suffering, I could understand; but on the contrary, sin often consists in avoiding needless suffering. Some years ago, in the English House of Lords, a bill was introduced to legalize euthanasia in cases of painful and incurable disease. The patient's consent was to be necessary, as well as several medical certificates. To me, in my simplicity, it would seem natural to require the patient's consent, but the late Archbishop of Canterbury, the English official expert on Sin, explained the erroneousness of such a view. The patient's consent turns euthanasia into suicide, and suicide is sin. Their Lordships listened to the voice of authority, and rejected the bill. Consequently, to please the Archbishop—and his God, if he reports truly—victims of cancer still have to endure months of wholly useless agony, unless their doctors or nurses are sufficiently humane to risk a charge of murder. I find difficulty in the conception of a God who gets pleasure from contemplating such tortures; and if there were a God capable of such wanton cruelty, I should certainly not think Him worthy of worship. But that only proves how sunk I am in moral depravity.

I am equally puzzled by the things that are sin and by the things that are not. When the Society for the Prevention of Cruelty to Animals asked the pope for his support, he refused it, on the ground that human beings owe no duty to the lower animals, and that ill-treating animals is not sinful. This is because animals have no souls. On the other hand, it is wicked to marry your deceased wife's sister—so at least the Church teaches—however much you and she may wish to marry. This is not because of any unhappiness that might result, but because of certain texts in the Bible.

The resurrection of the body, which is an article of the Apostles' Creed, is a dogma which has various curious consequences. There was an author not very many years ago, who had an ingenious method of calculating the date of the end of the world. He argued that there must be enough of the necessary ingredients of a human body to provide everybody with the requisites at the Last Day. By carefully calculating the available raw material, he decided that it would all have been used up by a certain date. When that date comes, the world must end, since otherwise the resurrection of the body would become impossible. Unfortunately I have forgotten what the date was, but I believe it is not very distant.

St. Thomas Aquinas, the official philosopher of the Catholic Church, discussed lengthily and seriously a very grave problem, which, I fear, modern theologians unduly neglect. He imagines a cannibal who has never eaten anything but human flesh, and whose father and mother before him had like propensities. Every particle of his body belongs rightfully to someone else. We cannot suppose that those who have been eaten by cannibals are to go short through all eternity. But, if not, what is left for the cannibal? How is he to be properly roasted in hell, if all his body is restored to its original owners? This is a puzzling question, as the Saint rightly perceives.

In this connection the orthodox have a curious objection to cremation, which seems to show an insufficient realization of God's omnipotence. It is thought that a body which has been burnt will be more difficult for Him to collect together again than one which has been put underground and transformed into worms. No doubt collecting the particles from the air and undoing the chemical work of combustion would be somewhat laborious, but it is surely blasphemous to suppose such a work impossible for the Deity. I conclude that the objection to cremation implies grave heresy. But I doubt whether my opinion will carry much weight with the orthodox.

It was only very slowly and reluctantly that the Church sanctioned the dissection of corpses in connection with the study of medicine. The pioneer in dissection was Vesalius, who was Court physician to the Emperor Charles V. His medical skill led the emperor to protect him, but after the emperor was dead he got into trouble. A corpse which he was dissecting was said to have shown signs of life under the knife, and he was accused of murder. The Inquisition was induced by King Philip II to take a lenient view, and only sentenced him to a pilgrimage to the Holy Land. On the way home he was shipwrecked and died of exhaustion. For centuries after this time, medical students at the Papal University in Rome were only allowed to operate on lay figures, from which the sexual parts were omitted.

The sacredness of corpses is a widespread belief. It was carried furthest by the Egyptians, among whom it led to the practice of mummification. It still exists in full force in China. A French surgeon, who was employed by the Chinese to teach Western medicine, relates that his demand for corpses to dissect was received with horror, but he was assured that he could have instead an unlimited supply of live criminals. His objection to this alternative was totally unintelligible to his Chinese employers.

Although there are many kinds of sin, seven of which are

deadly, the most fruitful field for Satan's wiles is sex. The orthodox Catholic doctrine on this subject is to be found in St. Paul, St. Augustine, and St. Thomas Aquinas. It is best to be celibate, but those who have not the gift of continence may marry. Intercourse in marriage is not sin, provided it is motivated by desire for offspring. All intercourse outside marriage is sin, and so is intercourse within marriage if any measures are adopted to prevent conception. Interruption of pregnancy is sin, even if, in medical opinion, it is the only way of saving the mother's life; for medical opinion is fallible, and God can always save a life by miracle if He sees fit. (This view is embodied in the law of Connecticut.) Venereal disease is God's punishment for sin. It is true that, through a guilty husband, this punishment may fall on an innocent woman and her children, but this is a mysterious dispensation of Providence, which it would be impious to question. We must also not inquire why venereal disease was not divinely instituted until the time of Columbus. Since it is the appointed penalty for sin, all measures for its avoidance are also sin—except, of course, a virtuous life. Marriage is nominally indissoluble, but many people who seem to be married are not. In the case of influential Catholics, some ground for nullity can often be found, but for the poor there is no such outlet, except perhaps in cases of impotence. Persons who divorce and remarry are guilty of adultery in the sight of God.

The phrase "in the sight of God" puzzles me. One would suppose that God sees everything, but apparently this is a mistake. He does not see Reno, for you cannot be divorced in the sight of God. Registry offices are a doubtful point. I notice that respectable people, who would not call on anybody who lives in open sin, are quite willing to call on people who have had only a civil marriage; so apparently God does see registry offices.

Some eminent men think even the doctrine of the Catholic Church deplorably lax where sex is concerned. Tolstoy and Mahatma Gandhi, in their old age, laid it down that *all* sexual intercourse is wicked, even in marriage and with a view to offspring. The Manicheans thought likewise, relying upon men's native sinfulness to supply them with a continually fresh crop of disciples. This doctrine, however, is heretical, though it is equally heretical to maintain that marriage is as praiseworthy as celibacy. Tolstoy thinks tobacco almost as bad as sex; in one of his novels, a man who is contemplating murder smokes a cigarette first in order to generate the necessary homicidal fury. Tobacco, however, is not prohibited in the Scriptures, though, as Samuel Butler points out, St. Paul would no doubt have denounced it if he had known of it.

It is odd that neither the Church nor modern public opinion condemns petting, provided it stops short at a certain point. At what point sin begins is a matter as to which casuists differ. One eminently orthodox Catholic divine laid it down that a confessor may fondle a nun's breasts, provided he does it without evil intent. But I doubt whether modern authorities would agree with him on this point.

Modern morals are a mixture of two elements: on the one hand, rational precepts as to how to live together peaceably in a society, and on the other hand traditional taboos derived originally from some ancient superstition, but proximately from sacred books, Christian, Mohammedan, Hindu, or Buddhist. To some extent the two agree; the prohibition of murder and theft, for instance, is supported both by human reason and by Divine command. But the prohibition of pork or beef has only scriptural authority, and that only in certain religions. It is odd that modern men, who are aware of what science has done in the way of bringing new knowledge and altering the conditions of social life, should still be willing to accept the authority of texts embodying the outlook of very ancient and very ignorant pastoral or agricultural tribes. It is discouraging that many of the precepts whose sacred character is thus uncritically acknowledged should be such as to inflict much wholly unnecessary misery. If men's kindly impulses were stronger, they would find some way of explaining that these precepts are not to be taken literally, any more than the command to "sell all that thou hast and give to the poor."

There are logical difficulties in the notion of sin. We are told that sin consists in disobedience to God's commands, but we are also told that God is omnipotent. If He is, nothing contrary to His will can occur; therefore when the sinner disobeys His commands, He must have intended this to happen. St. Augustine boldly accepts this view, and asserts that men are led to sin by a blindness with which God afflicts them. But most theologians, in modern times, have felt that, if God causes men to sin, it is not fair to send them to hell for what they cannot help. We are told that sin consists in acting contrary to God's will. This, however, does not get rid of the difficulty. Those who, like Spinoza, take God's omnipotence seriously, deduce that there can be no such thing as sin. This leads to frightful results. What! said Spinoza's contemporaries, was it not wicked of

Nero to murder his mother? Was it not wicked of Adam to eat the apple? Is one action just as good as another? Spinoza wriggles, but does not find any satisfactory answer. *If* everything happens in accordance with God's will, God must have wanted Nero to murder his mother; therefore, since God is good, the murder must have been a good thing. From this argument there is no escape.

On the other hand, those who are in earnest in thinking that sin is disobedience to God are compelled to say that God is not omnipotent. This gets out of all the logical puzzles, and is the view adopted by a certain school of liberal theologians. It has, however, its own difficulties. How are we to know what really is God's will? If the forces of evil have a certain share of power, they may deceive us into accepting as Scripture what is really their work. This was the view of the Gnostics, who thought that the Old Testament was the work of an evil spirit.

As soon as we abandon our own reason, and are content to rely upon authority, there is no end to our troubles. Whose authority? The Old Testament? The New Testament? The Koran? In practice, people choose the book considered sacred by the community in which they are born, and out of that book they choose the parts they like, ignoring the others. At one time, the most influential text in the Bible was: "Thou shalt not suffer a witch to live." Now-a-days, people pass over this text, in silence if possible; if not, with an apology. And so, even when we have a sacred book, we still choose as truth whatever suits our own prejudices. No Catholic, for instance, takes seriously the text which says that a bishop should be the husband of one wife.

People's beliefs have various causes. One is that there is some evidence for the belief in question. We apply this to matters of fact, such as "what is so-and-so's telephone number?" or "who won the World Series?" But as soon as it comes to anything more debatable, the causes of belief become less defensible. We believe, first and foremost, what makes us feel that we are fine fellows. Mr. Homo, if he has a good digestion and a sound income, thinks to himself how much more sensible he is than his neighbor so-and-so, who married a flighty wife and is always losing money. He thinks how superior his city is to the one 50 miles away: it has a bigger Chamber of Commerce and a more enterprising Rotary Club, and its mayor has never been in prison. He thinks how immeasurably his country surpasses all others. If he is an Englishman, he thinks of Shakespeare and Milton, or of Newton and Darwin, or of Nelson and Wellington,

216 Bertrand Russell On God and Religion

according to his temperament. If he is a Frenchman, he congratulates himself on the fact that for centuries France has led the world in culture, fashions, and cookery. If he is a Russian, he reflects that he belongs to the only nation which is truly international. If he is a Yugoslav, he boasts of his nation's pigs; if a native of the Principality of Monaco, he boasts of leading the world in the matter of gambling.

But these are not the only matters on which he has to congratulate himself. For is he not an individual of the species *homo sapiens*? Alone among animals he has an immortal soul, and is rational; he knows the difference between good and evil, and has learnt the multiplication table. Did not God make him in His own image? And was not everything created for man's convenience? The sun was made to light the day, and the moon to light the night—though the moon, by some oversight, only shines during half the noctural hours. The raw fruits of the earth were made for human sustenance. Even the white tails of rabbits, according to some theologians, have a purpose, namely to make it easier for sportsmen to shoot them. There are, it is true, some inconveniences: lions and tigers are too fierce, the summer is too hot, and the winter too cold. But these things only began after Adam ate the apple; before that, all animals were vegetarians, and the season was always spring. If only Adam had been content with peaches and nectarines, grapes and pears and pineapples, these blessings would still be ours.

Self-importance, individual or generic, is the source of most of our religious beliefs. Even sin is a conception derived from self-importance. Borrow relates how he met a Welsh preacher who was always melancholy. By sympathetic questioning he was brought to confess the source of his sorrow: that at the age of seven he had committed the sin against the Holy Ghost. "My dear fellow," said Borrow, "don't let that trouble you; I know dozens of people in like case. Do not imagine yourself cut off from the rest of mankind by this occurrence; if you inquire, you will find multitudes who suffer from the same misfortune." From that moment, the man was cured. He had enjoyed feeling singular, but there was no pleasure in being one of a herd of sinners. Most sinners are rather less egotistical; but theologians undoubtedly enjoy the feeling that Man is the special object of God's wrath, as well as of His love. After the Fall—so Milton assures us—

The Sun
Had first his precept so to move, so shine,
As might affect the Earth with cold and heat
Scarce tolerable, and from the North to call
Decrepit Winter, from the South to bring
Solstitial summer's heat.

However disagreeable the results may have been, Adam could hardly help feeling flattered that such vast astronomical phenomena should be brought about to teach *him* a lesson. The whole of theology, in regard to hell no less than to heaven, takes it for granted that Man is what is of most importance in the Universe of created beings. Since all theologians are men, this postulate has met with little opposition.

Since evolution became fashionable, the glorification of Man has taken a new form. We are told that evolution has been guided by one great Purpose: through the millions of years when there were only slime, or trilobites, throughout the ages of dinosaurs and giant ferns, of bees and wild flowers, God was preparing the Great Climax. At last, in the fullness of time, He produced Man, including such specimens as Nero and Caligula, Hitler and Mussolini, whose transcendent glory justified the long painful process. For my part, I find even eternal damnation less incredible, and certainly less ridiculous, than this lame and impotent conclusion which we are asked to admire as the supreme effort of Omnipotence. And if God is indeed omnipotent, why could He not have produced the glorious result without such a long and tedious prologue?

Apart from the question whether Man is really so glorious as the theologians of evolution say he is, there is the further difficulty that life on this planet is almost certainly temporary. The earth will grow cold, or the atmosphere will gradually fly off, or there will be an insufficiency of water, or, as Sir James Jeans genially prophesies, the sun will burst and all the planets will be turned into gas. Which of those will happen first, no one knows; but in any case the human race will ultimately die out. Of course, such an event is of little importance from the point of view of orthodox theology, since men are immortal, and will continue to exist in heaven and hell when none are left on earth. But in that case why bother about terrestrial developments? Those who lay stress on the gradual progress from the primitive slime to Man attach an importance to this mundane sphere which should make them shrink from the conclusion that all life on earth is only a brief interlude between the

218 Bertrand Russell On God and Religion

nebula and the eternal frost, or perhaps between one nebula and another. The importance of Man, which is the one indispensable dogma of the theologians, receives no support from a scientific view of the future of the solar system.

There are many other sources of false belief besides self-importance. One of these is love of the marvelous. I knew at one time a scientifically-minded conjuror, who used to perform his tricks before a small audience, and then get them, each separately, to write down what they had seen happen. Almost always they wrote down something much more astonishing than the reality, and usually something which no conjuror could have achieved; yet they all thought they were reporting truly what they had seen with their own eyes. This sort of falsification is still more true of rumors. A tells B that last night he saw Mr.———, the eminent prohibitionist, slightly the worse for liquor; B tells C that A saw the good man reeling drunk, C tells D that he was picked up unconscious in the ditch, D tells E that he is well known to pass out every evening. Here, it is true, another motive comes in, namely malice. We like to think ill of our neighbors, and are prepared to believe the worst on very little evidence. But even where there is no such motive, what is marvelous is readily believed unless it goes against some strong prejudice. All history until the eighteenth century is full of prodigies and wonders which modern historians ignore, not because they are less well attested than facts which the historians accept, but because modern taste among the learned prefers what science regards as probable. Shakespeare relates how on the night before Caesar was killed,

> A common slave—you know him well by sight—
> Held up his left hand, which did flame and burn
> Like twenty torches join'd; and yet his hand,
> Not sensible of fire, remain'd unscorch'd.
> Besides—I have not since put up my sword—
> Against the Capitol I met a lion,
> Who glar'd upon me, and went surly by,
> Without annoying me; and there were drawn
> Upon a heap a hundred ghastly women,
> Transformed with their fear, who swore they saw
> Men all in fire walk up and down the streets.

Shakespeare did not invent these marvels; he found them in reputable historians, who are among those upon whom we depend for our knowledge concerning Julius Caesar. This sort of thing always used to happen at the death of a great man or the beginning of an important war. Even so recently as 1914 the "angels of Mons" encouraged the British troops. The evidence for such events is very seldom first-hand, and modern historians refuse to accept it—except, of course, where the event is one that has religious importance.

Every powerful emotion has its own myth-making tendency. When the emotion is peculiar to an individual, he is considered more or less mad if he gives credence to such myths as he has invented. But when an emotion is collective, as in war, there is no one to correct the myths that naturally arise. Consequently in all times of great collective excitement unfounded rumors obtain wide credence. In September, 1914, almost everybody in England believed that Russian troops had passed through England on the way to the Western Front. Everybody knew someone who had seen them, though no one had seen them himself.

This myth-making faculty is often allied with cruelty. Ever since the middle ages, the Jews have been accused of practicing ritual murder. There is not an iota of evidence for this accusation, and no sane person who has examined it believes it. Nevertheless it persists. I have met white Russians who were convinced of its truth, and among many Nazis it is accepted without question. Such myths give an excuse for the infliction of torture, and the unfounded belief in them is evidence of the unconscious desire to find some victim to persecute.

There was, until the end of the eighteenth century, a theory that insanity is due to possession by devils. It was inferred that any pain suffered by the patient is also suffered by the devils, so that the best cure is to make the patient suffer so much that the devils will decide to abandon him. The insane, in accordance with this theory, were savagely beaten. This treatment was tried on King George III when he was mad, but without success. It is a curious and painful fact that almost all the completely futile treatments that have been believed in during the long history of medical folly have been such as caused acute suffering to the patient. When anesthetics were discovered, pious people considered them an attempt to evade the will of God. It was pointed out, however, that when God extracted Adam's rib He put him into a deep sleep. This proved that anesthetics are all right for *men;* women, however, ought to suffer, because of the curse of Eve. In the West votes for women proved this doctrine mistaken, but in Japan, to this day, women in childbirth are not allowed any alleviation through anesthetics. As the Japanese do not believe in

Genesis, this piece of sadism must have some other justification.

The fallacies about "race" and "blood," which have always been popular, and which the Nazis have embodied in their official creed, have no objective justification; they are believed solely because they minister to self-esteem and to the impulse toward cruelty. In one form or another, these beliefs are as old as civilization; their forms change, but their essence remains. Herodotus tells how Cyrus was brought up by peasants, in complete ignorance of his royal blood; at the age of twelve his kingly bearing toward other peasant boys revealed the the truth. This is a variant of an old story which is found in all Indo-European countries. Even quite modern people say that "blood will tell." It is no use for scientific physiologists to assure the world that there is no difference between the blood of a Negro and the blood of a white man. The American Red Cross, in obedience to popular prejudice, at first, when America became involved in the present war, decreed that no Negro blood should be used for blood transfusion. As a result of an agitation, it was conceded that Negro blood might be used, but only for Negro patients. Similarly, in Germany, the Aryan soldier who needs blood transfusion is carefully protected from the contamination of Jewish blood.

In the matter of race, there are different beliefs in different societies. Where monarchy is firmly established, kings are of a higher race than their subjects. Until very recently, it was universally believed that men are congenitally more intelligent than women; even so enlightened a man as Spinoza decides against votes for women on this ground. Among white men, it is held that white men are by nature superior to men of other colors, and especially to black men; in Japan, on the contrary, it is thought that yellow is the best color. In Haiti, when they make statues of Christ and Satan, they make Christ black and Satan white. Aristotle and Plato considered Greeks so innately superior to barbarians that slavery is justified so long as the master is Greek and the slave barbarian. The Nazis and the American legislators who made the immigration laws consider the Nordics superior to Slavs or Latins or any other white men. But the Nazis, under the stress of war, have been led to the conclusion that there are hardly any true Nordics outside Germany; the Norwegians, except Quisling and his few followers, have been corrupted by intermixture with Finns and Laps and such. Thus politics are a clue to descent. The biologically pure Nordic loves Hitler, and if you do not love Hitler, that is proof of tainted blood.

All this is, of course, pure nonsense, known to be such by everyone who has studied the subject. In schools in America, children of the most diverse origins are subjected to the same educational system, and those whose business it is to measure intelligence quotients and otherwise estimate the native ability of students are unable to make any such racial distinctions as are postulated by the theorists of race. In every national or racial group there are clever children and stupid children. It is not likely that, in the United States, colored children will develop as successfully as white children, because of the stigma of social inferiority; but in so far as congenital ability can be detached from environmental influence, there is no clear distinction among different groups. The whole conception of superior races is merely a myth generated by the overweening self-esteem of the holders of power. It may be that, some day, better evidence will be forthcoming; perhaps, in time, educators will be able to prove (say) that Jews are on the average more intelligent than gentiles. But as yet no such evidence exists, and all talk of superior races must be dismissed as nonsense.

There is a special absurdity in applying racial theories to the various populations of Europe. There is not in Europe any such thing as a pure race. Russians have an admixture of Tartar blood, Germans are largely Slavonic, France is a mixture of Celts, Germans, and people of Mediterranean race, Italy the same with the addition of the descendants of slaves imported by the Romans. The English are perhaps the most mixed of all. There is no evidence that there is any advantage in belonging to a pure race. The purest races now in existence are the Pygmies, the Hottentots, and the Australian aborigines; the Tasmanians, who were probably even purer, are extinct. They were not the bearers of a brilliant culture. The ancient Greeks, on the other hand, emerged from an amalgamation of northern barbarians and an indigenous population; the Athenians and Ionians, who were the most civilized, were also the most mixed. The supposed merits of racial purity are, it would seem, wholly imaginary.

Superstitions about blood have many forms that have nothing to do with race. The objection to homicide seems to have been, originally, based on the ritual pollution caused by the blood of the victim. God said to Cain: "The voice of thy brother's blood crieth unto me from the ground." According to some anthropologists, the mark of Cain was a disguise to prevent Abel's blood from finding him; this appears also to be the original reason for wearing mourning. In many ancient communities no difference was made between murder and accidental homicide; in either case equally ritual ablution was necessary. The feeling that blood defiles still lingers, for example in the Churching of Women and in taboos connected with menstruation. The idea that a child is of his father's "blood" has the same superstitious origin. So far as actual blood is concerned, the mother's enters into the child, but not the father's. If blood were as important as is supposed, matriarchy would be the only proper way of tracing descent.

In Russia, where, under the influence of Karl Marx, people since the revolution have been classified by their economic origin, difficulties have arisen not unlike those of German race theorists over the Scandinavian Nordics. There were two theories that had to be reconciled: on the one hand, proletarians were good and other people were bad; on the other hand, communists were good and other people were bad. The only way of effecting a reconciliation was to alter the meaning of words. A "proletarian" came to mean a supporter of the government; Lenin, though born a Prince, was reckoned a member of the proletariat. On the other hand, the word "kulak," which was supposed to mean a rich peasant, came to mean any peasant who opposed collectivization. This sort of absurdity always arises when one group of human beings is supposed to be inherently better than another. In America, the highest praise that can be bestowed on an eminent colored man after he is safely dead is to say "he was a *white* man." A courageous woman is called "masculine": Macbeth, praising his wife's courage, says:

> Bring forth men children only,
> For thy undaunted mettle should compose
> Nothing but males.

All these ways of speaking come of unwillingness to abandon foolish generalizations.

In the economic sphere there are many widespread superstitions. Why do people value gold and precious stones? Not simply because of their rarity: there are a number of elements called "rare earths" which are much rarer than gold, but no one will give a penny for them except a few men of science. There is a theory, for which there is much to be said, that gold and gems were valued originally on account of their supposed magical properties. The mistakes of governments in modern times seem to show that this belief still exists among the sort of men who are called "practical." At the end of the last war, it was agreed that Germany should pay vast sums to England and France, and they in turn should pay vast sums to the United States. Every one wanted to be paid in money rather than goods; the "practical" men failed to notice that there is not that amount of money in the world. They also failed to notice that money is no use unless it is used to buy goods. As they would not use it in this way, it did no good to anyone. There was supposed to be some mystic virtue about gold that made it worth while to dig it up in the Transvaal and put it underground again in bank vaults in America. In the end, of course, the debtor countries had no more money, and, since they were not allowed to pay in goods, they went bankrupt. The Great Depression was the direct result of the surviving belief in the magical properties of gold. It is to be feared that some similar superstition will cause equally bad results after the end of the present war.

Politics is largely governed by sententious platitudes which are devoid of truth.

One of the most widespread popular maxims is, "human nature cannot be changed." No one can say whether this is true or not without first defining "human nature." But as used it is certainly false. When Mr. A utters the maxim, with an air of portentous and conclusive wisdom, what he means is that all men everywhere will always continue to behave as they do in his own home town. A little anthropology will dispel this belief. Among the Tibetans, one wife has many husbands, because men are too poor to support a whole wife; yet family life, according to travelers, is no more unhappy than elsewhere. The practice of lending one's wife to a guest is very common among uncivilized tribes. The Australian aborigines, at puberty, undergo a very painful operation which, throughout the rest of their lives, greatly diminishes sexual potency. Infanticide, which might seem contrary to human nature, was almost universal before the rise of Christianity, and is recommended by Plato to prevent over-population. Private property is not recognized among some savage tribes. Even among highly civilized people, economic considerations will override what is called "human nature." In Moscow, where there is an acute housing shortage, when an unmarried woman is pregnant, it often happens that a number of men contend for the legal right to be considered the father of the prospective child, because whoever is judged to be the father acquires the right to share the woman's room, and half a room is better than no roof.

In fact, adult "human nature" is extremely variable, according to the circumstances of education. Food and sex are very general requirements, but the hermits of the Thebaid eschewed sex altogether and reduced food to the lowest point compatible with survival. By diet and training, people can be made ferocious or meek, masterful or slavish, as may suit the educator. There is no nonsense so arrant that it cannot be made the creed of the vast majority by adequate governmental action. Plato intended his Republic to be founded on a myth which he admitted to be absurd, but he was rightly confident that the populace could be induced to believe it. Hobbes, who thought it important that people should reverence the government however unworthy it might be, meets the argument that it might be difficult to obtain general assent to anything so irrational by pointing out that people have been brought to believe in the Christian religion, and, in particular, in the dogma of transubstantiation. If he had been alive now, he would have found ample confirmation in the devotion of German youth to the Nazis.

The power of governments over men's beliefs has been very great ever since the rise of large States. The great majority of Romans became Christian after the Roman emperors had been converted. In the parts of the Roman Empire that were conquered by the Arabs, most people abandoned Christianity for Islam. The division of Western Europe into Protestant and Catholic regions was determined by the attitude of governments in the sixteenth century. But the power of governments over belief in the present day is vastly greater than at any earlier time. A belief, however untrue, is important when it dominates the actions of large masses of men. In this sense, the beliefs inculcated by the Japanese, Russian, and German governments are important. Since they are completely divergent, they cannot all be true, though they may well all be false. Unfortunately they are such as to inspire men with an ardent desire to kill one another, even to the point of almost completely inhibiting the impulse of self-preservation. No one can deny, in face of the evidence, that it is easy, given military power, to produce a population of fanatical lunatics. It would be equally easy to produce a population of sane and reasonable people, but many governments do not wish to do so, since such people would fail to admire the politicians who are at the head of these governments.

There is one peculiarly pernicious application of the doctrine that human nature cannot be changed. This is the dogmatic assertion that there will always be wars, because we are so constituted that we feel a need of them. What is true is that a man who has had the kind of diet and education that most men have will wish to fight when provoked. But he will not actually fight unless he has a chance of victory. It is very annoying to be stopped by a speed cop, but we do not fight him because we know that he has the overwhelming forces of the State at his back. People who have no occasion for war do not make any impression of being psychologically thwarted. Sweden has had no war since 1814, but the Swedes were, a few years ago, one of the happiest and most contented nations in the world. I doubt whether they are so still, but that is because, though neutral, they are unable to escape many of the evils of war. If political organization were such as to make war obviously unprofitable, there is nothing in human nature that would compel its occurrence, or make average people unhappy because of its not occurring. Exactly the same arguments that are now used about the impossibility of preventing war were formerly used in defense of duelling, yet few of us feel thwarted because we are not allowed to fight duels.

I am persuaded that there is absolutely no limit to the absurdities that can, by government action, come to be generally believed. Give me an adequate army, with power to provide it with more pay and better food than falls to the lot of the average man, and I will undertake, within thirty years, to make the majority of the population believe that two and two are three, that water freezes when it gets hot and boils when it gets cold, or any other nonsense that might seem to serve the interest of the State. Of course, even when these beliefs had been generated, people would not put the kettle in the ice-box when they wanted it to boil. That cold makes water boil would be a Sunday truth, sacred and mystical, to be professed in awed tones, but not to be acted on in daily life. What would happen would be that any verbal denial of the mystic doctrine would be made illegal, and obstinate heretics would be "frozen" at the stake. No person who did not enthusiastically accept the official doctrine would be allowed to teach or to have any position of power. Only the very highest officials, in their cups, would whisper to each other what rubbish it all is; then they would laugh and drink again. This is hardly a caricature of what happens under some modern governments.

The discovery that man can be scientifically manipulated, and that governments can turn large masses this way or that as they choose, is one of the causes of our misfortunes. There is as much difference between a collection of mentally free citizens and a community molded by modern methods of propaganda as there is between a heap of raw materials and a battleship. Education, which was at first made universal in order that all might be able to read and write, has been found capable of serving quite other purposes. By instilling nonsense it unifies populations and generates collective enthusiasm. If all governments taught the same nonsense, the harm would not be so great. Unfortunately each has its own brand, and the diversity serves to produce hostility between the devotees of different creeds. If there is ever to be peace in the world, governments will have to agree either to inculcate no dogmas, or all to inculcate the same. The former, I fear, is a Utopian ideal, but perhaps they could agree to teach collectively that all public men, everywhere, are completely virtuous and perfectly wise. Perhaps, when the war is over, the surviving politicians may find it prudent to combine on some such programme.

But if conformity has its dangers, so has nonconformity.

Some "advanced thinkers" are of the opinion that any one who differs from the conventional opinion must be in the right. This is a delusion; if it were not, truth would be easier to come by than it is. There are infinite possibilities of error, and more cranks take up unfashionable errors than unfashionable truths. I met once an electrical engineer whose first words to me were: "How do you do? There are two methods of faith-healing, the one practiced by Christ and the one practiced by most Christian Scientists. I practice the method practiced by Christ." Shortly afterwards, he was sent to prison for making out fraudulent balance-sheets. The law does not look kindly on the intrusion of faith into this region. I knew also an eminent lunacy doctor who took to philosophy, and taught a new logic which, as he frankly confessed, he had learnt from his lunatics. When he died he left a will founding a professorship for the teaching of his new scientific methods, but unfortunately he left no assets. Arithmetic proved recalcitrant to lunatic logic. On one occasion a man came to ask me to recommend some of my books, as he was interested in philosophy. I did so, but he returned next day saying that he had been reading one of them, and had found only one statement he could understand, and that one seemed to him false. I asked him what it was, and he said it was the statement that Julius Caesar is dead. When I asked him why he did not agree, he drew himself up and said: "Because I am Julius Caesar." These examples may suffice to show that you cannot make sure of being right by being eccentric.

Science, which has always had to fight its way against popular beliefs, now has one of its most difficult battles in the sphere of psychology.

People who think they know all about human nature are always hopelessly at sea when they have to do with any abnormality. Some boys never learn to be what, in animals, is called "house-trained." The sort of person who won't stand any nonsense deals with such cases by punishment; the boy is beaten, and when he repeats the offense he is beaten worse. All medical men who have studied the matter know that punishment only aggravates the trouble. Sometimes the cause is physical, but usually it is psychological, and only curable by removing some deep-seated and probably unconscious grievance. But most people enjoy punishing anyone who irritates them, and so the medical view is rejected as fancy nonsense. The same sort of thing applies to men who are exhibitionists; they are sent to prison over and over again, but as soon as they come out they repeat the offense. A medical man who specialized in such ailments assured me that the exhibitionist can be cured by the simple device of having trousers that button up the back instead of the front. But this method is not tried because it does not satisfy people's vindictive impulses.

Broadly speaking, punishment is likely to prevent crimes that are sane in origin, but not those that spring from some psychological abnormality. This is now partially recognized; we distinguish between plain theft, which springs from what may be called rational self-interest, and kleptomania, which is a mark of something queer. And homicidal maniacs are not treated like ordinary murderers. But sexual aberrations rouse so much disgust that it is still impossible to have them treated medically rather than punitively. Indignation, though on the whole a useful social force, becomes harmful when it is directed against the victims of maladies that only medical skill can cure.

The same sort of thing happens as regards whole nations. During the last war, very naturally, people's vindictive feelings were aroused against the Germans, who were severely punished after their defeat. Now many people are arguing that the Versailles Treaty was ridiculously mild, since it failed to teach a lesson; this time, we are told, there must be *real* severity. To my mind, we shall be more likely to prevent a repetition of German aggression if we regard the rank and file of the Nazis as we regard lunatics than if we think of them as merely and simply criminals. Lunatics, of course, have to be restrained; we do not allow them to carry firearms. Similarly the German nation will have to be disarmed. But lunatics are restrained from prudence, not as a punishment, and so far as prudence permits we try to make them happy. Everybody recognizes that a homicidal maniac will only become more homicidal if he is made miserable. In Germany at the present day, there are, of course, many men among the Nazis who are plain criminals, but there must also be many who are more or less mad. Leaving the leaders out of account (I do not urge leniency toward them), the bulk of the German nation is much more likely to learn cooperation with the rest of the world if it is subjected to a kind but firm curative treatment than if it is regarded as an outcast among the nations. Those who are being punished seldom learn to feel kindly toward the men who punish them. And so long as the Germans hate the rest of mankind peace will be precarious.

When one reads of the beliefs of savages, or of the ancient Babylonians and Egyptians, they seem surprising by their capricious absurdity. But beliefs that are just as absurd are still entertained by the uneducated even in the most modern and civilized societies. I have been gravely assured, in America, that people born in March are unlucky and people born in May are peculiarly liable to corns. I do not know the history of these superstitions, but probably they are derived from Babylonian or Egyptian priestly love. Beliefs begin in the higher social strata, and then, like mud in a river, sink gradually downward in the educational scale; they may take 3,000 or 4,000 years to sink all the way. You may find your colored help making some remark that comes straight out of Plato—not the parts of Plato that scholars quote, but the parts where he utters obvious nonsense, such as that men who do not pursue wisdom in this life will be born again as women. Commentators on great philosophers always politely ignore their silly remarks.

Aristotle, in spite of his reputation, is full of absurdities. He says that children should be conceived in the Winter, when the wind is in the North, and that if people marry too young the children will be female. He tells us that the blood of females is blacker then that of males; that the pig is the only animal liable to measles; that an elephant suffering from insomnia should have its shoulders rubbed with salt, olive-oil, and warm water; that women have fewer teeth than men, and so on. Nevertheless, he is considered by the great majority of philosophers a paragon of wisdom.

Superstitions about lucky and unlucky days are almost universal. In ancient times they governed the actions of generals. Among ourselves the prejudice against Friday and the number thirteen is very active; sailors do not like to sail on Friday, and many hotels have no thirteenth floor. The superstitions about Friday and thirteen were once believed by those reputed wise; now such men regard them as harmless follies. But probably 2,000 years hence many beliefs of the wise of our day will have come to seem equally foolish. Man is a credulous animal, and must believe *something;* in the absence of good grounds for belief, he will be satisfied with bad ones.

Belief in "nature" and what is "natural" is a source of many errors. It used to be, and to some extent still is, powerfully operative in medicine. The human body, left to itself, has a certain power of curing itself; small cuts usually heal, colds pass off, and even serious diseases sometimes disappear without medical treatment. But aids to nature are very desirable, even in these cases. Cuts may turn septic if not disinfected, colds may turn to pneumonia, and serious diseases are only left without treatment by explorers and travelers in remote regions, who have no option. Many practices which have come to seem "natural" were originally "unnatural," for instance clothing and washing. Before men adopted clothing they must have found it impossible to live in cold climates. Where there is not a modicum of cleanliness, populations suffer from various diseases, such as typhus, from which Western nations have become exempt. Vaccination was (and by some still is) objected to as "unnatural." But there is no consistency in such objections, for no one supposes that a broken bone can be mended by "natural" behavior. Eating cooked food is "unnatural"; so is heating our houses. The Chinese philosopher Lao-tse, whose traditional date is about 600 B.C., objected to roads and bridges and boats as "unnatural," and in his disgust at such mechanistic devices left China and went to live among the Western barbarians. Every advance in civilization has been denounced as unnatural while it was recent.

The commonest objection to birth control is that it is against "nature." (For some reason we are not allowed to say that celibacy is against nature; the only reason I can think of is that it is not new.) Malthus saw only three ways of keeping down the population; moral restraint, vice, and misery. Moral restraint, he admitted, was not likely to be practiced on a large scale. "Vice," i.e., birth control, he, as a clergyman, viewed with abhorrence. There remained misery. In his comfortable parsonage, he contemplated the misery of the great majority of mankind with equanimity, and pointed out the fallacies of reformers who hoped to alleviate it. Modern theological opponents of birth control are less honest. They pretend to think that God will provide, however many mouths there may be to feed. They ignore

230 Bertrand Russell On God and Religion

the fact that He has never done so hitherto, but has left mankind exposed to periodical famines in which millions died of hunger. They must be deemed to hold—if they are saying what they believe—that from this moment onward God will work a continual miracle of loaves and fishes which He has hitherto thought unnecessary. Or perhaps they will say that suffering here below is of no importance; what matters is the hereafter. By their own theology, most of the children whom their opposition to birth control will cause to exist will go to hell. We must suppose, therefore, that they oppose the amelioration of life on earth because they think it a good thing that many millions should suffer eternal torment. By comparison with them, Malthus appears merciful.

Women, as the object of our strongest love and aversion, rouse complex emotions which are embodied in proverbial "wisdom."

Almost everybody allows himself or herself some entirely unjustifiable generalization on the subject of woman. Married men, when they generalize on that subject, judge by their wives; women judge by themselves. It would be amusing to write a history of men's views on women. In antiquity, when male supremacy was unquestioned and Christian ethics were still unknown, women were harmless but rather silly, and a man who took them seriously was somewhat despised. Plato thinks it a grave objection to the drama that the playwright has to imitate women in creating his female roles. With the coming of Christianity woman took on a new part, that of the temptress; but at the same time she was also found capable of being a saint. In Victorian days the saint was much more emphasized than the temptress; Victorian men could not admit themselves susceptible to temptation. The superior virtue of women was made a reason for keeping them out of politics, where, it was held, a lofty virtue is impossible. But the early feminists turned the argument round, and contended tha the participation of women would ennoble politics. Since this has turned out to be an illusion, there has been less talk of women's superior virtue, but there are still a number of men who adhere to the monkish view of woman as the temptress. Women themselves, for the most part, think of themselves as the sensible sex, whose business it is to undo the harm that comes of men's impetuous follies. For my part I distrust *all* generalizations about women, favorable and unfavorable, masculine and feminine, ancient and modern; all alike, I should say, result from paucity of experience.

The deeply irrational attitude of each sex toward women may

be seen in novels, particularly in bad novels. In bad novels by men, there is the woman with whom the author is in love, who usually possesses every charm, but is somewhat helpless, and requires male protection; sometimes, however, like Shakespeare's Cleopatra, she is an object of exasperated hatred, and is thought to be deeply and desperately wicked. In portraying the heroine, the male author does not write from observation, but merely objectifies his own emotions. In regard to his other female characters, he is more objective, and may even depend upon his notebook; but when he is in love, his passion makes a mist between him and the object of his devotion. Women novelists, also, have two kinds of women in their books. One is themselves, glamorous and kind, and object of lust to the wicked and of love to the good, sensitive, high-souled, and constantly misjudged. The other kind is represented by all other women, and is usually portrayed as petty, spiteful, cruel, and deceitful. It would seem that to judge women without bias is not easy either for men or for women.

Generalizations about national characteristics are just as common and just as unwarranted as generalizations about women. Until 1870, the Germans were thought of as a nation of spectacled professors, evolving everything out of their inner consciousness, and scarcely aware of the outer world, but since 1870 this conception has had to be very sharply revised. Frenchmen seem to be thought of by most Americans as perpetually engaged in amorous intrigue; Walt Whitman, in one of his catalogues, speaks of "the adulterous French couple on the sly settee." Americans who go to live in France are astonished, and perhaps disappointed, by the intensity of family life. Before the Russian Revolution, the Russians were credited with a mystical Slav soul, which, while it incapacitated them for ordinary sensible behavior, gave them a kind of deep wisdom to which more practical nations could not hope to attain. Suddenly everything was changed: mysticism was taboo, and only the most earthly ideals were tolerated. The truth is that what appears to one nation as the national character of another depends upon a few prominent individuals, or upon the class that happens to have power. For this reason, all generalizations on this subject are liable to be completely upset by any important political change.

To avoid the various foolish opinions to which mankind are prone, no superhuman genius is required. A few simple rules will keep you, not from *all* error, but from silly error.

If the matter is one that can be settled by observation, make the observation yourself. Aristotle could have avoided the mistake of thinking that women have fewer teeth than men, by the simple device of asking Mrs. Aristotle to keep her mouth open while he counted. He did not do so because he thought he knew. Thinking that you know when in fact you don't is a fatal mistake, to which we are all prone. I believe myself that hedgehogs eat black beetles, because I have been told that they do; but if I were writing a book on the habits of hedgehogs, I should not commit myself until I had seen one enjoying this unappetizing diet. Aristotle, however, was less cautious. Ancient and medieval authors knew all about unicorns and salamanders; not one of them thought it necessary to avoid dogmatic statements about them because he had never seen one of them.

Many matters, however, are less easily brought to the test of experience. If, like most of mankind, you have passionate convictions on many such matters, there are ways in which you can make yourself aware of your own bias. If an opinion contrary to your own makes you angry, that is a sign that you are subconsciously aware of having no good reason for thinking as you do. If some one maintains that two and two are five, or that Iceland is on the equator, you feel pity rather than anger, unless you know so little of arithmetic or geography that his opinion shakes your own contrary conviction. The most savage controversies are those about matters as to which there is no good evidence either way. Persecution is used in theology, not in arithmetic, because in arithmetic there is knowledge, but in theology there is only opinion. So whenever you find yourself getting angry about a difference of opinion, be on your guard; you will probably find, on examination, that your belief is going beyond what the evidence warrants.

A good way of ridding yourself of certain kinds of dogmatism is to become aware of opinions held in social circles different from your own. When I was young, I lived much outside my own country— in France, Germany, Italy, and the United States. I found this very profitable in diminishing the intensity of insular prejudice. If you cannot travel, seek out people with whom you disagree, and read a newspaper belonging to a party that is not yours. If the people and the newspaper seem mad, perverse, and wicked, remind yourself that you seem so to them. In this opinion both parties may be right, but they cannot both be wrong. This reflection should generate a certain caution.

Becoming aware of foreign customs, however, does not always

have a beneficial effect. In the seventeenth century, when the Manchus conquered China, it was the custom among the Chinese for the women to have small feet, and among the Manchus for the men to wear-pigtails. Instead of each dropping their own foolish custom, they each adopted the foolish custom of the other, and the Chinese continued to wear pigtails until they shook off the dominion of the Manchus in the revolution of 1911.

For those who have enough psychological imagination, it is a good plan to imagine an argument with a person having a different bias. This has one advantage, and only one, as compared with actual conversation with opponents; this one advantage is that the method is not subject to the same limitations of time or space. Mahatma Gandhi deplores railways and steamboats and machinery; he would like to undo the whole of the industrial revolution. You may never have an opportunity of actually meeting any one who holds this opinion, because in Western countries most people take the advantage of modern technique for granted. But if you want to make sure that you are right in agreeing with the prevailing opinion, you will find it a good plan to test the arguments that occur to you by considering what Gandhi might say in refutation of them. I have sometimes been led actually to change my mind as a result of this kind of imaginary dialogue, and, short of this, I have frequently found myself growing less dogmatic and cocksure through realizing the possible reasonableness of a hypothetical opponent.

Be very wary of opinions that flatter your self-esteem. Both men and women, nine times out of ten, are firmly convinced of the superior excellence of their own sex. There is abundant evidence on both sides. If you are a man, you can point out that most poets and men of science are male; if you are a woman, you can retort that so are most criminals. The question is inherently insoluble, but self-esteem conceals this from most people. We are all, whatever part of the world we come from, persuaded that our own nation is superior to all others. Seeing that each nation has its characteristic merits and demerits, we adjust our standard of values so as to make out that the merits possessed by our nation are the really important ones, while its demerits are comparatively trivial. Here, again, the rational man will admit that the question is one to which there is no demonstrably right answer. It is more difficult to deal with the self-esteem of man as man, because we cannot argue out the matter with some nonhuman mind. The only way I know of dealing with this general human conceit is to remind ourselves that man is a brief episode in the life of a small planet in a little corner of the universe, and that, for aught we know, other parts of the cosmos may contain beings as superior to ourselves as we are to jellyfish.

Other passions besides self-esteem are common sources of error; of these perhaps the most important is fear. Fear sometimes operates directly, by inventing rumors of disaster in war-time, or by imagining objects of terror, such as ghosts; sometimes it operates indirectly, by creating belief in something comforting, such as the elixir of life, or heaven for ourselves and hell for our enemies. Fear has many forms—fear of death, fear of the dark, fear of the unknown, fear of the herd, and that vague generalized fear that comes to those who conceal from themselves their more specific terrors. Until you have admitted your own fears to yourself, and have guarded yourself by a difficult effort of will against their myth-making power, you cannot hope to think truly about many matters of great importance, especially those with which religious beliefs are concerned. Fear is the main source of superstition and one of the main sources of cruelty. To conquer fear is the beginning of wisdom, in the pursuit of truth as in the endeavor after a worthy manner of life.

There are two ways of avoiding fear: one is by persuading ourselves that we are immune from disaster, and the other is by the practice of sheer courage. The latter is difficult, and to everybody becomes impossible at a certain point. The former has therefore always been more popular. Primitive magic has the purpose of securing safety, either by injuring enemies, or by protecting oneself by talismans, spells, or incantations. Without any essential change, belief in such ways of avoiding danger survived throughout the many centuries of Babylonian civilization, spread from Babylon throughout the empire of Alexander, and was acquired by the Romans in the course of their absorption of hellenistic culture. From the Romans it descended to medieval Christendom and Islam. Science has now lessened the belief in magic, but many people place more faith in mascots than they are willing to avow, and sorcery, while condemned by the Church, is still officially a *possible* sin.

Magic, however, was a crude way of avoiding terrors, and, moreover, not a very effective way, for wicked magicians might always prove stronger than good ones. In the fifteenth, sixteenth, and seventeenth centuries, dread of witches and sorcerers led to the burning of hundreds of thousands convicted of these crimes. But newer beliefs, particularly as to the future life, sought more effective ways of combating fear. Socrates on the day of his death (if Plato is to be believed) expressed the conviction that in the next world he would live in the company of the gods and heroes, and surrounded by just spirits who would never object to his endless argumentation. Plato, in his "Republic," laid it down that cheerful views of the next world must be enforced by the State, not because they were true, but to make soldiers more willing to die in battle. He would have none of the traditional myths about Hades, because they represented the spirits of the dead as unhappy.

Orthodox Christianity, in the Ages of Faith, laid down very definite rules for salvation. First, you must be baptized; then, you must avoid all theological error; last, you must, before dying, repent of your sins and receive absolution. All this would not save you from purgatory, but it would insure your ultimate arrival in heaven. It was not necessary to *know* theology. An eminent cardinal stated authoritatively that the requirements of orthodoxy would be satisfied if you murmured on your death-bed: "I believe all that the Church believes; the Church believes all that I believe." These very definite directions ought to have made Catholics sure of finding the way to heaven. Nevertheless, the dread of hell persisted, and has caused, in recent times, a great softening of the dogmas as to who will be damned. The doctrine, professed by many modern Christians, that everybody will go to heaven, ought to do away with the fear of death, but in fact this fear is too instinctive to be easily vanquished. F. W. H. Myers, whom spiritualism had converted to belief in a future life, questioned a woman who had lately lost her daughter as to what she supposed had become of her soul. The mother replied: "Oh, well, I suppose she is enjoying eternal bliss, but I wish you wouldn't talk about such unpleasant subjects." In spite of all that theology can do, heaven remains, to most people, an "unpleasant subject."

The most refined religions, such as those of Marcus Aurelius and Spinoza, are still concerned with the conquest of fear. The Stoic doctrine was simple: it maintained that the only true good is virtue, of which no enemy can deprive me; consequently, there is no need to fear enemies. The difficulty was that no one could really believe virtue to be the only good, not even Marcus Aurelius, who, as emperor, sought not only to make his subjects virtuous, but to protect them against barbarians, pestilences, and famines. Spinoza taught a somewhat similar doctrine. According to him, our true good consists in indifference to our mundane fortunes. Both these men sought to escape from fear by pretending that such things as physical suffering are not really evil. This is a noble way of escaping from fear, but is still based upon false belief. And if genuinely accepted, it would have the bad effect of making men indifferent, not only to their own sufferings, but also to those of others.

Under the influence of great fear, almost everybody becomes superstitious. The sailors who threw Jonah overboard imagined his presence to be the cause of the storm which threatened to wreck their ship. In a similar spirit the Japanese, at the time of the Tokyo earthquake took to massacring Koreans and Liberals. When the Romans won victories in the Punic wars, the Carthaginians became persuaded that their misfortunes were due to a certain laxity which had crept into the worship of Moloch. Moloch liked having children sacrificed to him, and preferred them aristocratic; but the noble families of Carthage had adopted the practice of surreptitiously substituting plebeian children for their own offspring. This, it was thought, had displeased the god, and at the worst moments even the most aristocratic children were duly consumed in the fire. Strange to say, the Romans were victorious in spite of this democratic reform on the part of their enemies.

Collective fear stimulates herd instinct, and tends to produce ferocity toward those who are not regarded as members of the herd. So it was in the French Revolution, when dread of foreign armies produced the reign of terror. And it is to be feared that the Nazis, as defeat draws nearer, will increase the intensity of their campaign for exterminating Jews. Fear generates impulses of cruelty, and therefore promotes such superstitious beliefs as seem to justify cruelty. Neither a man nor a crowd nor a nation can be trusted to act humanely or to think sanely under the influence of a great fear. And for this reason poltroons are more prone to cruelty than brave men, and are also more prone to superstition. When I say this, I am thinking of men who are brave in all respects, not only in facing death. Many a man will have the courage to die gallantly, but will not have the courage to say, or even to think, that the cause for which he is asked to die is an unworthy one. Obloquy is, to most men, more painful than death; that is one reason why, in times of collective excitement, so few men venture to dissent from the prevailing opinion. No Carthaginian denied Moloch, because to do so would have required more courage than was required to face death in battle.

But we have been getting too solemn. Superstitions are not always dark and cruel; often they add to the gaiety of life. I received once a communication from the god Osiris, giving me his telephone number; he lived, at that time, in a suburb of Boston. Although I did not enroll myself among his worshipers, his letter gave me pleasure. I have frequently received letters from men announcing themselves as the Messiah, and urging me not to omit to mention this important fact in my lectures. During prohibition, there was a sect which maintained that the communion service ought to be celebrated in whiskey, not in wine; this tenet gave them a legal right to a supply of hard liquor, and the sect grew rapidly. There is in England a sect which maintains that the English are the lost ten tribes; there is a stricter sect, which maintains that they are only the tribes of Ephraim and Manasseh. Whenever I encounter a member of eitherof these sects, I profess myself an adherent of the other, and much pleasant argumentation results. I like also the men who study the Great Pyramid, with a view to deciphering its mystical lore. Many great books have been written on this subject, some of which have been presented to me by their authors. It is a singular fact that the Great Pyramid always predicts the history of the world accurately up to the date of publication of the book in question, but after that date it becomes less reliable. Generally the author expects, very soon, wars in Egypt, followed by Armageddon and the coming of Antichrist, but by this time so many people have been recognized as Antichrist that the reader is reluctantly driven to skepticism.

I admire especially a certain prophetess who lived beside a lake in Northern New York State about the year 1820. She announced to her numerous followers that she possessed the power of walking on water, and that she proposed to do so at 11 o'clock on a certain morning. At the stated time, the faithful assembled in their thousands beside the lake. She spoke to them, saying: "Are you all entirely persuaded that I can walk on water?" With one voice they replied: "We are." "In that case," she announced, "there is not need for me to do so." And they all went home much edified.

Perhaps the world would lose some of its interest and variety if such beliefs were wholly replaced by cold science. Perhaps we may allow ourselves to be glad of the Abecedarians, who were so-called because, having rejected all profane learning, they thought it wicked to learn the ABC. And we may enjoy the perplexity of the South American Jesuit who wondered how the sloth could have traveled, since the Flood, all the way from Mount Ararat to Peru—a journey which its extreme tardiness of locomotion rendered almost incredible. A wise man will enjoy the goods of which there is a plentiful supply, and of intellectual rubbish he will find an abundant diet, in our own age as in every other.

15

The Value of Free Thought
How to Become a Truth-Seeker and Break the Chains of Mental Slavery

The expression "free thought" is often used as if it meant merely opposition to the prevailing orthodoxy. But this is only a symptom of free thought, frequent, but invariable. "Free thought" means thinking freely—as freely, at least, as is possible for a human being. The person who is free in any respect is free *from* something; what is the free thinker free from? To be worthy of the name, he must be free of two things: the force of tradition, and the tyranny of his own passions. No one is *completely* free from either, but in the measure of a man's emancipation he deserves to be called a free thinker. A man is not to be denied this title because he happens, on some point, to agree with the theologians of his country. An Arab who, starting from the first principles of human reason, is able to deduce that the Koran was not created, but existed eternally in heaven, may be counted as a free thinker, provided he is willing to listen to counter arguments and subject his ratiocination to critical scrutiny. On the same conditions, a European who, from a definition of benevolence, is able to show that a benevolent Deity, will subject infants to an eternity of torment if they die before some one sprinkles them with water to the accompaniment of certain magical words, will have to be regarded as satisfying our definition. What makes a free thinker is not his beliefs, but the way in which he holds them. If he holds them because his elders told him they were true when he was young, or if he holds them because if he did not he would be unhappy, his thought is not free; but if he holds them because, after careful

First published by Haldeman-Julius in 1944.

thought, he finds a balance of evidence in their favor, then his thought is free, however odd his conclusions may seem.

Freedom from the tyranny of passion is as essential as freedom from the influence of tradition. The lunatic who thinks he is God or the governor of the Bank of England is not a free thinker, because he has allowed the passion of megalomania to get the better of his reason. The jealous husband, who suspects his wife of infidelity on inadequate grounds, and the complacent optimist, who refuses to suspect her when the evidence is overwhelming, are alike permitting passion to enslave their thought; in neither of them is thought free.

The freedom that the free thinker seeks is not the absolute freedom of anarchy; it is freedom within the intellectual law. He will not bow to the authority of others, and he will not bow to his own desires, but he will submit to evidence. Prove to him that he is mistaken, and he will change his opinion; supply him with a new fact, and he will if necessary abandon even his most cherished theories. This is not to him a slavery, since his desire is to *know,* not to indulge in pretty fancies. The desire for knowledge has an element of humility toward facts; in opinion, it submits to the universe. But toward mankind it is not humble; it will not accept as genuine knowledge the counterfeit coin that is too often offered with all the apparatus of authority. The free thinker knows that to control his environment he must understand it, and that the illusion of power to be derived from myths is no better than that of a boastful drunkard. He needs, toward his fellow men, independence; toward his own prejudices, a difficult self-discipline; and toward the world that he wishes to understand a clear untroubled outlook which endeavors to see without distortion.

Is the free thinker, as we have been describing him, a desirable member of society, or is he a menace to all that we ought to hold sacred? In almost all times and places, he has been held to be a menace, and he is still held to be so, in varying degrees, in almost every country. In Germany he is sent to a concentration camp, in Russia to a labor colony in the Arctic; in Japan he is imprisoned for "dangerous thoughts"; in the United States, though not subject to legal penalities, he is debarred from teaching in the great majority of schools and universities, and has no chance of a political career. Throughout a period of about 1,200 years, every Christian country in Europe condemned free thinkers to be burnt at the stake. In Mohammedan countries, though often protected by monarchs, they were subjects of abhorrence to the mob even in the greatest periods of Arabic and Moorish culture. A hostility so widespread and so nearly universal must have deep roots, partly in human nature, partly in the statecraft of governing cliques; in either case, the soil in which they flourish is fear.

Let us consider some of the arguments against free thought that are used by those who are not content with a mere appeal to prejudice.

There is first the appeal to modesty, which is used especially by the old in dealing with rebellious youth. Wise men throughout the ages, it is said, have all been agreed in upholding certain great truths, and who are you to set yourself up against their unanimous testimony? If you are prepared to reject St. Paul and St. Augustine will you be equally contemptuous of Plato and Aristotle? Or, if you despise all the ancients, what about Descartes and Spinoza, Kant and Hegel? Were they not great intellects, who probed matters more deeply than you can hope to do? And is not the pastor of your parents' church a virtuous and learned man, who has a degree in theology, and even spent some months in the study of Hebrew? Have you forgotten what [Francis] Bacon, that good and great man, said about a *little* knowledge inclining to atheism? Do you pretend that there are no mysteries before which the human intellect is dumb? Pride of intellect is a sin, and you commit it when you set up your own judgment against that of all the wisest men of many centuries.

This argument, expressed in Latin—which is held to make any nonsense respectable—has been erected by the Catholic Church into a first principle: that we cannot err in believing what has been believed always, everywhere, and by everybody. Those who use this argument conveniently forget how many once universal beliefs-are now discarded. It was held that there could not be men at the antipodes, because they would fall off, or at least grow dizzy from standing upside down. Everybody believed that the sun goes round the earth, that there are unicorns, and that toads are poisonous. Until the sixteenth century, no one questioned the efficacy of witchcraft; of those who first doubted the truth of this superstition, not a few were burnt at the stake. Who now accepts the doctrine, once almost universal throughout Christendom, that infants who die without being baptized will spend eternity in hell because Adam ate an apple? Yet all these now obsolete doctrines could formerly have been upheld by the appeal to the wisdom of the ages.

The appeal to authority is fallacious, but even so it is questionable whether, if admitted, it would work more in favor of Christianity than against it. I have spent most of my life in the society of authors and men of science; among them, free thought is taken for granted, and the few exceptions are noted as freaks. It is true that most of them have too much worldly wisdom to allow their opinions to become known to the orthodox, for even now a *known* free thinker suffers various disabilities, and has much more difficulty in making a living than a man who is reputed to accept the teachings of some Church. It is only by imposing this somewhat flimsy hypocrisy that believers are still able to deceive the young by appealing to authority.

The study of anthropology is useful in this respect. Savages at a certain stage of development are found to have very similar beliefs in all parts of the world, and to the modern mind these beliefs are almost all absurd. But if mankind continues to advance, we shall, 20,000 years hence, appear to our successors scarcely distinguishable from the savages to whom we feel ourselves so superior. It is customary to date anthropological epochs by the materials employed—the the stone age, the bronze age, the iron age. But one might equally describe a culture by its prevalent beliefs: the cannibal culture, the animal sacrifice culture, the transubstantiation culture, and so on into the future. To see our beliefs as one stage in this development is wholesome. It shows that there is nothing which has been believed "always, everywhere, and by everybody"; and that whatever has been believed by everybody in a certain stage of culture has seemed nonsense to everybody in the next stage.

The common body of wisdom to which the conventional and orthodox like to appeal is a myth; there is only the "wisdom" of one time and place. In every age and in every place, if you wish to be thought well of by influential citizens you must at least seem to share their prejudices, and you must close your mind to the fact that influential citizens in other times and places have quite different prejudices. If on the other hand, you wish to acquire knowledge, you must ignore the influential citizens, and rely upon your judgment, even when you accept the authority of those whom your own judgment pronounces worthy of respect. This degree of reliance upon yourself is the first step toward freedom of thought. Not that you need think yourself infallible, but that you must learn to think every one fallible, and to content yourself with such greater or less probability as the evidence may seem to you to warrant. This renunciation of absolute certainty is, to some minds, the most difficult step toward intellectual freedom.

Of all the arguments designed to show that free thought is wicked, the one most often used is that without religion people would not be virtuous. Their virtue, we are told, will fail for two reasons, first, that they will no longer fear personal punishment, and second, that they will no longer know what is virtue and what is sin. In using this argument, orthodox Catholics have in some ways a logical advantage over Protestants. Let us see how the argument looks from a Catholic point of view.

The theology of sin has always been somewhat intricate, since it has had to face the fundamental question: why did God permit sin? St. Augustine held that, from the moment when Adam ate the apple, men have not had free will; they could not, by their own efforts, abstain from sin. Since sin deserves punishment, God would have been entirely just if He had condemned the whole human race to hell. But mercy is also a virtue, and in order to exercise this virtue He had to send another portion of the human race to heaven. Nothing but pure caprice, St. Augustine maintained, determined His choice of the elect and the reprobate. But on the elect, when He had chosen them, He bestowed grace, so that they were able, within limits, to abstain from sin. They were virtuous because they were saved, not saved because they were virtuous. For some obscure reason, grace was never bestowed on the unbaptized.

A certain kindly Welshman named Morgan, who translated his name into Pelagius, was a contemporary of St. Augustine, and combated his doctrine as too severe. Pelagius held that men still have free will, in spite of Adam's sin. He thought it even possible that a human being might be entirely without sin. He thought that the wicked are damned because they sin, whereas St. Augustine thought that they sin because they are damned. Pelagius held that each man had the power to live so virtuously as to deserve heaven, and that his use of his own free will determined the issue between salvation and damnation. St. Augustine's authority secured the condemnation of this doctrine, which remained heretical until the Reformation. But at the Reformation Luther and Calvin espoused the theory of predestination with such ardor that the Catholic Church, without formal change, turned increasingly toward the doctrine of Pelagius. This doctrine is now held, in practice if not in theory, not only by he Catholic Church, but also by the great majority of the Protestants. It has, however, been still further softened by the belief that fewer people go to hell than was formerly thought. Indeed, among Protestants, a complete rejection of hell has become very common.

A belief in either hell of purgatory ought, one would suppose, to have a powerful influence in promoting whatever the theologians consider to be virtue. If you accept St. Augustine's doctrine, you will hold that, although it is not virtue that causes you to go to heaven, virtue is a *mark* of the elect; if you live a sinful life, you will be forced to conclude that you are among the reprobate. You will therefore live virtuously in order to hope that you will go to heaven. If you accept the more usual view that you will be punished hereafter for your sins, either by spending eternity in hell or by a longer or shorter period of purgatorial fires, you will, if you are prudent, consider that, on the balance, the virtuous enjoy more pleasure than the wicked, and that therefore, as a rational hedonist, you had better abstain from sin. If, on the other hand, you do not believe in the life hereafter, you will sin whenever no earthly penalty is to be feared—so at least orthodox theologians seem to think. Whether from introspection or for some other reason, they seem to be all agreed that *disinterested* virtue is impossible.

However that may be, the views of the early Church on sin were found to be too severe for ordinary human nature, and were softened in various ways which, incidentally, increased the power of the priesthood. The sacrament of absolution secures sinners against the extreme penalty of damnation; you may commit all the sins you have a mind to, provided you repent on your deathbed and receive extreme unction. True, you may suffer for a while in purgatory, but your sojourn there can be shortened if masses are said for your soul, and priests will say masses for you if you leave them money for the purpose. Thus the power of wealth extends beyond the grave, and bribery is effective even in heaven. This comfortable doctrine left the rich and powerful free to indulge their passions as they saw fit. In the ages of faith, murder and rape were far commoner than they have since become. The supposed efficacy of orthodox belief in curbing sin is not borne out by history. Not only have believers been prone to sin, but unbelievers have often been exceptionally virtuous; it would be difficult to point to any set of men more impeccable than the earnest free thinkers of the nineteenth century.

But, the champion of orthodoxy will object, when free thinkers are virtuous, it is because they live in a Christian community and have imbibed its ethic in youth; without this influence, they would question the moral law and see no reason to abstain from any infamy. The sins of the Nazis and the Bolsheviks are pointed out as the fruits of free thought. But they are not free thinkers according to our definition: they are fanatical adherents of absurd creeds, and their crimes spring from their fanaticism. They are, in fact, the same crimes as those committed by men like Charles V or Philip II, who were champions of the faith. Charles V, after spending the day conquering a Protestant city, felt that he had earned a little relaxation; he sent his servants out to find a virgin, and they found one of seventeen. Presumably she got syphilis, but the emperor got absolution. This is the system which is supposed to preserve men from sin.

On the other hand, many who are now universally acknowledged to have been quite exceptionally virtuous incurred obloquy, if not worse, for their opposition to the orthodoxy of their day. Socrates, on the ground that he was guilty of impiety, was condemned to drink the hemlock. Giordano Bruno was burnt by the Inquisition and Servetus was burnt by Calvin, both because, though men of the highest moral excellence, they had fallen into heresy. Spinoza, one of the noblest men known to history, was excommunicated by the Jews and execrated by the Christians; for a hundred years after his death, hardly any one dared to say a good word for him. The English and American free thinkers of the eighteenth and early nineteenth centuries were, for the most part, men of quite exceptional moral excellence; in some cases, such as the Founding Fathers, this is so evident that the orthodox have been driven to conceal the fact that men so universally admired had shocking opinions. In our day free thought still leads men into trouble, but less for attacks on dogma than for criticism of the superstitious parts of religious ethics.

There are, it is true, some actions labelled "sin" which are likely to be promoted by free thought. A Jew, when he ceases to be orthodox, may eat pork; a Hindu may commit the offense of eating beef. The Greek Orthodox Church considers it sin for godparents of the same child to marry; I will not deny that free thought may encourage this enormity. Protestants condemn amusements on Sunday, and Catholics condemn birth control; in these respects, also, free thought may be inimical to what bigots choose to call virtue. Moral codes which are irrational, and have no basis except in superstition, cannot long survive the habit of disinterested thinking. But if a moral code seems to promote human well-being in this terrestrial existence, it has no need of supernatural sanctions. Kindliness and intelligence are the chief sources of useful behavior, and neither is promoted by causing people to believe, against all reason, in a capricious and vindictive deity who practices a degree of cruelty which, in the strictest mathematic sense, surpasses infinitely that of the worst human beings who have ever existed. Modern liberal Christians may protest that this is not the sort of God in whom they believe, but they should realize that only the teachings of persecuted free thinkers have caused this moral advance in their beliefs.

I come now to another class of arguments against free thought, namely those which may be called political. In former times, these arguments took a very crude form: it is all very w ll (it was said) for the rich and powerful to be skeptics, but the poor need some theological belief to make them contented with their lot. If they can be induced to think that this life of tribulation is only a brief prelude to eternal bliss, and that rewards in heaven are much more likely to go to the poor than to the rich, they will be less inclined to listen to subversive propaganda, particularly if heaven is only to be the reward of the submissive. This point of view existed in antiquity and throughout the Middle Ages, but it was especially prevalent in the early nineteenth century, when the preaching of Methodism induced acquiescence among the victims of the atrocious industrial system of that period. This frank defense of earthly injustice as a preface to celestial justice has now been pretty generally abandoned, but not, for the most part, through the initiative of champions of religion. It was mainly men like Tom Paine, Robert Owen, and Karl Marx, free thinkers all, who shamed the orthodox rich out of this complacent attempt to interpret God as the Supreme Capitalist.

There is, however, a generalized form of the same argument, which deserves more respect, and calls for serious discussion. In this form, the argument maintains that social cohesion, without which no community can survive, is only rendered possible by some unifying creed or moral code, and that no such creed or code can long survive the corrosive effect of skeptical criticism. There have been periods—so it is alleged—when denial of traditional orthodoxies caused political disaster; of these the most notable are the great age of Greece and the epoch of the Italian Renaissance. It is customary among the ignorant to bring up the fall of Rome in this connection, and to link it with the wickedness of Nero. But as the fall of Rome did not occur until 400 years after the time of Nero, and as meanwhile the Romans had undergone a great moral purification, culminating in the adoption of Christianity, this example is ill chosen. The other two deserve more serious discussion.

The Greek cities lost their independence, first to the Macedonians, and then, more completely, to the Romans, and this loss occurred at a time when the ancient pieties had been dissolved by free inquiry. But there is no reason to connect their fall with their skepticism. They fell because they could not unite, and their failure to unite was due to ordinary political causes, such as, in our own day, prevented the smaller neutrals from uniting against Hitler. No intensity of religious belief could have saved them; only a rare degree of political sagacity would have been of any service. Carthage fell equally, though at the crisis the Carthaginians sacrificed their children to Moloch as religiously as any champion of religion could wish.

Much the same considerations apply to Italy in the Renaissance. France and Spain were great powers, to which the small Italian states could offer no effective opposition. In the face of traditional enmities unity was difficult, as it always is in such circumstances; its most forceful advocate was the wicked Machiavelli, and, as he points out, its most powerful opponent was the pope. No serious historical student can maintain that the enslavement of Italy was due to lack of religion.

We may however concede one thing to those who urge that religion is socially necessary. Where the Church has been a very powerful organization, and has played a great part in regulating men's lives, its sudden dissolution may leave them without the accustomed external guidance, and render society somewhat chaotic until new organizations grow up. But in this respect the Church is no different from any other important organization. Social cohesion is important, and the Church has been one of the ways of securing it, but there are innumerable other ways which do not demand so high a price in mental bondage.

Some men argue that the question whether religious dogmas are true or false is unimportant; the important thing, they say, is that these beliefs are comforting. How could we face life, they ask, if this world were all, and if we had no assurance that its apparent evil serves some great purpose? Will not belief in immortality promote courage in the face of death? Will not the belief that the course of history is ordained by an all-wise beneficient Providence help us to stand firm in times when evil appears to be triumphant? Why rob ourselves or others of this source of happiness by listening to the dubious arguments of those who refuse to believe in anything that cannot be demonstrated by the cold intellect? Has not the heart its rights? Why should it submit to the head? As the poet Tennyson exclaims in rebutting the contentions of skeptics:

> Like a man in wrath the heart
> Stood up and answered: I have felt.

There is to my mind something pusillanimous and sniveling about this point of view, which makes me scarcely able to consider it with patience. To refuse to face facts merely because they are unpleasant is considered the mark of a weak character, except in the sphere of religion. I do not see how it can be ignoble to yield to the tyranny of fear in all ordinary terrestrial matters, but noble and virtuous to do exactly the same thing when God and the future life are concerned.

But, the defenders of orthodoxy may argue, you do not *know* that religious beliefs are untrue. Where all is doubtful, why not accept the more cheerful alternative? This is the argument of William James's "Will to Believe." The duty of veracity, he says, has two parts: first, to believe what is true; second, to disbelieve what is false. To these two parts he attaches equal authority. The skeptic, who suspends judgment in the absence of adequate evidence, is certainly failing to believe what is true, whereas, if he adopted either alternative, he *might* be succeeding in believing what is true. On this ground, in the name of veracity, William James condemns the skeptic.

His argument, however, is shockingly sophistical. The virtue of veracity does not consist in believing all sorts of things at a venture, on the off chance that they may happen to be true. No one would for a moment take this point of view except as regards religion. Suppose I get into conversation with a stranger, am I to believe that his name is Wilkinson on the ground that, if it is, I shall be believing truly whereas if I admit that I do not yet know his name I forfeit the chance of a true belief? You will say that there are known to be many surnames, and therefore each is improbable. But there are also many religions. If I am to believe at a venture, shall I believe what I am told by the Buddhists, or the Hindus, or the Christians? And if I choose the Christians, shall I prefer the Catholics, or the Lutherans, or the Calvinists, or the Muggletonians, or the Particular Baptists? On William James's principle I ought to believe them all, so as to have the greatest possible chance of believing something true.

The inconclusive character of the arguments *against* this or that theological dogma, even when fully admitted, does not justify belief in any one of the mutually inconsistent systems that human fantasy has created. I cannot *prove* that the Hindus are mistaken in attributing a peculiar sacredness to the cow, or that the Mohammendans are wrong in thinking that only the followers of the Prophet will enjoy the delights of paradise. Perhaps Mr. Muggleton was as great a man as the Muggletonians contend; perhaps the Seventh Day Adventists are right in thinking that it is on Saturdays that God wants us to do no work. But if we are going to adopt all these beliefs, as William James's principles would lead us to do, we shall find life somewhat difficult. We must not eat beef because the Hindus may be right, or pork because the Jews may be right, or beans because Pythagoras forbad them. We must not work on Fridays, Saturdays, or Sundays, to obey Mohammedan, Jewish and Christian precepts; the remaining days will mostly be sacred days in some religion. Perhaps in the end a general skepticism may seem less inconvenient than the consolations of all the religions at once. But how is a fair-minded man to choose among them?

The virtue of veracity, as I conceive it, consists in giving to every suggested belief the degree of credence that the evidence warrants. We give whole-hearted credence to our perceptions, almost complete credence to what is well established in science, such as predictions of eclipses, but much less to what is still somewhat tentative, such as the weather forecast. We do not doubt that there was a famous man called Julius Caesar, but about Zoroaster we are not so sure. Veracity does not consist simply in believing or disbelieving, but also in suspending judgment, and in thinking some things probable and others improbable.

But, says William James, you must, in any doubtful situation, act either on belief or disbelief, and whichever you act upon the other alternative is practically rejected. This is an undue simplification. Many hypotheses are worth acting upon in certain ways, but not in others. If I am healthy, I may act upon the hypothesis that the weather is going to be fine, but if I have a peculiar sensibility to chills I may require very strong evidence before it becomes wise to adopt this hypothesis. I may act upon the hypothesis that only the good can go to heaven to the extent of being good myself, without being justified in acting on it to the extent of burning those whom I think not good.

We are all obliged constantly to act upon doubtful hypotheses, but when we do so we ought to take care that the results will not be very disastrous if the hypotheses are false. And when we act upon a doubtful hypothesis, we ought not to persuade ourselves that it is certain, for then we close our minds against new evidence, and also venture on actions (such as persecution) which are very undesirable if the hypothesis is false. And for this reason praise and blame ought not to be attached to beliefs or disbeliefs, but only to rational or irrational ways of holding them.

The importance of free thought is the same thing as the importance of veracity. Veracity does not necessarily consist in believing what is in fact true, because sometimes the available evidence may point to a wrong conclusion. Occasions may arise when the most conscientious jury will condemn a man who is in fact innocent, because unfortunate circumstances have made him seem guilty. To be always right is not possible for human beings, but it is possible always to *try* to be right. Veracity consists in trying to be right in matters of belief, and also in doing what is possible to insure that others are right.

Why should veracity be regarded as important? The reasons are partly personal, partly social. Let us begin with the social reasons.

Every powerful individual or group depends upon the existence of certain beliefs in others. The Dalai Lama is powerful in Tibet, the caliph used to be powerful in the Muslim world, the pope is powerful among Catholics, and the power of these men depends upon the belief of their followers that they have some peculiar holiness. The Dalai Lama makes (or made) large sums of money be selling pills made out of his excrement. What the caliph used to make out of being holy is familiar to every reader of the Arabian Nights. The pope has been shorn of some of his glory by the wickedness of Protestants and free thinkers, but in the great days of the Italian renaissance he enjoyed immense splendor. Is it to be supposed that men in such a position will encourage a rational examination of their claims? The Dalai Lama, like the vendors of patent medicines among ourselves, would obviously stick at nothing to prevent a scientific investigation of the efficacy of various pills, or at any rate to prevent its results from becoming known. He may himself, like some of the Renaissance popes, be completely skeptical, but he will not wish his disciples to resemble him in this respect.

Wherever there is power, there is a temptation to encourage irrational credulity in those who are subject to the power in question. Kings have been supposed to be sacred beings; the Mikado is still a divinity descended from the sun-goddess. Sometimes the business of sacredness is overdone. The king of Dahomey had such majesty that whenever he looked toward any part of his dominions tempests arose in that part; he therefore had to look always at the ground, which made him easy to assassinate. But when the king as an individual is hampered in this way, certain people in his entourage can use his magical powers for their own ends, so that there is no gain to the public.

When superstition is needed to promote tyranny, free thought is likely to cause revolution. But when the population has been accustomed to irrational reverence, it is likely to transfer its reverence to the leader of a successful revolution. Icons are still habitual in Russia, but of Lenin or Stalin instead of Our Lady. The chief gain in such a case is that the new superstition is not likely to have such a firm hold as the old one had; Stalin-worship could be upset by a less terrific upheaval than the revolution of 1917.

If a population is to escape tyranny, it must have a free-thinking attitude toward its government and the theories upon which its government is based, that is to say, it must demand that the government shall act in the general interest, and must not be deceived by a superstitious theology into the belief that what is in fact only the interest of the governing clique is identical with the general interest. For obedience to a tolerable government there are abundant rational motives, but when obedience is given for irrational reasons the resulting slavishness encourages the government to become tyrannical.

Ever since the Reformation, the state has increasingly replaced the Church as the object of superstitious reverence. At first, the state was embodied in the king: Henry VIII in England and Louis XIV in France were able to do abominable things because of the divinity that doth hedge a king. But in Germany and Russia it has been found possible, by means of a fanatical creed, to generate a similar feeling of awe toward a revolutionary leader, and in order to achieve this end free thought has been suppressed more vigorously than at any time since the seventeenth century. Only a general growth of free thought can, in the long run, save these countries from a self-imposed despotism.

The use of control over opinion to promote the power of a dominant class is best shown in the growth of Catholic theology. The power of the priesthood depends upon its ability to decide whether you shall go to heaven or to hell, and, in the former event, how long you shall spend in purgatory. What must you do in order to be among the fortunate? Must you lead a virtuous life? Must you love your neighbor, as Christ ordained? Or must you obey the still more difficult precept to sell all you have and give to the poor? No, you need do none of these things. Getting to heaven is a matter of red tape, like getting to a foreign country in war time.

First, you must avoid heresy, that is to say, you must believe everything that the Church tells you to believe. You need not know what the dogmas of the Church are, because that is difficult except for educated theologians, but you must hold no opinions contrary to these dogmas, and, if you ever feel tempted to do so, you must abandon the dangerous opinions as soon as you are officially informed that they are not orthodox. In a word, on all the most important subjects you must never think for yourself.

As regards conduct, you need not avoid sin; indeed, it is heretical to suppose that you can. You are sure to sin, but that need not trouble you provided you take the proper steps. There are seven deadly sins; if you commit any of these, and die before taking the proper steps, you will go to hell, but all can be forgiven to those who go through the correct routine. You must first tell some priest all about it, and profess due penitence. He can then absolve you, but may impose a penance as the condition of absolution. You are now safe from hell, so far as that particular sin is concerned, but to shorten your time in purgatory there are various things that it is wise to do, most of which increase either the power or the income of the priesthood. If you have enough money, you can commit a great many sins and nevertheless get to heaven pretty soon. The more sins you commit, the more the Church profits by the steps you have to take to mitigate the punishment. The system is convenient both for priests and for sinners, but it is preposterous to pretend that it promotes virtue. What it does promote is mental docility and abject fear.

I do not wish to suggest that these defects are peculiarly characteristic of the Catholic Church. They exist equally under the tyranny of the Nazi party and the Communist party. The sins to which these parties object are somewhat different from those to which the Church objects: in particular, they are less obsessed by sex. And the punishment of sin, under their regime, is in this world, not in the next. But otherwise there is much similarity, except for the differences that must exist between what is new and what is old and tried and established. What is in common is the power of one group, based on irrational beliefs. And the ultimate cure, in all these forms of mental tyranny, is freedom of thought.

It is odd that the orthodox, while decrying free thought in their own day, are quite willing to admit a host of truths which would never have become known but for the free thinkers of earlier ages. It was free thinkers in early Greece who persuaded their compatriots, in spite of the opposition of the priests of Delphi, to abandon the practice of human sacrifice. Anaxagoras, who taught that the sun and moon are not gods, only escaped death for impiety by flight from Athens. Those who disbelieved in witchcraft were told, quite truly, that to question witchcraft is to question the Bible. Galileo, for holding that the earth goes round the sun, was forced under threat of torture to recant, was kept in prison, and was ordered to repeat daily the seven penitential psalms to show his contrition for having used his mind. Darwin, fortunately for himself, lived in an age when persecution was in abeyance, but he was denounced by the orthodox, and they would have suppressed his teaching if they had had the power. Every intellectual advance, and a great many moral reforms, have had to fight for victory against the forces of obscurantism. Nevertheless, in what the obscurantists still defend, they are as obstinate as they ever were. Progress, now as in the past, is only possible in the teeth of their bitter hostility.

The personal and private reasons in favor of veracity in thinking are no less cogent than the public reasons. We all know the kind of person who cannot bear any unpalatable fact, and we know that, to those who live with them, they appear irritating and contemptible. In Shakespeare's "Antony and Cleopatra" Cleopatra orders the messenger who brings news of Antony's marriage to Octavia to be scourged. After this, people are wary of telling her anything that may annoy her, and, hugging her illusions, she goes straight to disaster. In regard to mundane affairs, the capacity to assimilate what is unpleasant is a condition of success, and for this reason, if for no other, it is a mistake to wrap oneself around with comfortable fairy tales.

But, it will be said, beliefs about the next world are in quite a different category. However false they may be, they will not be refuted by any experience during this life. Even if there is no such place as heaven, the man who expects to go there will have a happier life than the man who regards death as annihiliation. What advantage is there, then, in thinking truly about such a matter?

Now to begin with, veracity consists, as we have already said, not in having true beliefs, but in trying to have them. The man who, after a dispassionate examination of the evidence, has decided that there is a future life, is not lacking in veracity; this lack exists only in the believer who refuses to examine the evidence because he fears that it may prove inadequate. This man is like one who refuses to open a letter because it may contain bad news. When a man allows one kind of fear to dominate him, he soon comes to be dominated by other kinds also. The world in which we live is full of unpleasant things, some of which are pretty sure to happen to ourselves. If we are to preserve self-respect, and to merit the respect of others, we must learn to endure such things, not only when they happen, but in prospect. The man who fears that there is no evidence for immortality, but nevertheless clings to the belief by closing his mind, is no better than a man who fears he has cancer, but refuses a medical examination lest his fears should be confirmed. Each alike is on a level with the soldier who runs away in battle.

One of the worst aspects of orthodox Christianity is that it sanctifies fear, both personal and impersonal. Fear of hell, fear of extinction, fear lest the universe should be purposeless, are regarded as noble emotions, and men who allow themselves to be dominated by such fears are thought superior to men who face what is painful without flinching. But human nature cannot be so completely departmentalized that fear can be exalted in one direction without acquiring a hold in other directions also. The man who thinks himself virtuous in fearing an angry God will soon begin to see virtue in submission to earthly tyrants. In the best character there is an element of pride—not the sort of pride that despises others, but the sort that will not be deflected from what it thinks good by outside pressure. The man who has this sort of pride will wish, as far as may be, to know the truth about matters than concern him, and will feel himself a slave if, in his thought, he yields to fear. But this kind of pride is condemned by the Church as a sin, and is called "pride of intellect." For my part, so far from regarding it as a sin, I hold it to be one of the greatest and most desirable of virtues.

But it is time to tackle the more specific questions: Is there evidence in favor of Christian dogmas, either in the old rigid forms or in the vaguer forms favored by modernists? And, if there is not such evidence, is there nevertheless reason to think that belief in Christian dogmas does good?

The old orthodoxy has now fallen into almost universal disfavor, even among Catholics. Catholics still believe in hell, but by means of the doctrine of invincible ignorance they escape the necessity of believing that their Protestant friends will go there. Indeed there is hardly anybody they know to be damned, except Judas

Iscariot. Nevertheless, they are still, theoretically, in favor of persecution, of which the justification was that heresy leads to damnation. In this as in various other respects, Catholic ethics has not yet drawn all the inferences that follow from the liberalizing of Catholic theology. Perhaps in time these inferences will be drawn. But as in purely theological matters, the driving force will have to come from free thinkers. But for their influence, Catholic theology would still be as rigid as in the middle ages.

I think we may say that what is essential to Christianity as conceived by modern theologians is belief in God and immortality, together with a moral code which is more traditional than that of most free thinkers.

What reasons are there for belief in God? In old days, there were a variety of purely intellectual arguments, which were thought to make it irrational to doubt the existence of God. The chief of these was the argument of the First Cause: in tracing events backward from effects to causes, we must, it was thought, come to an end somewhere, since an infinite series is impossible. Wherever we come to an end, we have reached a Cause which is not an effect, and this Cause is God. This and other purely intellectual arguments were criticized by free thinkers, and in the end most theologians came to admit that they are invalid. The arguments upon which most modern theologians rely are less precise and more concerned with moral issues. In the main, they result from examination of what is called the religious consciousness or the religious experience. I do not think they are any more cogent than the old arguments, but because of their vagueness they are less susceptible to precise refutations.

We are told that we have a moral sense which must have had a supernatural origin. We are told also that certain people have religious experiences in which they become aware of God with the same certainty with which we become aware of tables and chairs. It is thought to be irrational to question this evidence merely on the ground that only certain people have the mystical experiences in question. We accept a host of things in science on the word of certain skilled observers; why not accept things in religion on the word of the skilled observers in this field?

To the mystic, who is persuaded that he himself has seen God, it is useless to argue about the matter. If he has moments when he is amenable to reason, one may point out that innumerable people have seen Satan, in whom most modern mystics do not believe. We may point out that Mr. So-and-So, who is a devotee of the worship of Bacchus, has seen pink rats, but has not been able to persuade other zoologists of their reality. We may trace the history of visions and hallucinations, pointing out how they are colored by the previous beliefs of the seers or lunatics concerned. St. Anthony in the desert was constantly troubled by apparitions of naked ladies; are we to infer that the Koran is right in promising abundance of such sights in Paradise? Perish the thought!

Such things, I say, we may point out, but probably in vain. A lady of my acquaintance took to fasting, and recommended the practice on the ground that it gave rise to visions. "Yes," I said, "if you drink too much you see snakes, and if you eat too little you see angels." But alas! she was only annoyed. She held, as many mystics do, that a vision must be veridical if it is edifying and results from virtuous living. This view is only justified if we already know that the world is governed by a beneficent Providence which rewards those who obey its laws by allowing them glimpses of the felicity to come. What if, as some heretics have thought, this world is the empire of Satan, who rewards the wicked not only with riches and power, but with hidden magical lore? In that case, the visions of the wicked will deserve more-credence than those of the good, and we shall listen with more respect to the revelations of the drunkard than to those of the ascetic. Before we can decide, therefore, what weight to attach to the testimony of the mystics, we must first inquire whether there are any grounds for believing in a good God.

God, in orthodox theology, is the omnipotent Creator, who made the world out of nothing. There are some liberal theologians nowadays who deny His omnipotence; I shall consider their view presently, but first let us examine the more usual and correct opinion.

This view has been most clearly and exactly expressed by the philosopher Leibniz. According to him, God, before creating the world, surveyed all the worlds that are logically possible, and compared them as the amount of good and evil that they severally contained. Being beneficent, He decided to create that one of the possible worlds that contained the greatest excess of good over evil. This world happened to contain a good deal of evil, but the evil was logically bound up with the greater good. In particular, sin is an evil, but free will is a good. Not even omnipotence can confer free will without the possibility of sin, but free will is so great a good that God decided to create a world containing both free will and sin rather than a world containing neither. He did so, and Adam ate the apple. Hence all our sorrows.

This is a pretty fable, and I will not deny that it is logically possible, but that is the utmost that I will concede. It is exactly equally possible that the world was created by a wholly malicious devil, who allowed a certain amount of good in order to increase the sum of evil. Let us suppose his ethical valuations to be entirely orthodox, but his will to be toward what is bad. He would agree with the theologians in thinking sin the greatest of evils, and would perceive that sin is impossible without free will. He would therefore create things possessed of free will, in spite of the fact that free will made virtue possible. He would be consoled, however, by the fore-knowledge that virtue would be very rare. And so this actual world, which he created, is the worst of all possible worlds, although it contains some things that are good.

I am not advocating this fable, any more than Leibniz's. Both seem to me to be equally fantastic. The only difference between them is that one is pleasant, the other unpleasant, but this difference has sufficed to make Christians accept the one and reject the other. No one asked: Why should the truth be pleasant? What reason have we to think our wishes a key to reality? The only rational answer is: None whatever.

The shifts to which theologians have been put to prove the world such as a good God could have created are sometimes very curious. In 1755 there was a great earthquake in Lisbon, which shook Voltaire's faith. But Rousseau pointed out that the loss of life was due to people living in high houses; if they had run wild in the woods, like the noble savage, they would not have suffered; they were therefore justly punished for their sins. Bernard Bosanquet, the leading British philosopher of my youth, went so far as to argue that, on purely logical grounds, earthquakes, though possible in second-rate capitals such as Lisbon, could not occur in a really great city like London. The Tokyo earthquake occurred after his book was published, but then the Japanese, as we know, are wicked.

In the eighteenth century it was held that all suffering, even that of animals, is due to Adam's sin, and did not exist before the fall. Until that fatal moment, mosquitoes did not sting, snakes were not venomous, and lions were strictly vegetarian. Unfortunately, in the early nineteenth century geologists discovered fossils of carnivorous animals which, it was rightly held, must have existed before man appeared on the earth. We can all see how right and just it is that animals eaten by other animals should suffer because Adam and Eve were wicked, but why should they have suffered *before* our parents first sinned? This problem caused agonies of perplexity to the pious biologists of a hundred years ago.

Some forms of punishment here on earth are specially reserved for sinners. Persecutors of the early Church, as Lactantius pointed out, were apt to be eaten of worms. The death of Arius, who held shocking opinions on the Trinity, was a warning to sinners: his bowels gushed out, as did those of some less famous heretics. But Montaigne pointed out that the same fate had befallen men of undoubted virtue; it only remained, therefore, to fall back on the mysterious dispensations of Providence.

The favorite argument was, and perhaps still is, the argument from design. Could this universe, obedient as it is to natural laws, have come about without a Lawgiver? Could the sublimity of the starry heavens, the majesty of the ocean, the song of the skylark, and the loveliness of spring flowers, have come about by chance? As the poet sings:

> Behold the snowflake exquisite in form,
> Was it made perfect by unwilling norm?

The argument from design has, however, a logical weakness when used by those who believe the Creator to be omnipotent. Design implies the necessity of using means, which does not exist for omnipotence. When we desire a house, we have to go through the labor of building it, but Aladdin's genie could cause a palace to exist by magic. The long process of evolution might be necessary to a divine Artificer who found matter already in existence, and had to struggle to bring order out of chaos. But to the God of Genesis and of orthodox theology no such laborious process was needed; no gradual process, no adaptation of means to ends, was required by the Being who could say: Let there be light, and there was light. The vast astronomical and geological ages before life existed may have been inevitable for a finite Deity working in a reluctant material, but for Omnipotence they would have been a gratuitous waste of time.

Let us then consider the hypothesis (which now has influential advocates) of a God who is not omnipotent, who is well meaning, but has constantly to struggle against obstacles put in his way by preexisting Nature.

This hypothesis, it must be said, cannot be disproved. There is nothing known about the universe that proves it to be false. But it is open to the same objection that we formerly used against Leibniz, that is to say, that a nonomnipotent devil is as least as plausible as a nonomnipotent God. On this hypothesis, we shall suppose that the universe originally consisted only of matter, with the sole exception of Satan, who studied it scientifically with a view to discovering its potentialities of evil. He soon saw that there could be no evil without life, and he therefore set to work to discover how to create life. He had to wait a long time, till the nebula had condensed into stars, the stars had thrown out planets, and the planets had cooled. At last, when the moment had arrived so far as physics was concerned, he set to work to study chemistry, and discovered that a certain compound, if he could synthesize it, would be at once sentient and self-perpetuating. After many efforts, he succeeded in making the germ of life; then, with the sense of labor rewarded, he mumbled: "Mischief, thou are afoot! Now let it work."

At first the process was regrettably slow. Sea slime had only the rudiments of feeling, and even when evolution had got as far as oysters their pangs were still regrettably dim. But after that things began to go better. Sharks kept humbler fishes in a state of terror, hawks made litle birds miserable, and cats brought tragedy into the lives of mice. But there was still something lacking: in between times, animals would persist in being happy, and forgetting the horrors that the next moment might bring. At last, to Satan's infinite delight, man was evolved, with the fatal gifts of memory and foresight. Each horror that happened to man left its indelible mark in his mind; he could not forget that what had occurred might occur again, and in warding off misfortune he lost the joy of life. Furious at this own misery, he sought the cause in the misdeeds of other men, and turned upon them in savage battle, thus magnifying a thousand times the ills that Nature has provided. With increasing glee, Satan watched the dismal process. At last, to crown his joy, men appeared who suffered not only from their own suffering, but from that of all mankind. Their preaching roused their followers to anger against those who refused to accept it, and so in the end increased the sum of human misery. When Satan saw this, his happiness was at last complete.

But all this is nothing but a pleasant fancy. Men, as is natural, have an intense desire to humanize the universe: God and Satan, alike are essentially human figures, the one a projection of ourselves, the other of our enemies. Both alike have purposes, and their activities, like ours, spring from desire. A somewhat difficult effort of imagination is required before we can conceive a universe without purpose, developing blindly in accordance with aimless habits. We feel an impulse to ask why? meaning not from what causes, but to what end. The Greeks thought that the sun and moon and planets were each moved about by a god, who was actuated by an aesthetic love of regularity such as inspired the Parthenon. This view made the heavens feel cozy. But gradually it was discovered that the regularity is only approximate: the planets move in ellipses, not in circles, and even the ellipses are inaccurate. The only thing that seemed to remain precise and exact was Newton's law of gravitation, though now we know that this too was only roughly true. However, there certainly seemed to be laws of nature, and where there are laws (we are told) there must be a Lawgiver.

In the period immediately following Newton this point of view had much plausibility, and convinced even such temperamental skeptics as Voltaire. But alas! The laws of nature are not what they used to be; they have become mere statistical averages. There is no longer anything in physics to suggest the Almighty Watchmaker, who made such a superlative watch that it only had to be wound up once. The laws of nature, like the laws of chance, are only verified when large numbers of instances are concerned, and then only approximately. Moreover, the universe, like humanly made watches, and unlike the superlative watch of eighteenth-century theology, is running down; energy is only useful when it is unevenly distributed, and it is continually approaching nearer and nearer to complete equality of distribution. When once this perfection of cosmic democracy has been achieved, nothing of the slightest interest to man or God or devil can ever happen again, unless omnipotence sees fit to wind the watch up once more.

But after all, the champion of cosmic purpose will say, it is *Life* that exhibits the important part of the divine plan; the rest is only stage scenery. Before Darwin, the marvellous adaptation of animals to their environment was regarded as evidence of benevolent purpose on the part of the Deity, but the theory of natural selection provided a scientific explanation of a vast collection of facts which had been serviceable to the theologians. We can now see, in a general way, how, given the chemical properties of living substance, ordinary physical and chemical forces were likely to set the process of evolution in motion. True, we cannot manufacture life in the laboratory, and until we have done so it is open to the orthodox to maintain that we shall never be able to do so. But for my part I see no reason why organic chemists could not, within the next hundred years, manufacture living micro-organisms. It may take some time—say a million years—to cause these to develop by artificial selection into giraffes and hippopotamuses and tigers. When this has been achieved, no doubt the theologians will still maintain that MAN can only be made by the Deity, but I fear the biologists will soon refute this last hope. Whether artificial man will be better or worse than the natural sort I do not venture to predict.

There would seem, therefore, to be no evidence that the course of events has been planned either by an omnipotent or by a non-omnipotent Deity; there is also no evidence that it has not been planned. Nor, if there be a Deity, is there any evidence as to his moral attributes. He may be doing His best under difficulties; He may be doing His worst, but be unable to prevent the accidental emergence of a little bit of good now and then, Or, again, His purposes may be purely aesthetic; He may not care whether His creatures are happy or unhappy, but only whether they provide a pleasing spectacle. All these hypotheses are equally probable, in the sense that there is not a shred of evidence for or against any of them. Nor should we neglect the Zoroastrian hypothesis of two Great Spirits, one good and one bad, the good one to achieve final victory when Persia conquers all the world. Aristotle thought there were forty-seven or fifty-five gods; this view also deserves our charitable respect. Of possible hypotheses there is no end, but in the absence of evidence we have no right to incline toward those that we happen to find agreeable.

What are we to think of immortality? To most modern Christians this question seems to be bound up with that of the existence of God, but both historically and logically the questions are quite distinct. Buddhists, though in their early days they were Atheists, believed that the soul survives death, except when such a pitch of virtue has been achieved as to deserve Nirvana. The Jews of the Old Testament, though they believed in God, did not (for the most part) believe in immortality. Clearly both these views are possible; the question of immortality is therefore, at least in some degree, distinct from that of the existence of God.

In the natural theology that has grown up in Christian civilizations the two questions are connected through Divine justice. The good, in this life, are not always happy, nor are the wicked always unhappy. Therefore, if the world is governed by a just God, there must be a future life, where the good will enjoy eternal bliss and the wicked will suffer eternal torment—or at any rate such purifying pains as may ultimately make them good. *If* there is a just God, and *if* there is free will (without which sin becomes meaningless), there is some force in this argument. Are there any others that should convince us of the immortality of the soul?

First of all, what is meant by "the soul"? We are supposed to consist of two things, one called a body, the other called the mind or soul. The body can be weighed on a weighing machine, it can move about, fall downstairs, have pieces cut of by a surgeon, and so on. The mind, meanwhile, does quite other things: it thinks and feels and wills. If my leg is amputated, no part of my soul is cut off; conversely, when I sleep my body remains intact. Among the movements of my body, we can distinguish those that spring from the mind from those that have a purely physical origin: if I walk along a street, I do so because my mind has so chosen, but if I slip on a piece of orange peel my mind has no part in causing the consequent collapse. These distinctions are so familiar that we take them as a matter of course, but their origin is in fact theological rather than scientific. They begin with Plato, so far as explicit philosophy is concerned, but were taken over by him from the Orphic religion. From Plato, and also from some other sources, the separation of soul and body was taken over by Christianity, and in time people came to think of it as an unquestionable truth.

But in fact both soul and body are metaphysical abstractions; what we know from experience are occurrences. We know thoughts, but not the supposed thinker; we know particular volitions, but not the will *per se*. Nor are we in any better case as regards the body. Physicists, who are supposed to know most about matter, say the oddest things about it. According to them, it is merely a convenient fiction; what really goes on in the physical world, they say, in a perpetual redistribution of energy, sometimes by sudden explosions, sometimes in gradually spreading waves. The body, which seems so solid and familiar, consists, they say, mainly of holes in waves of probability. If you do not understand what this means, I will confess that I do not either. But however that may be, it is clear that my body, which is described on my passport, and my mind, which is described by other philosophers, are alike mainly convenient ways of grouping phenomena, and that phenomena, so far as we know them, have not the characteristics that we associate either with mind or with body, since they are brief and evanescent. The phenomena, in fact, are not specially mental or specially material; they are the raw material out of which, for convenience of discourse, we construct the systems that we call minds and bodies.

The question of the immortality of the soul can, however, be restated so as to take account of these modern theories. Our thoughts and feelings, while we live, are linked together by memory and experience. We can inquire whether, after we are dead, there will still be thoughts and feelings that remember those we had when we lived on earth, for, if there will be, they may be regarded as still belonging to us, in the only sense in which our thoughts and feelings in this life belong to us.

Stated in this way, it must be said that immortality appears exceedingly improbable. Memory is clearly associated with the brain, and there is nothing to suggest that memory can survive after the brain has disintegrated. This seems as improbable as that a fire will survive after it has burnt everything combustible in its neighborhood. It would be going too far to say that we *know* such things to be impossible; we seldom know enough to say that this or that *cannot* happen. But on ordinary scientific grounds, seeing the intimate correlation of mental and cerebral organization, we can say that the survival of the one without the other must remain no more than a bare possibility, with much evidence against it and none in its favor.

But, even supposing the dogmas of religion to be false, it may be urged that they afford comfort to believers and do little harm. That they do little harm is not true. Opposition to birth control makes it impossible to solve the population problem, and therefore postpones indefinitely all chance of world peace; it also secures, wherever the law is what the Catholic vote has made it in Connecticut, that women incapable of surviving childbirth shall die in futile confinements. The influence of the Anglican Church in England suffices to insure that victims of cancer shall suffer agonies as long as possible, however much they themselves may desire euthanasia. Orthodox Protestantism in Tennessee suffices to prevent honest teaching of biology. Not only, however, where the law intervenes does orthodoxy do harm. I was myself at one time officially concerned in the appointment of a philosophy professor in an important American university; all the others agreed that of course he must be a good Christian. Practically all philosophers of any intellectual eminence are openly or secretly free thinkers; the insistence on orthodoxy therefore necessitated the appointment of a nonentity or a humbug.

On many important moral issues of modern times, the Church has thrown its influence on the side of cruelty or illegality. I will give two examples. Leopold, king of the Belgians, was also king of the Congo "Free" state. His rule involved what were probably the worst and most systematic atrocities in the long blood-stained annals of the oppression of Negroes by white men. When the facts became known, the Belgian Socialist Party, which consisted of free thinkers, did everything in its power to mitigate the horrors of the king's personal tyranny; the Church, on the contrary, was obstructive and tried in every possible way to interefere with the publicity of those who were denouncing the horrors. The Church failed, but if the natives of the Belgian Congo no longer suffer as they did it is no thanks to the professed followers of Christ who occupied the important posts in the Catholic hierarchy.

The other example is more recent. It is supposed that we are fighting to secure the reign of law and the victory of democracy. Spain had a legally elected democratic government, but the Church disliked it. Pious generals who were orthodox sons of the Church made a military insurrection against the legal and democratic government, and in the end the Church, with the help of Hitler and Mussolini, was successful in reimposing tyranny on the gallant Spanish champions of freedom. In this contest America officially refused to lift a finger to help the Loyalists, and even strained the interpretation of the law so as to prevent help from being given to the Loyalists by private American citizens. The government took this line in order to please American Catholics, with the result, not only that the Spaniards suffer, but that we have lost a possible ally in the war. The British government, perhaps for somewhat different reasons, was at least equally culpable.

Christian orthodoxy, however, is no longer the chief danger to free thought. The greatest danger in our day comes from new religions, Communism and Nazism. To call these religions may perhaps be objectionable both to their friends and to their enemies, but in fact they have all the characteristics of religions. They advocate a way of life on the basis of irrational dogmas; they have a sacred history, a Messiah, and a priesthood. I do not see what more could be demanded to qualify a doctrine as a religion. But let us examine each of them a little more narrowly.

When I speak of communism in this connection, I do not mean the doctrine that men's goods ought to be held in common. This is an ancient doctrine, advocated by Plato, apparently held by the primitive Church, revived constantly by religious sects during the middle ages, and condemned by one of the thirty-nine Articles of the Church of England. With its truth or falsehood I am not concerned; what I am concerned with is the doctrine of the modern Communistic Party, and of the Russian government to which it owes allegiance.

According to this doctrine, the world develops on the lines of a plan called Dialectical Materialism, first discovered by Karl Marx, embodied in the practice of a great state by Lenin, and now expounded from day to day by a church of which Stalin is the pope. Those who disagree with the pope either as to doctrine or as to church government are to be liquidated if possible; if that is not possible, they are to be bamboozled. Free discussion is to be prevented wherever the power to do so exists; revelation is to be interpreted, without argument, not by democratic process, but by the dicta of ecclesiastical dignitaries. It has already become apparent that the original ethic of the early communists, like that of the early Christians, while still treated with verbal respect, is not to be followed in actual life; indeed those who would *practice* communism, like the Franciscans who practiced apostolic poverty, are heretics, to be suppressed with the utmost rigor of persecution. If this doctrine and this organization prevail, free inquiry will become as impossible as it was in the middle ages, and the world will relapse into bigotry and obscurantism.

The theory of the Nazis, however, is definitely worse. Let us consider its salient points. There is a master race, the Germans, which is divinely ordained to rule the rest of mankind, not for their good, but for its own. Originally it was thought that races akin to the Germans shared some of their merits, but this turned out to be a mistake; in Norway, for instance, there are no genuine Nordics except Quisling and a handful of followers. Non-Aryans are specially wicked, and the most wicked of non-Aryans are the Jews. The Japanese, on the other hand, are so virtuous that they may count as honorary Aryans.

The Germans, alas, have been corrupted by Jewish influences, notably Christ and Marx. What they were before this unfortunate poison got into their blood may be seen in the pages of Tacitus. When it has been eliminated, they will again perceive that war is the noblest of human activities, and the opportunity of tyranny its most splendid reward. Other nations, strange to say, seem blind to the superiority of the Germans, but it was hoped that tanks and planes would prove efficient missionaries of the new creed. This hope, however, is now rapidly fading.

No such tissue of nonsense could have been believed by any population trained to examine evidence scientifically, and to base its opinions on rational grounds. Self-esteem, personal, national, or human, is one of the great sources of irrational belief; in the case of the Nazis, the self-esteem is national. Education should be directed, in part, to teaching the young to think independently of their prejudices, especially their collective prejudices, which are politically the most harmful. But this is not done anywhere; every national government finds national self-esteem useful, every rich government finds admiration of the plutocracy useful, every obscurantist government finds credulity useful. Nowhere, therefore, except among the esoteric elite of a few universities, is anything done to promote an honest attempt to decide questions according to the evidence. And so credulous populations are left defenseless against the wiles of clever politicians, who lead them through inflated self-esteem to hatred, from hatred to war, from war to universal misery. The modern advances in the art of propaganda have been met with no corresponding advances in training to resist propaganda. And so the populations of the world, one by one as "civilization" reaches them, go down into a dark pit of madness, where all that is worth preserving perishes in aimless slaughter.

The creed that I am preaching, if it can be called a creed, is a simple one: that, if you have an opinion about any matter, it should be based on ascertained facts, not upon hope or fear or prejudice. There is a known educational technique by which pupils of average intelligence can be taught to discount their passions when they think, but almost everywhere the authorities prevent the use of this technique. The authorities, almost everywhere, are convinced that they would be overthrown if the public were to examine their claims dispassionately; they therefore encourage passionate as opposed to rational thinking. Sooner or later, they become so tyrannical that they are overthrown, passionately, not rationally. After the pot of passion has boiled long enough, a new crust forms, and the new authorities are usually no better than the old. Louis XVI is executed, and is succeeded, first by Robespierre, then by Napoleon. Tsar Nicholas is assassinated, and a stricter tyranny follows under Lenin and Stalin. To this rule the American Revolution is one of the rare exceptions, and it was led by free thinkers; Washington and Adams, just as much as Jefferson, rejected the orthodoxy that most of their followers accepted.

Few modern obscurantists have the courage to say that it is better to believe what is false than what is true. In antiquity and in the seventeenth and eighteenth centuries it was commonly held that religion was necessary to keep the poor submissive, and should therefore be believed by them although aristocrats might have seen through it. Even in the nineteenth century, many French free thinkers liked their wives to be believers, in the hope that it would keep them chaste. But democracy and votes for women have made these points of view obsolete; now-a-days, if you wish to advocate religion for the masses, you must advocate it for every one, and if you are to advocate it for everyone you must do so, at least nominally, on the ground that you believe it to be true.

The insincerity of this appeal to truth is shown by the unwillingness to trust to free discussion or to allow the scientific habit of mind to be taught in education. If you think that a doctrine can only be rendered acceptable by the stake or the concentration camp, you evidently have not much confidence in the rational grounds in its favor. If you think it is necessary to forbid the publication or sale of books which contradict your opinions, you evidently hold that such books, in a free intellectual competition, would be likely to get the best of the argument.

You may, of course, fall back on an anti-democratic point of view. You may say: We, the Censors, or we the dignitaries of the Church, or we the agents for government propaganda, are wise men and trained investigators; we have examined all the evidence, and reached a conclusion, which happens, by a mere coincidence, to be in line with the interest of the authorities. But the populace have not the time to study such questions deeply; subversive agitators will, if we leave them free, make appeals to vulgar passions, which it would require much time and work to combat. Since we know the truth, is it not better that we should impart it, and should forbid all attempts to cause the dissemination of what our wisdom shows to be falsehood? Let us teach humility to the public, and then tell them from time to time what we deem it good that they should know. In this way all the time spent on futile and vexatious argumentation will be saved.

Where the truth really is known, there is something to be said for this view. The multiplication table is taught dogmatically; a teacher who held heretical opinions about it would hardly get a job. But in such matters there is no need of censorship; no one in fact holds heretical views about the multiplication table. Heretical views arise when the truth is uncertain, and it is only when the truth is uncertain that censorship is invoked. In fact, it is difficult to find anything really certain outside the realm of pure mathematics and some facts of history and geography. If suppression of free discussion is necessary in order to cause an opinion to be believed, that in itself is evidence that the rational grounds in favor of the opinion are inadequate, for if they were adequate free discussion would be the best way of making the opinion prevail. When the authorities profess to *know* something which to the unprejudiced person seems doubtful or false, they are either themselves the victims of prejudice, or they are dishonestly trying to represent the interest of their class or creed or nation as coinciding with the general interest. In either case, interference with free discussion can only do harm.

Some one may object that, while free thought may be all very well in the abstract, it won't do in this actual world, because fanaticism is needed for victory in battle. Other things being equal, we may be told, the holders of an irrational warlike creed will always win the victory over peaceful folk who only want a quiet life. There is no doubt an element of truth in this argument, but it is a small element, and what truth it contains is only for the short run. The Germans and Japanese, by means of their fanaticism, were able to win initial victories; but their very fanaticism roused the hostility of the world, and is leading to their downfall. Fanatics, just because they lack the scientific temper, cannot weigh risks calmly, and are prone to overestimate the chances of victory. In the long run, fanaticism is incompatible with scientific excellence, which is the most important source of strength in modern war. In a war between a scientific and a fanatical nation, given equal material resources, the scientific nation is pretty sure to be victorious.

We have wandered into political and social questions, but the core of the argument for free thought lies in the individual life. It is good to ask ourselves, from time to time, what sort of person we should wish to be. When I ask myself this question, I find that I desire at once a kind of pride and a kind of humility. As for pride: I do not wish to be forced or cajoled into any opinion because others desire that I should hold it, nor do I wish to be the victim of my own hopes and fears to the extent of allowing myself to live in an unreal world of pleasant make-believe. I respect, in myself and others, the power of thought and of scientific investigation, by means of which we have acquired whatever knowledge we possess of the universe in which we live. And thought, when it is genuine thought, has its own intrinsic morality and its own brand of asceticism. But it has also its rewards: a happiness, amounting at moments to ecstasy, in understanding what had been obscure, and surveying in a unified vision what had seemed detached and chaotic fragments.

But the pursuit of truth, when it is profound and genuine, requires also a kind of humility which has some affinity to submission to the will of God. The universe is what it is, not what I choose that it should be. If it is indifferent to human desires, as it seems to be; if human life is a passing episode, hardly noticeable in the vastness of cosmic processes; if there is no superhuman purpose, and no hope of ultimate salvation, it is better to know and acknowledge this truth than to endeavor, in futile self-assertion, to order the universe to be what we find comfortable.

Toward facts, submission is the only rational attitude, but in the realm of ideals there is nothing to which to submit. The universe is neither hostile nor friendly; it neither favors our ideals nor refutes them. Our individual life is brief, and perhaps the whole life of mankind will be brief if measured on an astronomical scale. But that is no reason for not living it as seems best to us. The things that seem to us good are none the less good for not being eternal, and we should not ask of the universe an external approval of our own ethical standards.

The free thinker's universe may seem bleak and cold to those who have been accustomed to the comfortable indoor warmth of the Christian cosmology. But to those who have grown accustomed to it, it has its own sublimity, and confers its own joys. In learning to think freely we have learnt to thrust fear out of our thoughts, and this lesson, once learnt, brings a kind of peace which is impossible to the slave of hesitant and uncertain credulity.

16

Sin

The sense of sin has been one of the dominant psychological facts in history, and is still at the present day of great importance in the mental life of a large proportion of mankind. But although the *sense* of sin is easy to recognize and define, the *concept* of "sin" is obscure, especially if we attempt to interpret it in nontheological terms. In this article I wish to consider the sense of sin psychologically and historically, and then to examine whether there is any nontheological concept in terms of which this emotion can be rationalized.

Some "enlightened" persons believe themselves to have seen through "sin," and to have discarded the whole complex of beliefs and emotions with which it is associated. But most of these persons, if scrutinized, will be found to have only rejected some prominent part of the received moral code—e.g., the prohibition of adultery— but to have retained, none the less, a moral code of their own, to which they give complete adherence. A man may, for instance, be a conspirator in a left-wing movement in a fascist country; in the pursuit of his public objects he may consider himself justified in deceiving and hoodwinking half-hearted "fellow-travellers," in stealing from the funds of reactionaries, in making love insincerely with a view to discovering secrets, and in committing murder when the situation seems to demand it. He may at all times express himself with a devastating moral cynicism. Yet this very man, if he is caught and tortured with a view to discovering his confederates,

---

From *Horizon* 17 (January 1948): 7-15.

may display a heroic endurance beyond the capacity of many who would consider him ethically vile. If he does at last give way and betray his comrades, he is likely to feel a burning sense of shame which may drive him to suicide. Or, to take a very different example, a man may, like the hero of Shaw's *Doctor's Dilemma*, be morally contemptible in all respects except where his artistic conscience is involved, but in this one matter may be capable of very painful sacrifices. I am not prepared to maintain that to all men there are some acts that are felt as "sin"; I am willing to believe that there are human beings who are utterly shameless. But I am convinced that they are few, and that they are not to be found among those who most loudly proclaim their own emancipation from moral scruples.

Most psychoanalysts make much of the sense of guilt or sin, which they seem to regard as innate. I cannot agree with them in this. I believe the psychological origin of the sense of guilt in the young to be fear of punishment or disapproval by parents or whoever is in authority. If a feeling of guilt is to result from punishment or disapproval, it is necessary, however, that authority should be respected, and not merely feared; where there is only fear, the natural reaction is an impulse to deceit or rebellion. It is natural to young children to respect their parents, but school boys are less apt to respect their teachers, with the result that only fear of punishment, not sense of sin, restrains them from many acts of disobedience. Disobedience, if it is to *feel* sinful, must be disobedience to an authority inwardly respected and acknowledged. A dog caught stealing a leg of mutton may have this feeling if he is caught by his master, but not if he is caught by a stranger.

The psychoanalysts, however, are certainly right in tracing the origins of a man's sense of sin to the very early years of childhood. In those years parental precepts are unquestioningly accepted, but impulse is too strong for them to be always obeyed; hence experience of disapproval is frequent and painful, and so is temptation which may be successfully resisted. In later life the parental disapproval may come to be almost forgotten, and yet there may still be a feeling of something painful associated with certain kinds of acts, and this feeling may translate itself into the conviction that such acts are sinful. For those who believe that sin consists in disobedience to God the Father, the change of emotional pattern is very slight.

However, many men who do not believe in God nevertheless have a sense of sin. This may be merely a subconscious association with parental disapproval, or it may be fear of the bad opinion of a man's own herd, when the man is not a rebel against the herd's standards. Sometimes it is the sinner's own disapproval, quite independently of what others think, that makes him feel wicked. This is not likely to happen except to men who are unusually self-reliant or have exceptional gifts. If Columbus had abandoned the attempt to find the Indies, no one else would have blamed him, but one can imagine that he would have felt degraded in his own eyes. Sir Thomas More was removed from Oxford in his youth, on account of his determination to learn Greek in spite of the disapproval of his father and the university authorities. No doubt if he had yielded to the advice of his elders and betters he would have had a sense of sin, though everyone would have praised him.

The sense of sin has played a very important part in religion, more especially the Christian religion. In the Catholic Church it was one of the main sources of the power of the priesthood, and did much to facilitate the victory of the popes in their long struggle with the emperors. Psychologically and doctrinally, the sense of sin reached its acme in St. Augustine. But its origin lies far back in prehistoric times; in all the civilized nations of antiquity it was already well developed. In its earlier forms it was connected with ritual defilement and with breaches of taboo. Among the Greeks it was especially emphasized by the Orphics and by the philosophers whom they influenced. By the Orphics, as in India, sin was connected with transmigration: the sinful soul passed, after death, into the body of an animal, but after many purgative ages at last achieved emancipation from bondage to "the wheel of life." As Empedocles says: "Whenever one of the daemons, whose portion is length of days, has sinfully polluted his hands with blood, or followed strife and foresworn himself, he must wander thrice ten thousand years from the abodes of the blessed, being born throughout the time in all manners of mortal forms. . . . One of these I now am, an exile and a wanderer from the gods for that I put my trust in insensate strife."

In another fragment he says: "Ah, woe is me that the pitiless day of death did not destroy me ere ever I did evil deeds of devouring with my lips!" It seems probable that these "evil deeds" consisted of munching beans and laurel leaves for he says: "Abstain wholly from laurel leaves," and again: "Wretches, utter wretches! keep your hands from beans." These passages illustrate the fact that sin, as originally conceived, was not essentially something that injured someone else, but merely something forbidden. This attitude persists to our own day in much of orthodox doctrine on sexual morality.

The Christian conception of sin owes more to the Jews than to the Greeks. The Prophets attributed the Babylonian captivity to the wrath of God, which was kindled by the heathen practices that were still prevalent while Judea was independent. At first the sin was collective and the punishment collective, but gradually, as the Jews became accustomed to the absence of political independence, a more individualistic view came to prevail: it was the individual who sinned, and the individual who would be punished. For a long time punishment was expected in this life, with the corollary that prosperity was a proof of virtue. But during the persecution at the time of the Maccabees it became evident that the most virtuous were, in this life, the most unfortunate. This stimulated belief in a future life of rewards and punishments, in which Antiochus would suffer and his victims would triumph—a point of view which, with appropriate modifications, passed over into the early Church and sustained it during the persecutions.

Sin, however, is psychologically very different when imputed to our enemies from what it is when thought of as our own shortcoming, for the one involves pride and the other humility. The extreme of humility is reached in the doctrine of original sin, of which the best exposition is to be found in St. Augustine. According to this doctrine, Adam and Eve were created with free will, and had the power of choice between good and evil. When they ate the apple they chose evil, and in that moment corruption entered into their souls. They and all their progeny were thenceforth unable to choose the good by the strength of their own unaided wills; only Divine Grace enabled the elect to live virtuously. Divine Grace is bestowed, without any guiding principle, upon some of those who have been baptized, but upon no one else, with the exception of certain of the Patriarchs and Prophets, and a small number of miraculously enlightened pagans. The rest of mankind, although, since Grace is withheld, they are fatally predestined to sin, yet, because of their sin, are justly objects of God's wrath, and as such will suffer eternal perdition. St. Augustine enumerates the sins committed by infants at the breast, and does not shrink from the conclusion that infants who die unbaptized go to hell. The elect go to heaven because God chooses to make them the objects of His mercy: they are virtuous because they are elect, not elect because they are virtuous.

This ferocious doctrine, though accepted by Luther and Calvin, has not, since their time, been the orthodox teaching of the Catholic Church, and is now accepted by very few Christians, of whatever denomination. Nevertheless hell is still part of Catholic dogma, though fewer people suffer damnation than was formerly supposed. And hell is justified as the appropriate punishment for sin.

The doctrine of original sin, according to which we shall all deserve punishment because of Adam's transgression, is one which strikes most people at the present day as unjust, although there are many who see no injustice when analogous doctrines are proclaimed in politics—for example, when it is thought right that German children born since 1939 should starve because their parents did not oppose the Nazis. This, however, even by its supporters, is recognized as rough human justice, and not of a sort to be ascribed to the Deity. The standpoint of modern liberal theologians is well set forth by Dr. Tennant in his book *The Concept of Sin*. According to him sin consists in acts of will that are in conscious opposition to a known moral law, the moral law being known by revelation as God's will. It follows that a man destitute of religion cannot sin:

> If we press the indispensableness of the religious element in the concept of sin, and if we adopt the psychical definition of religion, then it will follow that persons, if any there by, possessing no religion—who would confess, that is to say, to entertaining no ideas of deity or of the supernatural, and to feeling no religious sentiment of any sort—cannot be accounted sinners at all, in the sense in which we agree to use that term, however morally evil, even from their own point of view, may be their lives (p. 216).

It is difficult to know exactly what is meant by this statement, owing to the qualifications with which it is introduced. By the "psychical" definition of religion the author means, as he has previously explained, whatever a man accepts in the way of religion, and not only what Christians regard as true religion. But it is not clear what is meant by "feeling no religious sentiment of any sort." I myself have "sentiments"—emotions and moral convictions—which are apt to be associated with Christian beliefs, but I have no "ideas of deity or of the supernatural." I am not quite sure, therefore, whether, in Dr. Tennant's view, I am or am not capable of "sin." Nor am I sure whether, in my own view, there is a valid concept deserving to be called "sin." I know that certain acts, if I perform them, fill me with shame. I know that I find cruelty detestable and that I wish it did not exist; I know that failure to use to the full such talents as I may possess would feel to me like treachery to an ideal. But I am by no means certain how to rationalize these feelings, nor whether, if I suceeded in rationalizing them, the result would afford a definition of "sin."

If "sin" means "disobedience to the known will of God," then clearly sin is impossible for those who do not believe in God or do not think that they know His will. But if "sin" means "disobedience to the voice of conscience," then it can exist independently of theological beliefs. If it means only this, however, it lacks some properties commonly associated with the word "sin." Sin is usually thought of as deserving punishment, not only as a deterrent or as an incentive to reform, but on grounds of abstract justice. The sufferings of hell, theologians assure us, do not make tortured souls morally better; on the contrary, they persist in sin through all eternity, and have no power to do otherwise. The belief in "sin" as something meriting the purely retributive infliction of pain is one which cannot be reconciled with any ethic at all analogous to that which I believe in, though it has been advocated independently of theology, for instance in G. E. Moore's *Principia Ethica*. When retribution for its own sake is not thought good, the concepts of "justice" and "punishment" need reinterpretation.

"Justice," in its legalistic interpretation, might be taken to mean "reward according to desert." But when retributive punishment for its own sake is no longer advocated, this can only mean "reward and punishment on the system most likely to promote socially desirable conduct." It might happen, on occasion, that a man who expected punishment would undergo a change of heart if he were given a free pardon; in that case, it would be right to pardon him. It might also happen that a man who had acted in a socially desirable manner might have set an example which ought not to be followed in apparently similar cases, and on this account, it might be proper to punish him. (Nelson's blind eye.) In short, rewards and punishments should be awarded according to the desirability of their social effects, and not according to some supposed absolute standard of merit or demerit. No doubt it will , as a rule, be wise to reward those whose conduct is socially desirable and punish those whose conduct is harmful, but exceptions are conceivable and are likely actually to occur from time to time. Such a conception of 'justice' as underlies the belief in heaven and hell is not defensible if 'right' conduct is that which promotes the satisfaction of desire.

The conception of "sin" is closely connected with the belief in free will, for, if our actions are determined by causes over which we have no control, retributive punishment can have no justification. I think the ethical importance of free will is sometimes exaggerated, but it cannot be denied that the question is relevant in relation to "sin," and something must therefore be said about it.

"Free will" must be taken to mean that a volition is not always, or not necessarily, the result of previous causes. But the word "cause" has not as clear a meaning as could be wished. The first step toward clarity is to substitute "causal law" for "cause." We shall say that an event is "determined" by previous events if there is a law by means of which it can be inferred if a sufficient number of previous events are known. We can predict the movements of the planets because they follow from the law of gravitation. Sometimes, human actions are equally predictable; it may be that Mr. So-and-So, on meeting a stranger, never fails to mention his acquaintance with Lord Such-and-Such. But, as a general rule, we are not able to predict with any accuracy what people will do. This may be only from inadequate knowledge of the relevant laws, or it may be because there are no laws that invariably connect a man's action with his past and present circumstances. The latter possibility, which is that of free will, is always unhesitatingly rejected except when people are thinking about the free-will problem. No one says: "It is useless to punish theft, because perhaps people henceforth will like punishment." No one says: "It is useless to address a letter, because the postman, having free will, may decide to deliver it somewhere else." No one says: "It is useless to offer wages for work that you wish done, because people may prefer starvation." If free will were common, all social organization would be impossible, since there would be no way of influencing men's actions.

While, therefore, as a philosopher I hold the principle of universal causation to be open to question, as a common-sense individual I hold that it is an indispensable postulate in the conduct of affairs. For practical purposes we must assume that our volitions have causes, and our ethics must be compatible with this assumption.

Praise and blame, rewards and punishments, and the whole apparatus of the criminal law, are rational on the deterministic hypothesis, but not on the hypothesis of free will, for they are all mechanisms designed to cause volitions that are in harmony with

278 Bertrand Russell On God and Religion

the interests of the community, or what are believed to be its interests. But the conception of "sin" is only rational on the assumption of free will, for, on the deterministic hypothesis, when a man does something that the community would wish him not to do, that is because the community has not provided adequate motives to cause him not to do it, or perhaps could not have provided adequate motives. We all recognize this second possibility in the case of insanity: a homicidal lunatic would not be deterred from murder even if he were certain to be hanged for it, and therefore it is useless to hang him. But sane people, when they commit a murder, usually do so in the hope of escaping detection, and it is this fact that makes it worth while to punish them when they are detected. Murder is punished, not because it is a sin and it is good that sinners should suffer, but because the community wishes to prevent it, and fear of punishment causes most people to abstain from it. This is completely compatible with the deterministic hypothesis, and completely incompatible with the hypothesis of free will.

I conclude that free will is not essential to any rational ethic, but only to the vindictive ethic that justifies hell and holds that "sin" should be punished regardless of any good that punishment may do. I conclude, also, that "sin," except in the sense of conduct toward which the agent, or the community, feel an emotion of disapproval, is a mistaken concept calculated to promote needless cruelty and vindictiveness when it is others that are thought to sin, and a morbid self-abasement when it is ourselves whom we condemn.

But it must not be supposed that, in rejecting the concept of "sin," we are maintaining that there is no difference between right and wrong actions. "Right" actions are those that it is useful to praise, "wrong" actions are those that it is useful to blame. Praise and blame remain as powerful incentives, tending to promote conduct which serves the general interest. Rewards and punishments also remain. But with regard to punishment, the rejection of "sin" makes a difference that has some practical importance, for, on the view which I advocate, the punishment is always *per se* an evil, and is only justified by its deterrent or reformative effect. If it were possible to keep the public persuaded that burglars go to prison, while in fact they are made happy in some remote South Sea island, that would be better than punishment; the only objection to the scheme is that it would inevitably leak out sooner or later, and then there would be a general outbreak of burglary.

What applies to punishment applies also to blame. The fear of being blamed is a very powerful deterrent, but actual blame, when the blameworthy action has been performed, is, as a rule, painful without being morally helpful. The person blamed is likely to become sullen and defiant, to despair of the good opinion of the community, and to acquiesce in the position of an Ishmael. This result is especially probable when it is not an individual, but a large group, that is blamed. After the First World War the victors told the Germans that the guilt was wholly Germany's, and even forced them to sign a document by which they pretended to acknowledge their sole culpability. After the Second World War Montgomery issued a proclamation telling German parents to explain to their children that British soldiers could not smile at them because of the wickedness of their fathers and mothers. This was, on both occasions, bad psychology and bad politics, of a sort that is encouraged by belief in the doctrine of "sin." We are all what our circumstances have made us, and if that is unsatisfactory to our neighbors, it is for them to find ways of improving us. It is very seldom that moral reprobation is the best way of achieving this object.

17

Are the World's Troubles
Due to Decay of Faith?

There is a theory, which is winning widespread acceptance in the Western World, to the effect that what is afflicting the nations is due to the decay of religious faith. I think this theory completely contrary to the truth. In so far as faith has anything to do with the matter, there is a great deal more faith in the world than there was at a somewhat earlier time. But, in actual fact, the chain of causation which has led to the perilous position in which we find ourselves, is, as I shall try to show, almost wholly independent of men's beliefs, which are an effect rather than a cause of what is amiss.

What has happened in the world since 1914 has proceeded with a kind of inevitability that is like that of Greek tragedy. It is an inevitability derived, not from external circumstances, but from the characters of the actors. Let us briefly trace the steps in this development.

The Germans in 1914 thought themselves strong enough to secure by force an empire comparable to those of Britain, France, and Russia. Britain, France, and Russia combined to thwart this ambition. Russia was defeated and, in the revolution of 1917, abandoned its traditional imperialistic policy. The West had promised Constantinople to the Russians, but, when the Russians made a separate peace, this promise fell through. Britain and France, with the help of America, defeated the Germans after the Germans had defeated the Russians. The Germans were compelled to accept the humiliating treaty of Versailles and to profess a belief in their sole

First published in *The Rationalist Annual* (1956) by Watts and Company for the Rationalist Press Association. Reprinted by permission of the Rationalist Press Association.

282 Bertrand Russell On God and Religion

war-guilt. They were "wicked" because they had made war. The Russians were "wicked" because they had made a separate peace and, still more, because they had repudiated their war debts. All the victorious nations combined to fight the Bolsheviks, but were defeated and were somewhat surprised to find that Russia no longer loved them. The Germans meanwhile suffered great distress, which was much aggravated when the folly of the American Republican government brought about the Great Depression. Suffering produced hysteria, and hysteria produced Hitler. The Western nations, hoping that Hitler would attack Russia, did not oppose him. They had opposed the comparatively blameless Weimar Republic, but, in befriending Hitler, they proved to all mankind that they were totally destitute of moral standards. Hitler, fortunately, was mad, and, owing to madness, brought about his own downfall. The West had been delighted to accept Russia's help in bringing about this result and, whereas at the end of the First World War Russia and Germany had been alike weak, Russia at the end of the Second World War was strong. Britain was traditionally hostile to Russia, but from 1907 to 1917 had been forced into a semblance of friendship with that country by fear of Germany. At the end of the Second World War a quite new international pattern developed. Western Europe had ceased to count. Russia and the United States were alone powerful. As has always happened in the past in more or less similar situations, these two great powers were mutually hostile. Each saw a chance of world hegemony. Russia inherited the policy of Philip II, Napoleon, and the Kaiser. America inherited the policy which England had pursued throughout the eighteenth and nineteenth centuries.

In all this there was nothing new except technique. The conflicts of great powers were just what they had always been, except that technique had made great powers greater and war more destructive. The situation would be exactly what it is if Russia still adhered to the Orthodox Church. We in the West should, in that case, be pointing out what we consider heretical in the Greek Church. What our propaganda would be can be seen by anybody who reads the records of the Crimean War. I am not in any way defending the present Russian régime any more than I should defend the tsarist régime. What I am saying is that the two are closely similar, although the one was Christian and the other is not. I am saying also that, if the present government of Russia were Christian, the situation would be exactly what it is. The cause of conflict is the ancient clash of power politics. It is not fundamentally a clash between faith and un-faith, or between one faith and another, but between two mighty empires, each of which sees a chance of world supremacy.

Nobody can pretend that the First World War was in any degree due to lack of Christian faith in the rulers who brought it about. The tsar, the kaiser, and the emperor of Austria were all earnest Christians. So was Sir Edward Grey, and so was President Wilson. There was only one prominent politician at that time who was not a Christian. That was Jean Jaurès, a Socialist who opposed the war and was assassinated with the approval of almost all French Christians. In England the only member of the Cabinet who resigned from disapproval of the war was Lord Morley, a noted atheist. In Germany likewise the only opposition came from atheists under the leadership of Liebknecht. In Russia, when the atheists acquired power, their first act was to make peace. The Bolsheviks, it is true, did not remain peaceful, but that is hardly surprising in view of the fact that the victorious Christian nations attacked them.

But let us leave the details of politics and consider our question more generally. Christians hold that their faith does good, but other faiths do harm. At any rate, they hold this about the Communist faith. What I wish to maintain is that *all* faiths do harm. We may define "faith" as a firm belief in something for which there is no evidence. Where there is evidence, no one speaks of "faith." We do not speak of faith that two and two are four or that the earth is round. We only speak of faith when we wish to substitute emotion for evidence. The substitution of emotion for evidence is apt to lead to strife, since different groups, substitute different emotions. Christians have faith in the resurrection, Communists have faith in Marx's theory of value. Neither faith can be defended rationally, and each therefore is defended by propaganda and, if necessary, by war. The two are equal in this respect. If you think it immensely important that people should believe something which cannot be rationally defended, it makes no difference what the something is. Where you control the government, you teach the something to the immature minds of children and you burn or prohibit books which teach the contrary. When you do not control the government you will, if you are strong enough, build up armed forces with a view to conquest. All this is an inevitable consequence of any strongly-held faith unless, like the Quakers, you are content to remain forever a tiny minority.

It is completely mysterious to me that there are apparently sane people who think that a belief in Christianity might prevent war. Such people seem totally unable to learn anything from history. The Roman state became Christian at the time of Constantine and was almost continually at war until it ceased to exist. The Christian states which succeeded to it continued to fight each other, though it must be confessed, they also from time to time fought states which were not Christian. From the time of Constantine to the present day there has been no shred of evidence to show that Christian states are less warlike than others. Indeed, some of the most ferocious wars have been due to disputes between different kinds of Christianity. Nobody can deny that Luther and Loyola were Christians; nobody can deny that their differences were associated with a long period of ferocious wars.

There are those who argue that Christianity, though it may not be true, is very useful as promoting social cohesion, and, though it may not be perfect, is better than any other faith that has the same social effectiveness. I will admit that I would rather see the whole world Christian than Marxist. I find the Marxist faith more repellent than any other that has been adopted by civilized nations (except perhaps the Aztecs). But I am quite unwilling to accept the view that social cohesion is impossible except by the help of useful lies. I know that this view has the sanction of Plato and of a long line of practical politicians, but I think that even from a practical point of view it is mistaken. It is not necessary for purposes of self defense, where rational arguments suffice. It is necessary for a crusade, but I cannot think of any case in which a crusade has done any good whatever. When people regard Christianity as part of rearmament they are taking out of it whatever spiritual merit it may have. And, in order that it may be effective as rearmament, it is generally thought that it must be pugnacious, dogmatic, and narrow-minded. When people think of Christianity as a help in fighting the Russians, it is not the Quaker type of Christianity that they have in view, but something more in the style of Senator [Joseph] McCarthy. What makes a creed effective in war is its negative aspect—that is to say, its hatred of those who do not adopt it. Without this hatred it serves no bellicose purpose. But, as soon as it is used as a weapon of war, it is the hatred of unbelievers that becomes prominent. Consequently, when two faiths fight each other each develops its worst aspects and even copies whatever it imagines to be effective in the faith that it is combating.

The belief that fanaticism promotes success in war is one that is not borne out by history, although it is constantly assumed by those who cloak their ignorance under the name of "realism." When the Romans conquered the Mediterranean world, fanaticism played no part in their success. The motives of Roman generals were either to acquire the gold reserves of temples with a view to keeping half for themselves and giving half to their soldiers, or, as in the case of Caesar, to gain the prestige which would enable them to win elections in Rome and defy their creditors. In the early contests of Christians and Mohammedans it was the Christians who were fanatical and the Mohammedans who were successful. Christian propaganda has invented stories of Mohammedan intolerance, but these are wholly false as applied to the early centuries of Islam. Every Christian has been taught the story of the Caliph destroying the Library of Alexandria. As a matter of fact, this library was frequently destroyed and frequently recreated. Its first destroyer was Julius Caesar; and its last antedated the Prophet. The early Mohammedans, unlike the Christians, tolerated those whom they called "people of the Book," provided they paid tribute. In contrast to the Christians, who persecuted not only pagans but each other, the Mohammedans were welcomed for their broad-mindedness, and it was largely this that facilitated their conquests. To come to later times, Spain was ruined by fanatical hatred of Jews and Moors; France was disastrously impoverished by the persecution of Huguenots; and one main cause of Hitler's defeat was his failure to employ Jews in atomic research. Ever since the time of Archimedes war has been a science, and proficiency in science has been a main cause of victory. But proficiency in science is very difficult to combine with fanaticism. We all know how, under the orders of Stalin, Russian biologists were compelled to subscribe to Lysenko's errors. It is obvious to every person capable of free scientific inquiry that the doctrines of Lysenko are less likely to increase the wheat supply of Russia than those of orthodox geneticists are to increase the wheat supply of the West. I think it is also very doubtful whether nuclear research can long continue to flourish in such an atmosphere as Stalin produced in Russia. Perhaps Russia is now going to become liberal, and perhaps it will be in the United States that bigotry will hamper atomic research. As to this, I express no opinion. But, however this may be, it is clear that, without intellectual freedom, scientific warfare is not likely to remain long successful.

But let us look at this matter of fanaticism somewhat more broadly. The contention of those who advocate fanaticism without being fanatics is, to my mind, not only false, but ignoble. It seems to be thought that unless everybody in a nation is compelled, either by persecution or by an education which destroys the power of thought, to believe things which no rational man can believe, that nation would be so torn by dissensions or so paralyzed by hesitant doubts that it would inevitably come to grief. Not only, as I have already argued, is there no historical evidence for this view, but it is also quite contrary to what ought to be expected. When a British military expedition marched to Lhasa in 1905, the Tibetan soldiers at first opposed it bravely, because the priests had pronounced charms which afforded protection against lead. When the soldiers neverthe-less were killed, the priests excused themselves on the ground that the bullets contained nickel, against which their charms had been powerless. After this, the British troops encountered little opposition. Philip II of Spain was so persuaded that Heaven must bless his warfare against the heretics that he neglected entirely to consider the difference between fighting the English and fighting the Turks, and so he was defeated. There is a very widespread belief that people can be induced to believe what is contrary to fact in one domain while remaining scientific in another. This is not the case. It is by no means easy to keep one's mind open to fresh evidence, and it is almost impossible to achieve this in one direction if, in another, one has a carefully fostered blindness.

There is something feeble, and a little contemptible, about a man who cannot face the perils of life without the help of com-fortable myths. Almost inevitably some part of him is aware that they are myths and that he believes them only because they are comforting. But he dare not face this thought, and he therefore cannot carry his own reflections to any logical conclusion. More-over, since he is aware, however dimly, that his opinions are not rational, he becomes furious when they are disputed. He therefore adopts persecution, censorship, and a narrowly cramping education as essentials of statecraft. In so far as he is successful, he produces a population which is timid and unadventurous and incapable of progress. Authoritarian rulers have always aimed at producing such a population. They have usually succeeded, and by their success have brought their countries to ruin.

Many of the objections to what is called "faith" do not depend in any way upon what the faith in question may be. You may believe in the verbal inspiration of the Bible or of the Koran or of Marx's *Kapital*. Whichever of these beliefs you entertain, you have to close your mind against evidence; and if you close your mind against evidence in one respect, you will also do so in another, if the temptation is strong. The Duke of Wellington never allowed himself to doubt the value of the playing fields of Eton, and was therefore never able to accept the superiority of the rifle to the old-fashioned musket. You may say that belief in God is not as harmful as belief in the playing fields of Eton. I will not argue on this point, except to say that it becomes harmful in proportion as you secretly doubt whether it is in accordance with the facts. The important thing is not what you believe, but how you believe it. There was a time when it was rational to believe that the earth is flat. At that time this belief did not have the bad consequences belonging to what is called "faith." But the people who, in our day, persist in believing that the earth is flat, have to close their minds against reason and to open them to every kind of absurdity in addition to the one from which they start. If you think that your belief is based upon reason, you will support it by argument, rather than by persecution, and will abandon it if the argument goes against you. But if your belief is based on faith, you will realize that argument is useless, and will therefore resort to force either in the form of persecution or by stunting and distorting the minds of the young in what is called "education." This last is peculiarly dastardly, since it takes advantage of the defenselessness of immature minds. Unfortunately it is practiced in a greater or less degree in the schools of every civilized country.

In addition to the general argument against faith, there is something peculiarly odious in the contention that the principles of the Sermon on the Mount are to be adopted with a view to making atom bombs more effective. If I were a Christian, I should consider this the absolute extreme of blasphemy.

18

Ideas that Have Harmed Mankind

The misfortunes of human beings may be divided into two classes: First, those inflicted by the nonhuman environment, and, second, those inflicted by other people. As mankind have progressed in knowledge and technique, the second class has become a continually increasing percentage of the total. In old times, famine, for example, was due to natural causes, and, although people did their best to combat it, large numbers of them died of starvation. At the present moment large parts of the world are faced with the threat of famine, but although natural causes have contributed to the situation, the principal causes are human. For six years the civilized nations of the world devoted all their best energies to killing each other, and they find it difficult suddenly to switch over to keeping each other alive. Having destroyed harvests, dismantled agricultural machinery, and disorganized shipping, they find it no easy matter to relieve the shortage of crops in one place by means of a superabundance in another, as would easily be done if the economic system were in normal working order. As this illustration shows, it is now man that is man's worst enemy. Nature, it is true, still sees to it that we are mortal, but with the progress in medicine it will become more and more common for people to live until they have had their fill of life. We are supposed to wish to live forever and to look forward to the unending joys of heaven, of which, by miracle, the monotony will never grow stale. But in fact, if you question any candid person who is no longer young, he is very likely to tell you

First published by Haldeman-Julius in 1946.

that, having tasted life in this world, he has no wish to begin again as a "new boy" in another. For the future, therefore, it may be taken that much the most important evils that mankind have to consider are those which they inflict upon each other through stupidity or malevolence or both.

I think that the evils that men inflict on each other, and by reflection upon themselves, have their main source in evil passions rather than in ideas or beliefs. But ideas and principles that do harm are, as a rule, though not always, cloaks for evil passions. In Lisbon when heretics were publicly burnt, it sometimes happened that one of them, by a particularly edifying recantation, would be granted the boon of being strangled before being put into the flames. This would make the spectators so furious that the authorities had great difficulty in preventing them from lynching the penitent and burning him on their own account. The spectacle of the writhing torments of the victims was, in fact, one of the principal pleasures to which the populace looked forward to enliven a somewhat drab existence. I cannot doubt that this pleasure greatly contributed to the general belief that the burning of heretics was a righteous act. The same sort of thing applies to war. People who are vigorous and brutal often find war enjoyable, provided that it is a victorious war and that there is not too much interference with rape and plunder. This is a great help in persuading people that wars are righteous. Dr. Arnold, the hero of *Tom Brown's Schooldays,* and the admired reformer of Public Schools, came across some cranks who thought it a mistake to flog boys. Anyone reading his outburst of furious indignation against this opinion will be forced to the conclusion that he enjoyed inflicting floggings, and did not wish to be deprived of this pleasure.

It would be easy to multiply instances in support of the thesis that opinions which justify cruelty are inspired by cruel impulses. When we pass in review the opinions of former times which are now recognized as absurd, it will be found that nine times out of ten they were such as to justify the infliction of suffering. Take, for instance, medical practice. When anaesthetics were invented they were thought to be wicked as being an attempt to thwart God's will. Insanity was thought to be due to diabolic possession, and it was believed that demons inhabiting a madman could be driven out by inflicting pain upon him, and so making them uncomfortable. In pursuit of this opinion, lunatics were treated for years on end with systematic and conscientious brutality. I cannot think of any instance of an erroneous medical treatment that was agreeable rather than disagreeable to the patient. Or again, take moral education. Consider how much brutality has been justified by the rhyme:

> A dog, a wife, and a walnut tree,
> The more you beat them the better they be.

I have no experience of the moral effect of flagellation on walnut trees, but no civilized person would now justify the rhyme as regards wives. The reformative effect of punishment is a belief that dies hard, chiefly I think, because it is so satisfying to our sadistic impulses.

But although passions have had more to do than beliefs with what is amiss in human life, yet beliefs, especially where they are ancient and systematic and embodied in organizations, have a great power of delaying desirable changes of opinion and of influencing in the wrong direction people who otherwise would have no strong feelings either way. Since my subject is *"ideas* that have harmed mankind," it is especially harmful systems of beliefs that I shall consider.

The most obvious case as regards past history is constituted by the beliefs which may be called religious or superstitious, according to one's personal bias. It was supposed that human sacrifice would improve the crops, at first for purely magical reasons, and then because the blood of victims was thought pleasing to the gods, who certainly were made in the image of their worshippers. We read in the Old Testament that it was a religious duty to exterminate conquered races completely, and that to spare even their cattle and sheep was an impiety. Dark terrors and misfortunes in the life to come oppressed the Egyptians and Etruscans, but never reached their full development until the victory of Christianity. Gloomy saints who abstained from all pleasures of sense, who lived in solitude in the desert, denying themselves meat and wine and the society of women, were, nevertheless, not obliged to abstain from *all* pleasures. The pleasures of the mind were considered to be superior to those of the body, and a high place among the pleasures of the mind was assigned to the contemplation of the eternal tortures to which the pagans and heretics would hereafter be subjected. It is one of the drawbacks to asceticism that it sees no harm in pleasures other than those of sense, and yet, in fact, not only the best pleasures, but also the very worst, are purely mental. Consider the pleasures of Milton's Satan when he contemplates the harm that he could do to man. As Milton makes him say:

> The mind is its own place, and of itself
> Can make a hell of heaven, a heaven of hell,

and his psychology is not so very different from that of Tertullian, exulting in the thought that he will be able to look out from heaven at the sufferings of the damned. The ascetic depreciation of the pleasures of sense has not promoted kindliness or tolerance, or any of the other virtues that a nonsuperstitious outlook on human life would lead us to desire. On the contrary, when a man tortures himself he feels that it gives him a right to torture others, and inclines him to accept any system of dogma by which this right is fortified.

The ascetic form of cruelty is, unfortunately, not confined to the fiercer forms of Christian dogma, which are now seldom believed with their former ferocity. The world has produced new and menacing forms of the same psychological pattern. The Nazis in the days before they achieved power lived laborious lives, involving much sacrifice of ease and present pleasure in obedience to the belief in strenuousness and Nietzsche's maxim that one should make oneself hard. Even after they achieved power, the slogan "guns rather than butter" still involved a sacrifice of the pleasures of sense for the mental pleasures of prospective victory—the very pleasures, in fact, with which Milton's Satan consoles himself while tortured by the fires of hell. The same mentality is to be found among earnest Communists, to whom luxury is an evil, hard work the principal duty, and universal poverty the means to the millennium. The combination of asceticism and cruelty has not disappeared with the softening of Christian dogma, but has taken on new forms hostile to Christianity. There is still much of the same mentality: mankind are divided into saints and sinners; the saints are to achieve bliss in the Nazi or Communist heaven, while the sinners are to be liquidated, or to suffer such pains as human beings can inflict in concentration camps—inferior, of course, to those which Omnipotence was thought to inflict in hell, but the worst that human beings with their limited powers are able to achieve. There is still, for the saints, a hard period of probation followed by "the shout of them that triumph, the song of them that feast," as the Christian hymn says in describing the joys of heaven.

As this psychological pattern seems so persistent and so capable of clothing itself in completely new mantles of dogma, it must have its roots somewhat deep in human nature. This is the kind of matter that is studied by psychoanalysts, and while I am very far from subscribing to all their doctrines, I think that their general methods are important if we wish to seek out the source of evil in our innermost depths. The twin conceptions of sin and vindictive punishment seem to be at the root of much that is most vigorous, both in religion and politics. I cannot believe, as some psychoanalysts do, that the feeling of sin is innate, though I believe it to be a product of very early infancy. I think that, if this feeling could be eradicated, the amount of cruelty in the world would be very greatly diminished. Given that we are all sinners and that we all deserve punishment, there is evidently much to be said for a system that causes the punishment to fall upon others than ourselves. Calvinists, by the fiat of undeserved mercy, would go to heaven, and their feelings that sin deserved punishment would receive a merely vicarious satisfaction. Communists have a similar outlook. When we are born we do not choose whether we are to be born capitalists or proletarians, but if the latter we are among the elect, and if the former we are not. Without any choice on our own parts, by the working of economic determinism, we are fated to be on the right side in the one case, and on the wrong side in the other. Marx's father became a Christian when Marx was a little boy, and some, at least, of the dogmas he must have then accepted seem to have borne fruit in his son's psychology.

One of the odd effects of the importance which each of us attaches to himself, is that we tend to imagine our own good or evil fortune to be the purpose of other people's actions. If you pass in a train a field containing grazing cows, you may sometimes see them running away in terror as the train passes. The cow, if it were a metaphysician, would argue: "Everything in my own desires and hopes and fears has reference to myself; hence by induction I conclude that everything in the universe has reference to myself. This noisy train, therefore, intends to do me either good or evil. I cannot suppose that it intends to do me good, since it comes in such a terrifying form, and therefore, as a prudent cow, I shall endeavor to escape it." If you were to explain to this metaphysical ruminant that the train has no intention of leaving the rails, and is totally indifferent to the fate of the cow, the poor beast would be bewildered by anything so unnatural. The train that wishes her neither well nor ill would seem more cold and more abysmally horrifying than a train that wished her ill. Just this has happened with human beings. The course of nature brings them sometimes good fortune, sometimes evil. They cannot believe that this happens by accident. The cow, having known of a companion which had strayed on to the railway line and been killed by a train, would pursue her philosophical reflections, if she were endowed with that moderate degree of intelligence that characterizes most human beings, to the point of concluding that the unfortunate cow had been punished for sin by the god of the railway. She would be glad when his priests put fences along the line, and would warn younger and friskier cows never to avail themselves of accidental openings in the fence, since the wages of sin is death. By similar myths men have succeeded, without sacrificing their self-importance, in explaining many of the misfortunes to which they are subject. But sometimes misfortune befalls the wholly virtuous, and what are we to say in this case? We shall still be prevented by our feeling that we must be the center of the universe from admitting that misfortune has merely happened to us without anybody's intending it, and since we are not wicked by hypothesis, our misfortune must be due to somebody's malevolence, that is to say, to somebody wishing to injure us from mere hatred and not from the hope of any advantage to himself. It was this state of mind that gave rise to demonology, and the belief in witchcraft and black magic. The witch is a person who injures her neighbors from sheer hatred, not from any hope of gain. The belief in witchcraft, until about the middle of the seventeenth century, afforded a most satisfying outlet for the delicious emotion of self-righteous cruelty. There was biblical warrant for the belief, since the Bible says: "Thou shalt not suffer a witch to live." And on this ground the Inquisition punished not only witches, but those who did not believe in the possibility of witchcraft, since to disbelieve it was heresy. Science, by giving some insight into natural causation, dissipated the belief in magic, but could not wholly dispel the fear and sense of insecurity that had given rise to it. In modern times, these same emotions find an outlet in fear of foreign nations, an outlet which, it must be confessed, requires not much in the way of superstitious support.

One of the most powerful sources of false belief is envy. In any small town you will find, if you question the comparatively well-to-do, that they all exaggerate their neighbors' incomes, which gives them an opportunity to justify an accusation of meanness. The jealousies of women are proverbial among men, but in any large office you will find exactly the same kind of jealousy among male officials. When one of them secures promotion the others will say: "Humph! So-and-So knows how to make up to the big men. I could have risen quite as fast as he has if I had chosen to debase myself by using the sycophantic arts of which he is not ashamed. No doubt his work has a flashy brilliance, but it lacks solidity, and sooner or later the authorities will find out their mistake." So all the mediocre men will say if a really able man is allowed to rise as fast as his abilities deserve, and that is why there is a tendency to adopt the rule of seniority, which, since it has nothing to do with merit, does not give rise to the same envious discontent.

One of the most unfortunate results of our proneness to envy is that it has caused a complete misconception of economic self-interest, both individual and national. I will illustrate by a parable. There was once upon a time a medium-sized town containing a number of butchers, a number of bakers, and so forth. One butcher, who was exceptionally energetic, decided that he would make much larger profits if all the other butchers were ruined and he became a monopolist. By systematically under-selling them he succeeded in his object, though his losses meanwhile had almost exhausted his command of capital and credit. At the same time an energetic baker had had the same idea and had pursued it to a similar successful conclusion. In every trade which lived by selling goods to consumers the same thing had happened. Each of the successful monopolists had a happy anticipation of making a fortune, but unfortunately the ruined butchers were no longer in the position to buy bread, and the ruined bakers were no longer in the position to buy meat. Their employees had had to be dismissed and had gone elsewhere. The consequence was that, although the butcher and the baker each had a monopoly, they sold less than they had done in the old days. They had forgotten that while a man may be injured by his competitors he is benefited by his customers, and that customers become more numerous when the general level of prosperity is increased. Envy had made them concentrate their attention upon competitors and forget altogether the aspect of their prosperity that depended upon customers.

This is a fable, and the town of which I have been speaking never existed, but substitute for a town the world, and for individuals nations, and you will have a perfect picture of the economic policy universally pursued in the present day. Every nation is persuaded that its economic interest is opposed to that of every other nation, and that it must profit if other nations are reduced to destitution.

During the First World War, I used to hear English people saying how immensely British trade would benefit from the destruction of German trade, which was to be one of the principal fruits of our victory. After the war, although we should have liked to find a market on the Continent of Europe, and although the industrial life of Western Europe depended upon coal from the Ruhr, we could not bring ourselves to allow the Ruhr coal industry to produce more than a tiny fraction of what it produced before the Germans were defeated. The whole philosophy of economic nationalism, which is now universal throughout the world, is based upon the false belief that the economic interest of one nation is necessarily opposed to that of another. This false belief, by producing international hatreds and rivalries, is a cause of war, and in this way tends to make itself true, since when war has once broken out the conflict of national interests becomes only too real. If you try to explain to someone, say, in the steel industry, that possibly prosperity in other countries might be advantageous to him, you will find it quite impossible to make him see the argument, because the only foreigners of whom he is vividly aware are his competitors in the steel industry. Other foreigners are shadowy beings in whom he has no emotional interest. This is the psychological root of economic nationalism, and war, and man-made starvation, and all the other evils which will bring our civilization to a disastrous and disgraceful end unless men can be induced to take a wider and less hysterical view of their mutual relations.

Another passion which gives rise to false beliefs that are politically harmful is pride—pride of nationality, race, sex, class, or creed. When I was young France was still regarded as the traditional enemy of England, and I gathered as an unquestionable truth that one Englishman could defeat three Frenchmen. When Germany became the enemy this belief was modified and English people ceased to mention derisively the French propensity for eating frogs. But in spite of governmental efforts, I think few Englishmen succeeded in genuinely regarding the French as their equals. Americans and Englishmen, when they become acquainted with the Balkans, feel an astonished contempt when they study the mutual enmities of Bulgarians and Serbs, or Hungarians and Rumanians. It is evident to them that these enmities are absurd and that the belief of each little nation in its own superiority has no objective basis. But most of them are quite unable to see that the national pride of a great power is essentially as unjustifiable as that of a little Balkan country.

Pride of race is even more harmful than national pride. When I was in China I was struck by the fact that cultivated Chinese were perhaps more highly civilized than any other human beings that it has been my good fortune to meet. Nevertheless, I found numbers of gross and ignorant white men who despised even the best of the Chinese solely because their skins were yellow. In general, the British were more to blame in this than the Americans, but there were exceptions. I was once in the company of a Chinese scholar of vast learning, not only of the traditional Chinese kind, but also of the kind taught in Western universities, a man with a breadth of culture which I scarcely hoped to equal. He and I went together into a garage to hire a motor car. The garage proprietor was a bad type of American, who treated my Chinese friend like dirt, contemptuously accused him of being Japanese, and made my blood boil by his ignorant malevolence. The similar attitude of the English in India, exacerbated by their political power, was one of the main causes of the friction that arose in that country between the British and the educated Indians. The superiority of one race to another is hardly ever believed in for any good reason. Where the belief persists it is kept alive by military supremacy. So long as the Japanese were victorious, they entertained a contempt for the white man, which was the counterpart of the contempt that the white man had felt for them while they were weak. Sometimes, however, the feeling of superiority has nothing to do with military prowess. The Greeks despised the barbarians, even at times when the barbarians surpassed them in warlike strength. The more enlightened among the Greeks held that slavery was justifable so long as the masters were Greek and the slaves barbarian, but that otherwise it was contrary to nature. The Jews had, in antiquity, a quite peculiar belief in their own racial superiority; ever since Christianity became the religion of the state gentiles have had an equally irrational belief in their superiority to Jews. Beliefs of this kind do infinite harm, and it should be, but is not, one of the aims of education to eradicate them. I spoke a moment ago about the attitude of superiority that Englishmen have permitted themselves in their dealings with the inhabitants of India, which was naturally resented in that country, but the caste system arose as a result of successive invasions by "superior" races from the North, and is every bit as objectionable as white arrogance.

The belief in the superiority of the male sex, which has now officially died out in Western nations, is a curious example of the sin of pride. There was, I think, never any reason to believe in any innate superiority of the male, except his superior muscle. I remember once going to a place where they kept a number of pedigree bulls, and what made a bull illustrious was the milk-giving qualities of his female ancestors. But if bulls had drawn up the pedigrees they would have been very different. Nothing would have been said about the female ancestors, except that they were docile and virtuous, whereas the male ancestors would have been celebrated for their supremacy in battle. In the case of cattle we can take a disinterested view of the relative merits of the sexes, but in the case of our own species we find this more difficult. Male superiority in former days was easily demonstrated, because if a woman questioned her husband's he could beat her. From superiority in this respect others were thought to follow. Men were more reasonable than women, more inventive, less swayed by their emotions, and so on. Anatomists, until the women had the vote, developed a number of ingenious arguments from the study of the brain to show that men's intellectual capacities must be greater than women's. Each of these arguments in turn was proved to be fallacious, but it always gave place to another from which the same conclusion would follow. It used to be held that the male foetus acquires a soul after six weeks, but the female only after three months. This opinion also has been abandoned since women have had the vote. Thomas Aquinas states parenthetically, as something entirely obvious, that men are more rational than women. For my part, I see no evidence of this. Some few individuals have some slight glimmerings of rationality in some directions, but so far as my observations go, such glimmerings are no commoner among men than among women.

Male domination has had some very unfortunate effects. It made the most intimate of human relations, that of marriage, one of master and slave, instead of one between equal partners. It made it unnecessary for a man to please a woman in order to acquire her as his wife, and thus confined the arts of courtship to irregular relations. By the seclusion which it forced upon respectable women it made them dull and uninteresting; the only women who could be interesting and adventurous were social outcasts. Owing to the dullness of respectable women, the most civilized men in the most civilized countries often became homosexual. Owing to the fact that there was no equality in marriage men became confirmed in domineering habits. All this has now more or less ended in civilized countries, but it will be a long time before either men or women learn to adapt their behavior completely to the new state of affairs. Emancipation always has at first certain bad effects; it leaves former superiors sore and former inferiors self-assertive. But it is to be hoped that time will bring adjustment in this matter as in others.

Another kind of superiority which is rapidly disappearing is that of class, which now survives only in Soviet Russia. In that country the son of a proletarian has advantages over the son of a bourgeois, but elsewhere such hereditary privileges are regarded as unjust. The disappearance of class distinctions is, however, far from complete. In America everybody is of the opinion that he has no social superiors, since all men are equal, but he does not admit that he has no social inferiors, for, from the time of Jefferson onward, the doctrine that all men are equal applies only upwards, not downwards. There is on this subject a profound and widespread hypocrisy whenever people talk in general terms. What they really think and feel can be discovered by reading second-rate novels, where one finds that it is a dreadful thing to be born on the wrong side of the tracks, and that there is as much fuss about a *mésalliance* as there used to be in a small German Court. So long as great inequalities of wealth survive it is not easy to see how this can be otherwise. In England, where snobbery is deeply ingrained, the equalization of incomes which has been brought about by the war has had a profound effect, and among the young the snobbery of their elders has begun to seem somewhat ridiculous. There is still a very large amount of regrettable snobbery in England, but it is connected more with education and manner of speech than with income or with social status in the old sense.

Pride of creed is another variety of the same kind of feeling. When I had recently returned from China I lectured on that country to a number of women's clubs in America. There was always one elderly woman who appeared to be sleeping throughout the lecture, but at the end would ask me, somewhat portentously, why I had omitted to mention that the Chinese, being heathen, could of course have no virtues. I imagine that the Mormons of Salt Lake City must have had a similar attitude when non-Mormons were first admitted among them. Throughout the Middle Ages, Christians and Mohammedans were entirely persuaded of each other's wickedness and were incapable of doubting their own superiority.

All these are pleasant ways of feeling "grand." In order to be happy we require all kinds of supports to our self-esteem. We are human beings, therefore human beings are the purpose of creation.

We are Americans, therefore America is God's own country. We are white, and therefore God cursed Ham and his descendants who were black. We are Protestant or Catholic, as the case may be, therefore Catholics or Protestants, as the case may be, are an abomination. We are male, and therefore women are unreasonable; or female, and therefore men are brutes. We are Easterners, and therefore the West is wild and woolly; or Westerners, and therefore the East is effete. We work with our brains, and therefore it is the educated classes that are important; or we work with our hands, and therefore manual labor alone gives dignity. Finally, and above all, we each have one merit which is entirely unique, we are ourself. With these comforting reflections we go out to do battle with the world; without them our courage might fail. Without them, as things are, we should feel inferior because we have not learnt the sentiment of equality. If we could feel genuinely that we are the equals of our neighbors, neither their betters nor their inferiors, perhaps life would become less of a battle, and we should need less in the way of intoxicating myth to give us Dutch courage.

One of the most interesting and harmful delusions to which men and nations can be subjected, is that of imagining themselves special instruments of the Divine Will. We know that when the Israelites invaded the Promised Land it was they who were fulfilling the Divine Purpose, and not the Hittites, the Girgashites, the Amorites, the Canaanites, the Perizzites, the Hivites, or the Jebbusites. Perhaps if these others had written long history books the matter might have looked a little different. In fact, the Hittites did leave some inscriptions, from which you would never guess what abandoned wretches they were. It was discovered, "after the fact," that Rome was destined by the gods for the conquest of the world. Then came Islam with its fanatical belief that every soldier dying in battle for the True Faith went straight to a Paradise more attractive than that of the Christians, as houris are more attractive than harps. Cromwell was persuaded that he was the Divinely appointed instrument of justice for suppressing Catholics and malignants. Andrew Jackson was the agent of Manifest Destiny in freeing North America from the incubus of Sabbath-breaking Spaniards. In our day, the sword of the Lord has been put into the hands of the Marxists. Hegel thought that the Dialectic with fatalistic logic had given supremacy to Germany. "No," said Marx, "not to Germany, but to the Proletariat." This doctrine has kinship with the earlier doctrines of the Chosen People and Manifest Destiny. In its character of fatalism it has viewed the struggle of opponents as one against destiny, and argued that therefore the wise man would put himself on the winning side as quickly as possible. That is why this argument is such a useful one politically. The only objection to it is that it assumes a knowledge of the Divine purposes to which no rational man can lay claim, and that in the execution of them it justifies a ruthless cruelty which would be condemned if our program had a merely mundane origin. It is good to know that God is on our side, but a little confusing when you find the enemy equally convinced of the opposite. To quote the immortal lines of the poet during the First World War:

> Gott strafe England, and God save the King.
> God this, and God that, and God the other thing.
> "Good God," said God, "I've got my work cut out."

Belief in a Divine mission is one of the many forms of certainty that have afflicted the human race. I think perhaps one of the wisest things ever said was when Cromwell said to the Scotch before the battle of Dunbar: "I beseech you in the bowels of Christ, think it possible that you may be mistaken." But the Scotch did not, and so he had to defeat them in battle. It is a pity that Cromwell never addressed the same remark to himself. Most of the greatest evils that man has inflicted upon man have come through people feeling quite certain about something which, in fact, was false. To know the truth is more difficult than most men suppose, and to act with ruthless determination in the belief that truth is the monopoly of their party is to invite disaster. Long calculations that certain evil in the present is worth inflicting for the sake of some doubtful benefit in the future are always to be viewed with suspicion, for, as Shakespeare says: "What's to come is still unsure." Even the shrewdest men are apt to be wildly astray if they prophesy so much as ten years ahead. Some people will consider this doctrine immoral, but after all it is the Gospel which says "take no thought for the morrow."

In public, as in private life, the important thing is tolerance and kindliness, without the presumption of a superhuman ability to read the future.

Instead of calling this essay "Ideas that have harmed mankind," I might perhaps have called it simply "Ideas have harmed mankind," for, seeing that the future cannot be foretold and that there is an almost endless variety of possible beliefs about it, the chance that any belief which a man may hold may be true is very slender. Whatever you think is going to happen ten years hence, unless it is something like the sun rising tomorrow that has nothing to do with human relations, you are almost sure to be wrong. I find this thought consoling when I remember some gloomy prophesies of which I myself have rashly been guilty.

But you will say: how is statesmanship possible except on the assumption that the future can be to some extent foretold? I admit that some degree of prevision is necessary, and I am not suggesting that we are completely ignorant. It is a fair prophecy that if you tell a man he is a knave and a fool he will not love you, and it is a fair prophecy that if you say the same thing to seventy million people they will not love you. It is safe to assume that cut-throat competition will not produce a feeling of good fellowship between the competitors. It is highly probable that if two states equipped with modern armament face each other across a frontier, and if their leading statesmen devote themselves to mutual insults, the population of each side will in time become nervous, and one side will attack for fear of the other doing so. It is safe to assume that a great modern war will not raise the level of prosperity even among the victors. Such generalizations are not difficult to know. What is difficult is to foresee in detail the long-run consequences of a concrete policy. Bismarck with extreme astuteness won three wars and unified Germany. The long-run result of his policy has been that Germany has suffered two colossal defeats. These resulted because he taught Germans to be indifferent to the interests of all countries except Germany, and generated an aggressive spirit which in the end united the world against his successors. Selfishness beyond a point, whether individual or national, is not wise. It may with luck succeed, but if it fails failure is terrible. Few men will run this risk unless they are supported by a theory, for it is only theory that makes men completely incautious.

Passing from the moral to the purely intellectual point of view, we have to ask ourselves what social science can do in the way of establishing such causal laws as should be a help to statesmen in making political decisions. Some things of real importance have begun to be known, for example how to avoid slumps and large-scale unemployment such as afflicted the world after the last war [World War II]. It is also now generally known by those who have taken the trouble to look into the matter that only an international government can prevent war, and that civilization is hardly likely to survive more than one more great war, if that. But although these things are known, the knowledge is not effective; it has not penetrated to the great masses of men, and it is not strong enough to control sinister interests. There is, in fact, a great deal more social science than politicians are willing or able to apply. Some people attribute this failure to democracy, but it seems to me to be more marked in autocracy than anywhere else. Belief in democracy, however, like any other belief, may be carried to the point where it becomes fanatical, and therefore harmful. A democrat need not believe that the majority will always decide wisely; what he must believe is that the decision of the majority, whether wise or unwise, must be accepted until such time as the majority decides otherwise. And this he believes not from any mystic conception of the wisdom of the plain man, but as the best practical device for putting the reign of law in place of the reign of arbitrary force. Nor does the democrat necessarily believe that democracy is the best system always and everywhere. There are many nations which lack the self-restraint and political experience that are required for the success of parliamentary institutions, where the democrat, while he would wish them to acquire the necessary political education, will recognize that it is useless to thrust upon them prematurely a system which is almost certain to break down. In politics, as elsewhere, it does not do to deal in absolutes; what is good in one time and place may be bad in another, and what satisfies the political instincts of one nation may to another seem wholly futile. The general aim of the democrat is to substitute government by general assent for government by force, but this requires a population that has undergone a certain kind of training. Given a nation divided into two nearly equal portions which hate each other and long to fly at each other's throats, the portion which is just less than half will not submit tamely to the domination of the other portion, nor will the portion which is just more than half show, in the moment of victory, the kind of moderation which might heal the breach.

The world at the present day stands in need of two kinds of things. On the one hand, organization—political organization for the elimination of wars, economic organization to enable men to work productively, especially in the countries that have been devastated by war, educational organization to generate a sane internationalism. On the other hand it needs certain moral qualities—the qualities which have been advocated by moralists for many ages, but hitherto with little success. The qualities most needed are charity and tolerance, not some form of fanatical faith such as is offered us by the various rampant isms. I think these two aims, the organizational and the ethical, are closely interwoven; given either the other would soon follow. But, in effect, if the world is to move in the right direction it will have to move simultaneously in both respects. There will have to be a gradual lessening of the evil passions which are the natural aftermath of war, and a gradual increase of the organizations by means of which mankind can bring each other mutual help. There will have to be a realization at once intellectual and moral that we are all one family, and that the happiness of no one branch of this family can be built securely upon the ruin of another. At the present time, moral defects stand in the way of clear thinking, and muddled thinking encourages moral defects. Perhaps, though I scarcely dare to hope it, the hydrogen bomb will terrify mankind into sanity and tolerance. If this should happen we shall have reason to bless its inventors.

19

Ideas that Have Helped Mankind

Before we can discuss this subject we must form some conception as to the kind of effect that we consider a help to mankind. Are mankind helped when they become more numerous? Or when they become less like animals? Or when they become happier? Or when they learn to enjoy a greater diversity of experiences? Or when they come to know more? Or when they become more friendly to one another? I think all these things come into our conception of what helps mankind, and I will say a preliminary word about them.

The most indubitable respect in which ideas have helped mankind is numbers. There must have been a time when *homo sapiens* was a very rare species, subsisting precariously in jungles and caves, terrified of wild beasts, having difficulty in securing nourishment. At this period the biological advantage of his greater intelligence, which was cumulative because it could be handed on from generation to generation, had scarcely begun to outweigh the disadvantages of his long infancy, his lessened agility as compared with monkeys, and his lack of hirsute protection against cold. In those days, the number of men must certainly have been very small. The main use to which, throughout the ages, men have put their technical skill has been to increase the total population. I do not mean that this was the intention, but that it was, in fact, the effect. If this is something to rejoice in, then we have occasion to rejoice.

We have also become, in certain respects, progressively less like animals. I can think in particular of two respects: first, that ac-

First published by Haldeman-Julius in 1946.

quired, as opposed to congenital, skills play a continually increasing part in human life, and, secondly, that forethought more and more dominates impulse. In these respects we have certainly become progressively less like animals.

As to happiness, I am not so sure. Birds, it is true, die of hunger in large numbers during the winter, if they are not birds of passage. But during the summer they do not foresee this catastrophe, or remember how nearly it befell them in the previous winter. With human beings the matter is otherwise. I doubt whether the percentage of birds that will have died of hunger during the present winter (1946-7) is as great as the percentage of human beings that will have died from this cause in India and central Europe during the same period. But every human death by starvation is preceded by a long period of anxiety, and surrounded by the corresponding anxiety of neighbors. We suffer not only the evils that actually befall us, but all those that our intelligence tells us we have reason to fear. The curbing of impulses to which we are led by forethought averts physical disaster at the cost of worry, and general lack of joy. I do not think that the learned men of my acquaintance, even when they enjoy a secure income, are as happy as the mice that eat the crumbs from their tables while the erudite gentlemen snooze. In this respect, therefore, I am not convinced that there has been any progress at all.

As to diversity of enjoyments, however, the matter is otherwise. I remember reading an account of some lions who were taken to a movie showing the successful depredations of lions in a wild state, but none of them got any pleasure from the spectacle. Not only music, and poetry, and science, but football, and baseball, and alcohol, afford no pleasure to animals. Our intelligence has, therefore, certainly enabled us to get a much greater variety of enjoyment than is open to animals, but we have purchased this advantage at the expense of a much greater liability to boredom.

But I shall be told that it is neither numbers nor multiplicity of pleasures that make the glory of man. It is his intellectual and moral qualities. It is obvious that we know more than animals do, and it is common to consider this one of our advantages. Whether it is, in fact, an advantage, may be doubted. But at any rate it is something that distinguishes us from the brutes.

Has civilization taught us to be more friendly toward one another? The answer is easy. Robins (the English, not the American species) peck an elderly robin to death, whereas men (the English, not the American species) give an elderly man an old-age pension. Within the herd we are more friendly to each other than are many species of animals, but in our attitude toward those outside the herd, in spite of all that has been done by moralists and religious teachers, our emotions are as ferocious as those of any animal, and our intelligence enables us to give them a scope which is denied to even the most savage beast. It may be hoped, though not very confidently, that the more humane attitude will in time come to prevail, but so far the omens are not very propitious.

All these different elements must be borne in mind in considering what ideas have done most to help mankind. The ideas with which we shall be concerned may be broadly divided into two kinds: those that contribute to knowledge and technique, and those that are concerned with morals and politics. I will treat first those that have to do with knowledge and technique.

The most important and difficult steps were taken before the dawn of history. At what stage language began is not known, but we may be pretty certain that it began very gradually. Without it it would have been very difficult to hand on from generation to generation the inventions and discoveries that were gradually made.

Another great step, which may have come either before or after the beginning of language, was the utilization of fire. I suppose that at first fire was chiefly used to keep away wild beasts while our ancestors slept, but the warmth must have been found agreeable. Presumably on some occasion a child got scolded for throwing the meat into the fire, but when it was taken out it was found to be much better, and so the long history of cookery began.

The taming of domestic animals, especially the cow and the sheep, must have made life much pleasanter and more secure. Some anthropologists have an attractive theory that the utility of domestic animals was not foreseen, but that people attempted to tame whatever animal their religion taught them to worship. The tribes that worshipped lions and crocodiles died out, while those to whom the cow or the sheep was a sacred animal prospered. I like this theory, and in the entire absence of evidence, for or against it, I feel at liberty to play with it.

Even more important than the domestication of animals was the invention of agriculture, which, however, introduced bloodthirsty practices into religion that lasted for many centuries. Fertility rites tended to involve human sacrifice and cannibalism. Moloch would not help the corn to grow unless he was allowed to feast on the blood of children. A similar opinion was adopted by the Evangelicals of Manchester in the early days of industrialism, when they kept six-year-old children working twelve to fourteen hours a day, in conditions that caused most of them to die. It has now been discovered that grain will grow, and cotton goods can be manufactured, without being watered by the blood of infants. In the case of the grain, the discovery took thousands of years; in the case of the cotton goods hardly a century. So perhaps there is some evidence of progress in the world.

The last of the great prehistoric inventions was the art of writing, which was indeed a prerequisite of history. Writing, like speech, developed gradually, and in the form of pictures designed to convey a message it was probably as old as speech, but from pictures to syllable writing and thence to the alphabet was a very slow evolution. In China the last step was never taken.

Coming to historic times, we find that the earliest important steps were taken in mathematics and astronomy, both of which began in Babylonia some millenia before the beginning of our era. Learning in Babylonia seems, however, to have become sterotyped and nonprogressive, long before the Greeks first came into contact with it. It is to the Greeks that we owe ways of thinking and investigating that have ever since been found fruitful. In the prosperous Greek commercial cities, rich men living on slave labor were brought by the processes of trade into contact with many nations, some quite barbarous, others fairly civilized. What the civilized nations—the Babylonians and Egyptians—had to offer the Greeks quickly assimilated. They became critical of their own traditional customs, by perceiving them to be at once analogous to, and different from, the customs of surrounding inferior peoples, and so by the sixth century B.C. some of them achieved a degree of enlightened rationalism which cannot be surpassed in the present day. Xenophanes observed that men make gods in their own image—"the Ethiopians make their gods black and snub-nosed; the Thracians say theirs have blue eyes and red hair: Yes, and if oxen and lions and horses had hands, and could paint with their hands, and produced works of art as men do, horses would paint the forms of gods like horses, and oxen like oxen, and make their bodies in the image of their several kinds."

Some Greeks used their emancipation from tradition in the pursuit of mathematics and astronomy, in both of which they made the most amazing progress. Mathematics was not used by the Greeks, as it is by the moderns, to facilitate industrial processes; it was a "gentlemanly" pursuit, valued for its own sake as giving eternal truth, and a supersensible standard by which the visible world was condemned as second-rate. Only Archimedes foreshadowed the modern use of mathematics by inventing engines of war for the defense of Syracuse against the Romans. A Roman soldier killed him and the mathematicians retired again into their ivory tower.

Astronomy, which the sixteenth and seventeeth centuries pursued with ardor, largely because of its usefulness in navigation, was pursued by the Greeks with no regard for practical utility, except when, in later antiquity, it became associated with astrology. At a very early stage they discovered the earth to be round and made a fairly accurate estimate of its size. They discovered ways of calculating the distance of the sun and moon, and Aristarchus of Samos even evolved the complete Copernican hypothesis, but his views were rejected by all his followers except one, and after the third century B.C. no very important progress was made. At the time of the Renaissance, however, something of what the Greeks had done became known, and greatly facilitated the rise of modern science.

The Greeks had the conception of natural law, and acquired the habit of expressing natural laws in mathematical terms. These ideas have provided the key to a very great deal of the understanding of the physical world that has been achieved in modern times. But many of them, including Aristotle, were misled by a belief that science could make a fruitful use of the idea of purpose. Aristotle distinguished four kinds of cause, of which only two concern us, the "efficient" cause and the "final" cause. The "efficient" cause is what *we* should call simply the cause. The "final" cause is the purpose. For instance, if, in the course of a tramp in the mountains, you find an inn just when your thirst has become unendurable, the efficient cause of the inn is the actions of the bricklayers that built it, while its final cause is the satisfaction of your thirst. If someone were to ask "why is there an inn there?" it would be equally appropriate to answer "because someone had it built there" or "because many thirsty travellers pass that way." One is an explanation by the "efficient" cause and the other by the "final" cause. Where human affairs are concerned, the explanation by "final" cause is often appropriate, since human actions have purposes. But where inanimate nature is concerned, only "efficient" causes have been found scientifically discoverable, and the attempt to explain phenomena by "final" causes has always led to bad science. There may, for aught we know, be a purpose in natural phenomena, but if so it has remained completely undiscovered, and all known scientific laws have to do only with "efficient" causes. In this respect Aristotle led the world astray, and it did not recover fully until the time of Galileo.

The seventeenth century, especially Galileo, Descartes, Newton, and Leibniz, made an advance in our understanding of nature more sudden and surprising than any other in history, except that of the early Greeks. It is true that some of the concepts used in the mathematical physics of that time had not quite the validity that was then ascribed to them. It is true also that the more recent advances of physics often require new concepts quite different from those of the seventeenth century. Their concepts, in fact, were not the key to *all* the secrets of nature, but they were the key to a great many. Modern technique in industry and war, with the sole exception of the atomic bomb, is still wholly based upon a type of dynamics developed out of the principles of Galileo and Newton. Most of astronomy still rests upon these same principles, though there are some problems such as "what keeps the sun hot?" in which the recent discoveries of quantum mechanics are essential. The dynamics of Galileo and Newton depended upon two new principles and a new technique.

The first of the new principles was the law of inertia, which stated that any body, left to itself, will continue to move as it is moving in the same straight line, and with the same velocity. The importance of this principle is only evident when it is contrasted with the principles that the scholastics had evolved out of Aristotle. Before Galileo it was held that there was a radical difference between regions below the moon and regions from the moon upwards. In the regions below the moon, the "sublunary" sphere, there was change and decay; the "natural" motion of bodies was rectilinear, but any body in motion, if left to itself, would gradually slow up and presently stop. From the moon upwards, on the contrary, the "natural" motion of bodies was circular, or compounded of circular motions, and in the heavens there was no such thing as change or decay, except the periodic changes of the orbits of the heavenly bodies. The movements of the heavenly bodies were not spontaneous, but were passed on to them from the *primum mobile*, which was the outermost of the moving spheres, and itself derived its motion from the Unmoved Mover, i.e., God. No one thought of making any appeal to observation; for instance, it was held that a projectile will first move horizontally for a while, and then suddenly begin to fall vertically, although it might have been supposed that anybody watching a fountain could have seen that the drops move in curves. Comets, since they appear and disappear, had to be supposed to be between the earth and the moon, for if they had been above the moon they would have had to be indestructible. It is evident that out of such a jumble nothing could be developed. Galileo unified the principles governing the earth and the heavens by his single law of inertia, according to which a body, once in motion, will not stop of itself, but will move with a constant velocity in a straight line whether it is on earth or in one of the celestial spheres. This principle made it possible to develop a science of the motions of matter, without taking account of any supposed influence of mind or spirit, and thus laid the foundations of the purely materialistic physics in which men of science, however pious, have ever since believed.

From the seventeenth century onwards, it has become increasingly evident that if we wish to understand natural laws, we must get rid of every kind of ethical and aesthetic bias. We must cease to think that noble things have noble causes, that intelligent things have intelligent causes, or that order is impossible without a celestial policeman. The Greeks admired the sun and moon and planets, and supposed them to be gods; Plotinus explains how superior they are to human beings in wisdom and virtue. Anaxagoras, who taught otherwise, was prosecuted for impiety and compelled to fly from Athens. The Greeks also allowed themselves to think that since the circle is the most perfect figure, the motions of the heavenly bodies must be, or be derived from, circular motions. Every bias of this sort had to be discarded by seventeenth-century astronomy. The Copernican system showed that the earth is not the center of the universe, and suggested to a few bold spirits that perhaps man was not the supreme purpose of the Creator. In the main, however, astronomers were pious folk, and until the nineteenth century most of them, except in France, believed in Genesis.

It was geology, Darwin, and the doctrine of evolution, that first upset the faith of British men of science. If man was evolved by insensible gradations from lower forms of life, a number of things became very difficult to understand. At what moment in evolution did our ancestors acquire free will? At what stage in the long journey from the ameba did they begin to have immortal souls? When did they first become capable of the kinds of wickedness that would justify a benevolent Creator in sending them into eternal torment?

312 Bertrand Russell On God and Religion

Most people felt that such punishment would be hard on monkeys, in spite of their propensity for throwing coconuts at the heads of Europeans. But how about *Pithecanthropus Erectus*? Was it really he who ate the apple? Or was it *Homo Pekiniensis*? Or was it perhaps the Piltdown man? I went to Piltdown once, but saw no evidence of special depravity in that village, nor did I see any signs of its having changed appreciably since prehistoric ages. Perhaps then it was the Neanderthal men who first sinned? This seems the more likely, as they lived in Germany. But obviously there can be no answer to such questions, and those theologians who do not wholly reject evolution have had to make profound readjustments.

One of the "grand" conceptions which have proved scientifically useless is the soul. I do not mean that there is positive evidence showing that men have no souls; I only mean that the soul, if it exists, plays no part in any discoverable causal law. There are all kinds of experimental methods of determining how men and animals behave under various circumstances. You can put rats in mazes and men in barbed wire cages, and observe their methods of escape. You can administer drugs and observe their effect. You can turn a male rat into a female, though so far nothing analogous has been done with human beings, even at Buchenwald. It appears that socially undesirable conduct can be dealt with by medical means, or by creating a better environment, and the conception of sin has thus come to seem quite unscientific, except, of course, as applied to the Nazis. There is real hope that, by getting to understand the science of human behavior, governments may be even more able than they are at present to turn mankind into rabbles of mutually ferocious lunatics. Governments could, of course, do exactly the opposite and cause the human race to cooperate willingly and cheerfully in making themselves happy, rather than in making others miserable, but only if there is an international government with a monopoly of armed force. It is very doubtful whether this will take place.

This brings me to the second kind of idea that has helped or may in time help mankind; I mean moral as opposed to technical ideas. Hitherto I have been considering the increased command over the forces of nature which men have derived from scientific knowledge, but this, although it is a precondition of many forms of progress, does not of itself ensure anything desirable. On the contrary, the present state of the world and the fear of an atomic war show that scientific progress without a corresponding moral and political progress may only increase the magnitude of the diasaster that misdirected skill may bring about. In superstitious moments I am tempted to believe in the myth of the Tower of Babel, and to suppose that in our own day a similar but greater impiety is about to be visited by a more tragic and terrible punishment. Perhaps—so I sometimes allow myself to fancy—God does not intend us to understand the mechanism by which He regulates the material universe. Perhaps the nuclear physicists have come so near to the ultimate secrets that He thinks it time to bring their activities to a stop. And what simpler method could He devise than to let them carry their ingenuity to the point where they exterminate the human race? If I could think that deer and squirrels, nightingales and larks, would survive, I might view this catastrophe with some equanimity, since man has not shown himself worthy to be the lord of creation. But it is to be feared that the dreadful alchemy of the atomic bomb will destroy all forms of life equally, and that the earth will remain forever a dead cloud senselessly whirling round a futile sun. I do not know the immediate precipitating cause of this interesting occurrence. Perhaps it will be a dispute about Persian oil, perhaps a disagreement as to Chinese trade, perhaps a quarrel between Jews and Mohommedans for the control of Palestine. Any patriotic person can see that these issues are of such importance as to make the extermination of mankind preferable to cowardly conciliation.

In case, however, there should be some among my readers who would like to see the human race survive, it may be worth while considering the stock of moral ideas that great men have put into the world and that might, if they were listened to, secure happiness instead of misery for the mass of mankind.

Man, viewed morally, is a strange amalgam of angel and devil. He can feel the splendor of the night, the delicate beauty of spring flowers, the tender emotion of parental love, and the intoxication of intellectual understanding. In moments of insight visions come to him of how life should be lived and how men should order their dealings one with another. Universal love is an emotion which many have felt and which many more could feel if the world made it less difficult. This is one side of the picture. On the other side are cruelty, greed, indifference and overweening pride. Men, quite ordinary men, will compel children to look on while their mothers are raped. In pursuit of political aims men will submit their opponents to long years of unspeakable anguish. We know what Nazis did to Jews at Auschwitz. In mass cruelty, the expulsions of Germans ordered by the Russians fall not very far short of the atrocities perpetuated by the Nazis. And how about our noble selves? We would not do such deeds, oh no! But we enjoy our juicy steaks and our hot rolls while German children die of hunger because our governments dare not face our indignation if they asked us to forgo some part of our pleasures. If there were a Last Judgment as Christians believe, how do you think our excuses would sound before that final tribunal?

Moral ideas sometimes wait upon political developments, and sometimes outrun them. The brotherhood of man is an ideal which owed its first force to political developments. When Alexander conquered the East he set to work to obliterate the distinction of Greek and barbarian, no doubt because his Greek and Macedonian army was too small to hold down so vast an empire by force. He compelled his officers to marry barbarian aristocratic ladies, while he himself, to set a doubly excellent example, married *two* barbarian princesses. As a result of this policy Greek pride and exclusiveness were diminished, and Greek culture spread to many regions not inhabited by Hellenic stock. Zeno, the founder of Stoicism, who was probably a boy at the time of Alexander's conquest, was a Phoenician, and few of the eminent Stoics were Greeks. It was the Stoics who invented the conception of the brotherhood of man. They taught that all men are children of Zeus and that the sage will ignore the distinctions of Greek and barbarian, bond and free. When Rome brought the whole civilized world under one government, the political environment was favorable to the spread of this doctrine. In a new form, more capable of appealing to the emotions of ordinary men and women, Christianity taught a similar doctrine. Christ said "Thou shalt love thy neighbor as thyself," and when asked "who is my neighbor?" went on to the parable of the Good Samaritan. If you wish to understand this parable as it was understood by his hearers, you should substitute "German" or "Japanese" for "Samaritan." I fear many present-day Christians would resent such a substitution, because it would compel them to realize how far they have departed from the teaching of the Founder of their religon. A similar doctrine had been taught much earlier by the Buddhists. According to them, the Buddha declared that he could not be happy so long as even one man remained miserable. It might seem as if these lofty ethical teachings had little effect upon the world; in India Buddhism died out, in Europe Christianity was emptied of most of the elements it derived form Christ. But I think this would be a superficial view.

Christianity, as soon as it conquered the state, put an end to gladiatorial shows, not because they were cruel, but because they were idolatrous. The result, however, was to diminish the widespread education in cruelty by which the populace of Roman towns were degraded. Christianity also did much to soften the lot of slaves. It established charity on a large scale, and inaugurated hospitals. Although the great majority of Christians failed lamentably in Christian charity, the ideal remained alive and in every age inspired some notable saints. In a new form, it passed over into modern liberalism, and remains the inspiration of much that is most hopeful in our sombre world.

The watchwords of the French Revolution, Liberty, Equality, and Fraternity, have religious origins. Of Fraternity I have already spoken. Equality was a characteristic of the Orphic Societies in ancient Greece, from which, indirectly, a great deal of Christian dogma took its rise. In these societies, slave and women were admitted on equal terms with citizens. Plato's advocacy of votes for women, which has seemed surprising to some modern readers, is derived from Orphic practices. The Orphics believed in transmigration and thought that a soul which in one life inhabits the body of a slave, may, in another, inhabit that of a king. Viewed from the standpoint of religion, it is therefore foolish to discriminate between a slave and a king; both share the dignity belonging to an immortal soul, and neither, in religion, can claim anything more. This point of view passed over from Orphism into Stoicism, and into Christianity. For a long time its practical effect was small, but ultimately, whenever circumstances were favorable, it helped in bringing about the diminution of the inequalities in the social system. Read, for instance, John Woolman's Journal. John Woolman was a Quaker, one of the first Americans to oppose slavery. No doubt the real ground of his opposition was humane feeling, but he was able to fortify this feeling and to make it controversially more effective by appeals to Christian doctrines, which his neighbors did not dare to repudiate openly.

Liberty as an ideal has had a very chequered history. In antiquity, Sparta, which was a totalitarian state, had as little use for it as the Nazis had. But most of the Greek city states allowed a degree of liberty which we should now think excessive, and, in fact, do think excessive when it is practiced by their descendants in the same part of the world. Politics was a matter of assassination and rival armies, one of them supporting the government, and the other composed of refugees. The refugees would often ally themselves with their city's enemies and march in in triumph on the heels of foreign conquerors. This sort of thing was done by everybody, and, in spite of much fine talk in the works of modern historians about Greek loyalty to the city state, nobody seemed to view such conduct as particularly nefarious. This was carrying liberty to excess, and led by reaction to admiration of Sparta.

The word "liberty" has had strange meanings at different times. In Rome, in the last days of the Republic and the early days of the empire, it meant the right of powerful senators to plunder provinces for their private profit. Brutus, whom most English-speaking readers know as the high-minded hero of Shakespeare's *Julius Caesar,* was, in fact, rather different from this. He would lend money to a munici- pality at sixty percent, and when they failed to pay the interest he would hire a private army to besiege them, for which his friend Cicero mildly expostulated with him. In our own day, the word "liberty" bears a very similar meaning when used by industrial magnates. Leaving these vagaries on one side, there are two serious meanings of the word "liberty." On the one hand the freedom of a nation from foreign domination, on the other hand, the freedom of the citizen to pursue his legitimate avocations. Each of these in a well-ordered world should be subject to limitations, but unfortun- ately the former has been taken in an absolute sense. To this point of view I will return presently; it is the liberty of the individual citizen that I now wish to speak about.

This kind of liberty first entered practical politics in the form of religious toleration, a doctrine which came to be widely adopted in the seventeenth century through the inability of either Protestants or Catholics to exterminate the opposite party. After they had fought each other for a hundred years, culminating in the horror of the thirty years' war, and after it had appeared that as a result of all this bloodshed the balance of parties at the end was almost exactly what it had been at the beginning, certain men of genius, mostly Dutchmen, suggested that perhaps all the killing had been unnecessary, and that people might be allowed to think what they chose on such matters as consubstantiation versus transubstantia- tion, or whether the cup should be allowed to the laity. The doctrine of religious toleration came to England with the Dutch King William, along with the Bank of England and the national debt. In fact all three were products of the commercial mentality.

The greatest of the theoretical advocates of liberty at that period was John Locke, who devoted much thought to the problem of reconciling the maximum of liberty with the indispensable minimum of government, a problem with which his successors in the liberal tradition have been occupied down to the present day.

In addition to religious freedom, free press, free speech, and freedom from arbitrary arrest came to be taken for granted during the nineteenth century, at least among the Western democracies. But their hold on men's minds was much more precarious than was at the time supposed, and now, over the greater part of the earth's surface, nothing remains of them, either in practice or in theory. [Joseph] Stalin could neither understand nor respect the point of view which led Winston Churchill to allow himself to be peaceably dispossessed as a result of a popular vote. I am a firm believer in democratic representative government as the best form for those who have the tolerance and self-restraint that is required to make it workable. But its advocates make a mistake if they suppose that it can be at once introduced into countries where the average citizen has hitherto lacked all training in the give-and-take that it requires. In a Balkan country, not so many years ago, a party which had been beaten by a narrow margin in a general election retrieved its fortunes by shooting a sufficient number of the representatives of the other side to give it a majority. People in the West thought this characteristic of the Balkans, forgetting that Cromwell and Robespierre had acted likewise.

And this brings me to the last pair of great political ideas to which mankind owes whatever little success in social organization it has achieved. I mean the ideas of law and government. Of these, government is the more fundamental. Government can easily exist without law, but law cannot exist without government—a fact which was forgotten by those who framed the League of Nations and the Kellogg Pact. Government may be defined as a concentration of the collective forces of a community in a certain organization which, in virtue of this concentration, is able to control individual citizens and to resist pressure from foreign states. War has always been the chief promoter of governmental power. The control of government over the private citizen is always greater where there is war or imminent danger of war than where peace seems secure. But when governments have acquired power with a view to resisting foreign aggression, they have naturally used it, if they could, to further their private interests at the expense of the citizens. Absolute monarchy was, until recently, the grossest form of this abuse of power. But in the modern totalitarian state the same evil has been carried much further than had been dreamt of by Xerxes or Nero or any of the tyrants of earlier times.

Democracy was invented as a device for reconciling government with liberty. It is clear that government is necessary if anything worthy to be called civilization is to exist, but all history shows that any set of men entrusted with power over another set will abuse their power if they can do so with impunity. Democracy is intended to make men's tenure of power temporary and dependent upon popular approval. In so far as it achieves this it prevents the worst abuses of power. The Second Triumvirate in Rome, when they wanted money with a view to fighting Brutus and Cassius, made a list of rich men and declared them public enemies, cut off their heads, and seized their property. This sort of procedure is not possible in America and England at the present day. We owe the fact that it is not possible not only to democracy, but also to the doctrine of personal liberty. This doctrine, in practice, consists of two parts, on the one hand that a man shall not be punished except by due process of law, and on the other hand that there shall be a sphere within which a man's actions are not to be subject to governmental control. This sphere includes free speech, free press and religious freedom. It used to include freedom of economic enterprise. All these doctrines, of course, are held in practice with certain limitations. The British formerly did not adhere to them in their dealings with India. Freedom of the press is not respected in the case of doctrines which are thought dangerously subversive. Free speech would not be held to exonerate public advocacy of assassination of an unpopular politician. But in spite of these limitations the doctrine of personal liberty has been of great value throughout the English-speaking world, as anyone who lives in it will quickly realize when he finds himself in a police state.

In the history of social evolution it will be found that almost invariably the establishment of some sort of government has come first and attempts to make government compatible with personal liberty have come later. In international affairs we have not yet reached the first stage, although it is now evident that international government is at least as important to mankind as national government. I think it may be seriously doubted whether the next twenty years would be more disastrous to mankind if all government were abolished than they will be if no effective international government is established. I find it often urged that an international government would be oppressive, and I do not deny that this might be the case, at any rate for a time, but national governments were oppressive when they were new and are still oppressive in most countries, and yet hardly anybody would on this ground advocate anarchy within a nation.

Ordered social life of a kind that could seem in any degree desirable rests upon a synthesis and balance of certain slowly developed ideas and institutions: government, law, individual liberty, and democracy. Individual liberty, of course, existed in the ages before there was government, but when it existed without government civilized life was impossible. When governments first arose they involved slavery, absolute monarchy, and usually the enforcement of superstition by a powerful priesthood. All these were very great evils, and one can understand Rousseau's nostalgia for the life of the noble savage. But this was a mere romantic idealization, and, in fact, the life of the savage was, as Hobbes said, "nasty, brutish, and short." The history of man reaches occasional great crises. There must have been a crisis when the apes lost their tails, and another when our ancestors took to walking upright and lost their protective covering of hair. As I remarked before, the human population of the globe, which must at one time have been very small, was greatly increased by the invention of agriculture, and was increased again in our own time by modern industrial and medical technique. But modern technique has brought us to a new crisis. In this new crisis we are faced with an alternative: either man must again become a rare species as in the days of *Homo Pekiniensis,* or we must learn to submit to an international government. Any such government, whether good, bad or indifferent, will make the continuation of the human species possible, and, as in the course of the past 5,000 years men have climbed gradually from the despotism of the Pharoes [sic] to the glories of the American Constitution, so perhaps in the next 5,000 they may climb from a bad international government to a good one. But if they do not establish an international government of some kind, new progress will have to begin at a lower level, probably at that of tribal savagery, and will have to begin after a cataclysmic destruction only to be paralleled by the biblical account of the deluge. When we survey the long development of mankind from a rare hunted animal, hiding precariously in caves from the fury of wild beasts which he was incapable of killing; subsisting doubtfully on the raw fruits of the earth which he did not know how to cultivate; reinforcing real terrors by the imaginary terrors of ghosts and evil spirits and malign spells; gradually acquiring the mastery of his environment by the invention of fire, writing, weapons, and at last science; building up a social organization which curbed private violence and gave a measure of security to daily life; using the leisure gained by his skill, not only in idle luxury, but in the production of beauty and the unveiling of the secrets of natural law; learning gradually, though imperfectly, to view an increasing number of his neighbors as allies in the task of production rather than enemies in the attempts at mutual depredation—when we consider this long and arduous journey, it becomes intolerable to think that it may all have to be made again from the beginning owing to failure to take one step for which past developments, rightly viewed, have been a preparation. Social cohesion, which among the apes is confined to the family, grew in prehistoric times as far as the tribe, and in the very beginnings of history reached the level of small kingdoms in upper and lower Egypt and Mesopotamia. From these small kingdoms grew the empires of antiquity, and then gradually the great states of our own day, far larger than even the Roman Empire. Quite recent developments have robbed the smaller states of any real independence, until now there remain only two that are wholly capable of independent self-direction: I mean, of course, the United States and the USSR. All that is necessary to save mankind from disaster is the step from two independent states to one—not by war, which would bring disaster, but by agreement.

If this step can be accomplished, all the great achievements of mankind will quickly lead to an era of happiness and well-being, such as has never before been dreamt of. Our scientific skill will make it possible to abolish poverty throughout the world without necessitating more than four or five hours a day of productive labor. Disease, which has been very rapidly reduced during the last hundred years, will be reduced still further. The leisure achieved through organization and science will no doubt be devoted very largely to pure enjoyment, but there will remain a number of people to whom the pursuit of art and science will seem important. There will be a new freedom from economic bondage to the mere necessities of keeping alive, and the great mass of mankind may enjoy the kind of carefree adventurousness that characterizes the rich young Athenians of Plato's *Dialogues*. All this is easily within the bounds of technical possibility. It requires for its realization only one thing: that the men who hold power, and the populations that support them, should think it more important to keep themselves alive than to cause the death of their enemies. No very lofty or difficult ideal, one might think, and yet one which so far has proved beyond the scope of human intelligence.

The present moment is the most important and most crucial that has ever confronted mankind. Upon our collective wisdom during the next twenty years depends the question whether mankind shall be plunged into unparalleled disaster, or shall achieve a new level of happiness, security, well-being, and intelligence. I do not know which mankind will choose. There is grave reason for fear, but there is enough possibility of a good solution to make hope not irrational. And it is on this hope that we must act.

Part Five

20

Mahatma Gandhi

Mahatma Gandhi was unquestionably a great man, both in personal force and in political effect. He molded the character of the struggle for freedom in India, and impressed his own ideals upon the new governing class that came into power when the English went home. There is, at the present day, a general awakening throughout Asia, but the spirit and policy of India, thanks largely to Gandhi, remains very different from that of any other Asiatic country.

Gandhi, like some other great men, developed slowly. Quite extraordinary psychological acumen would have been necessary to discern his future in the shy youth who studied law, first in India and then in England. His autobiography contains a picture of him as he was in his early days in England, and there is nothing in it to suggest the future loincloth; on the contrary, his costume is faultlessly correct and would pass inspection by the "Tailor and Cutter" without any criticism.

Some of the characteristics that he displayed throughout his life were already in evidence at this time. He had a wide and unsectarian interest in religion, and listened to Christian teaching without hostility, though without acceptance. He had already that scrupulous honesty which later distinguished him. He had been married, as was the custom of this country, while still a schoolboy, but

From *The Atlantic* (December 1952): 35–39. Reprinted by permission of the legal heir of Lord Russell.

when he came to England he left his wife in India and was not generally known by his English friends to be married. He believed, rightly or wrongly, that a certain young lady was becoming interested in him, and he therefore wrote a long letter to her chaperone explaining his matrimonial position. He had been brought up to be a vegetarian on religious grounds, but his brother, who wanted to become "modern," induced him on a few occasions to taste meat. He found it made him ill, and he disliked the deceiving of his parents that was involved. He therefore reverted to strict vegetarianism before his journey to England. All through his life he attached an importance to questions of diet which it is a little difficult for most modern Europeans to understand. But although in England he observed as far as he could the customs in which he had been brought up, he did not become in any degree a rebel, and did not apparently encounter the kind of treatment by which rebels are created.

After a year or so in India, he went on professional legal business to South Africa, and it was there that events soon pushed him into the career which made him famous. He landed at Durban and had to travel to Pretoria. The incidents of this journey are treated vividly and precisely in his autobiography. He took a first-class ticket at Durban, and apparently the railway authorities had no objection to selling it to him. But after he had been in the train some time, a railway official insisted that however much he might have a first-class ticket, he must travel in a third-class carriage. Gandhi refused to yield voluntarily, so he was pushed out of the train, which went on without him. He sat throughout the night in the station waiting-room, shivering with cold, because his overcoat was in the luggage of which the railway company had taken charge, and he would not ask of them the favor of being allowed to get it out.

"I began to think of my duty," he writes in his autobiography. "Should I fight for my rights or go back to India; or should I go on to Pretoria without minding the insults, and return to India after finishing the case? It would be cowardice to run back to India without fulfilling my obligation. The hardship to which I was subjected was only superficial. It was only a symptom of the deep disease of color prejudice. I should try, if possible, to root out the disease and suffer hardship in the process. Redress for wrongs I should seek only to the extent that would be necessary for the removal of the color prejudice. So I decided to take the next available train to Pretoria."

A part of his journey had to be done by stagecoach, as there was at that time no railway from the Natal frontier to Johannesburg. He had a ticket for the journey by coach of which the validity was not questioned, but as he was a "colored man," the conductor of the coach considered that he could not be allowed to travel inside.

For a time he was allowed to sit next to the driver while the conductor sat inside, but presently the conductor decided that he wanted to smoke, and ordered Gandhi to sit on the floor of the roof. Gandhi describes the incident: "So he took a piece of dirty sackcloth from the driver, spread it on the footboard and, addressing me, said, 'Sammy, you sit on this, I want to sit near the driver.' The insult was more than I could bear. In fear and trembling, I said to him, 'It was you who seated me here, though I should have been accommodated inside. That insult I put up with. Now that you want to sit outside and smoke, you would have me sit at your feet. I refuse to do so, but I am prepared to sit inside.' As I was struggling through these sentences the man came for me and began heavily to box my ears. He seized me by the arm and tried to drag me down. I clung to the brass rails of the coach-box and was determined to keep my hold even at the risk of breaking my wristbones. The passengers were witnessing the scene—the man swearing at me, dragging and belaboring me, and I remaining still. He was strong and I was weak."

It is difficult to guess how this scene would have ended but for the intervention of some of the passengers, who apparently had some inkling of humanity. Thanks to them, Gandhi was allowed to remain where he was, and a Hottentot, who had been sitting on the other side of the driver, was made to vacate his seat for the conductor. The feelings of Hottentots about this incident remain for a future page of history.

He had some further adventures on the journey, but of a less dramatic sort. No good hotel would give him lodging, and it was only with some difficulty that he procured a first-class ticket from Johannesburg to Pretoria. This he did by writing a long letter to the stationmaster, and then appearing at the station so faultlessly dressed that the stationmaster observed, "I see you are a gentleman." If he had met Gandhi in later life, clad in his loincloth, he would not have been able to say this.

At this time, as Gandhi's reflections show, although he was outraged by the color prejudice that he encountered, he had no conception of general human equality. He was aware of himself as an educated man, a man whose family in their own country had a certain social prominence. He was rendered indignant by the fact that all Hindus in South Africa were called "coolies," however little they might work with their hands. He had not yet thought of Negroes as having the same right to equality as he was claiming for himself, and at first he was not particularly interested in the wrongs of Indian indentured laborers. It was only step by step, through a number of years, that his outlook on human affairs developed to the point where the untouchables became his main preoccupation. I think, however, that the indignities which he suffered on his first journey in South Africa were what first awakened him to the intolerable humiliations to which classes and nations which are deemed "inferior" are subjected by the insolence of their "masters." I should therefore judge that it was this journey which was the turning point in Gandhi's life.

II

Gandhi returned to India in 1896, and while in India he gave large publicity to the bad treatment of Indians in South Africa. What he had to say on this subject was quoted in many Indian newspapers and brought him into contact with Indian leaders. This agitation had repercussions in South Africa, where the white population became filled with fury against Gandhi. His Indian friends in South Africa telegraphed to him to return to that country, which he did. All sorts of measures were adopted to prevent him from landing. First the ship on which he had come was kept in quarantine for a long time, without any medical justification. Then he was warned not to land with the other passengers, but to slip ashore surreptitiously after dark. He would not do this. His refusal nearly cost him his life. His own account in his autobiography is so vivid that it must be quoted:

> The number of persons present about the wharf was not larger than what it is to be usually seen there. As soon as we landed some young lads saw us. As I was the only Indian who wore a turban of a particular type, they at once recognized me, and began to shout, "Here's Gandhi! Here's Gandhi! Thrash him! Surround him!" and they came up towards me. Some began to throw stones. Then a few older Europeans joined the boys, and gradually the party of rioters began to grow. Mr. Laughton thought that there was danger in our going on

foot. He therefore beckoned for a rickshaw. Up to now I had never sat in a rickshaw, as it was thoroughly disgusting to me to sit in a vehicle pulled by human beings. But I then felt that it was my duty to use that vehicle. Five or six times in my life I have experienced that one whom God wished to save cannot fall even if he will. If I did not fall at that moment I cannot take any credit for it to myself. These rickshaws are pulled by Zulus. The older Europeans and the young lads threatened the rickshaw puller that if he allowed me to sit in his rickshaw they would beat him and smash his rickshaw to pieces. The rickshaw boy therefore said "Kha" (No), and went away. I was thus spared the shame of a rickshaw ride.

We had no alternative now but to proceed to our destination on foot. The mob followed us. With every step we advanced, it grew larger and larger. The gathering was enormous when we reached West Street. A man of powerful build caught hold of Mr. Laughton and tore him away from me. He was not therefore in a position to come up with me. The crowd began to abuse me and showered upon me stones and whatever else they could lay their hands on. They threw down my turban. Meanwhile a burly fellow came up to me, slapped me in the face and then kicked me. I was about to fall unconscious when I held on to the railings of a house near by. For a while I took breath, and when the fainting was over proceeded on my way. At that time I had almost given up any hope of reaching home alive. But I remember well that even then my heart did not arraign my assailants.

He was saved from further injury, perhaps even from death, by the wife of the superintendent of police, whose name was Mrs. Alexander. She had been a friend of his before, and insisted upon walking beside him so that the mob, even with the worst will in the world, could not injure him much without injuring her too, which they did not wish to do. Finally the police heard what was happening, and escorted him to the police station. From there he reached his destination without further injury.

It was not until many years later that Gandhi became in any general sense a rebel against authority. At the time of the Boer War he did war work for the British, and justified his doing so on the ground that Indians owed something to British protection. He argued at this time that "the authorities may not always be right, but so long as the subjects owe allegiance to a State, it is their clear duty generally to accommodate themselves, and to accord their support, to acts of the State." He did not think that arguments as to the injustice of the British case in the Boer War justified a British subject in disobedience, or even in an attitude of passivity. Many things are surprising in Gandhi's development, and this is certainly one of them.

III

Gandhi possessed every form of courage in the highest possible degree. We have already seen his courage in facing the Durban mob. He showed another sort when, shortly after the end of the Boer War, the pneumonic plague broke out. The pneumonic plague, as everyone knows, is even more deadly and more infectious than the bubonic plague, but without a moment's hesitation Gandhi devoted himself to the care of the victims, and did everything in his power for them until the outbreak had been adequately coped with. He was not under any kind of official obligation to do this work. I think that few men would have behaved with the wholehearted and immediate devotion which he displayed on this occasion.

The Boer War and its aftermath give more occasion for cynical disillusionment than most events in British history. The war was brought on by the intrigues of moneygrubbing financiers, who spread a network of corruption that descended far down in the social scale. It was fought by the British, first with incompetence and then with inhumanity. It was in this war that concentration camps were invented. Boer women and children were taken to these camps, where they died in large numbers of enteric fever, brought on by the sanitary carelessness of the authorities.

Throughout the war two arguments had been used by the British government to mitigate its imperialistic character. It was said that the Boers treated non-Europeans very much worse than the English colonists, and it was said that when the war was ended, British miners would find lucrative employment in the mines of South Africa. The British government, however, decided that Chinese indentured labor would be cheaper than the labor of British miners. A great wave of popular indignation swept out of power the government which had introduced Chinese labor. Those who had voted for the Liberals imagined that a victory had been won. The Chinese, it is true, were sent back to China, but their place was taken by Indian indentured labor. At the same time legislation was introduced to make the position of Indians in South Africa worse than it had been. At first the British government refused to sanction this legislation, but very soon it granted self-government to the

Transvaal, a measure which was universally hailed as a "noble gesture," and as allowing to the brave Boers the enjoyment of that liberty for which they had fought so well.

The brave Boers immediately saw to it that only they should enjoy the blessings of liberty. The oppressive measures which the British government had refused to sanction were immediately carried, and the British government no longer dared to use its legal power to veto. The country had been made safe for mineowners and slave drivers, and the vanquished had been generously given permission to persist in their slave-driving. This was the situation with which Gandhi had to contend.

The Transvaal government was faced with a dilemma which generally confronts governments in such a situation. On the one hand cheap colored labor was very convenient, while on the other hand there was a general hatred of Asians, and a desire, so far as possible, to have no non-Europeans except Negroes. With this end in view, acts were passed to compel a sifting of Indians, with a view to diminishing their numbers and to reducing those who remained to a much more subservient condition. Gandhi led the opposition, and it was in this campaign that he first developed the method of *Satyagraha.*

The essence of this method, which he gradually brought to greater and greater perfection, consisted in refusal to do things which the authorities wished to have done, while abstaining from any positive action of an aggressive sort. If the police could be provoked into brutalities, so much the better, but those who were brutally treated were to submit to the treatment with complete passivity. The method always had in Gandhi's mind a religious aspect. He came gradually to object more and more to violence, while at the same time preaching, with ever greater emphasis, the duty of not resisting violence with violence. As a rule this method depended upon moral force for its success. The authorities found it intensely repugnant to persist in ill-treating people who did nothing whatever in self-defense.

The method was, however, subject to two limitations. One of these, which led Gandhi to what he called a "Himalayan blunder," was the likelihood that excited crowds would be carried away and would forget to observe the limitations that Gandhi endeavored to impose. On some occasions in India Europeans and policemen were killed by the infuriated mob—occasions when the first impulse had come from Gandhi, but he was unable to restrain the subsequent fury. The other limitation to which the method is subject is one which did not arise either in South Africa or in India, but certainly would have arisen if the method had been employed against Nazis or Russian Communists. If the authorities are sufficiently brutal, they can exterminate nonviolent resisters without experiencing that moral repugnance from their acts which in the end paralyzed the British in India. During the Second World War, for example, disciples of Gandhi would lie down on the rails of railways and refuse to move. English drivers would not run over such men, and the result was that railway traffic was paralyzed. I cannot think that if the drivers had been Nazis and the men on the rails had been Jews, the result would have been the same. But in the circumstances with which Gandhi had to deal, his method was capable of bringing successes that probably no other method would have brought.

Take, for example, the "battle" which occurred during the campaign against the salt tax, which was described by an eyewitness, Webb Miller, in an account of which the following is a summary:

The raid which Gandhi had planned on the salt-pans at Dharsana was now carried out by 2,500 volunteers, led by his second son, Manilal. Before they advanced, Mrs. Naidu led them in prayer and appealed to them to be true to Gandhiji's inspiration and abstain from violence. "You will be beaten, but you must not resist; you must not even raise a hand to ward off blows." Round the depot a barrier of barbed wire had been erected and a ditch dug. As the first picked column of the volunteers went forward, police officers ordered them to disperse; they still advanced in silence. Suddenly scores of police fell upon them and rained blows on their heads. Not one man so much as raised his arm to fend off the blows. Soon the ground was carpeted with the prostrate bodies of men writhing in pain, with fractured skulls or broken shoulders, their white clothes stained with blood. Then a second column advanced, without wavering, knowing well what awaited it. There was no struggle; the volunteers simply marched forward until they, too, were struck down. Now the tactics were varied. Groups of twenty-five men advanced, sat down and waited. As they sat, the enraged police fell upon them, beat them on the head and kicked them in the abdomen or the testicles. Some were dragged along the ground and thrown into the ditches. Hour after hour this went on, while stretcher-bearers removed the inert, bleeding bodies. Over three hundred casualties were taken to hospital with fractured skulls and other serious injuries; two died. Mrs. Naidu and Manilal Gandhi were arrested.

This sort of thing filled every decent English person with a sense of intolerable shame, far greater than would have been felt if the Indian resistance had been of a military character.

There was, of course, also an opposite effect. The police and some of the British authorities in India were rendered furious as a reaction from their own shame, and became more brutal than they would have been against less passive opponents. But this was not the effect that was produced at a distance by those who read of what was being done. English people who were not familiar with India, and had no direct financial interest in maintaining the British raj, felt that something must be done to put an end to such atrocities. General Dwyer, who at Amritsar ordered soldiers to fire for ten minutes upon a packed, peaceful mob, unable to escape, killing many and wounding many more, was recalled, and a Conservative government even went so far as to deprive him of his pension. It is true that he had a number of admirers who presented him with a large sum of money and a Sword of Honor, but this did not represent average British feeling. People who were neither exceptionally rich nor exceptionally brutal began in the end to feel that if British rule could be preserved only by such methods, then it was not worth preserving.

But all this belongs to the later stages of Gandhi's career. To return now to South Africa, the next large campaign in which he was involved concerned the three-pound tax which was imposed upon indentured laborers when the period of their indenture terminated. Very few of them possessed three pounds, and if they were unable to pay the tax, it was remitted on condition of their serving a new period of indentured labor. This meant in practice for most of them that they had unintentionally and unwittingly incurred a life sentence. The conditions of indentured labor were semiservile, and by means of this tax it was transformed by a trick from being temporary to being probably permanent. The agitation which Gandhi conducted against the poll tax was spectcular, and had the political merit of bringing the indentured laborers into the campaign. Gandhi induced them to strike and to undertake a long march, in the course of which he himself was arrested. The movement was so successful as to produce a state of economic paralysis which compelled the government to capitulate. After this, the South African authorities behaved with a modicum of decency and enlightenment until Gandhi was dead.

IV

Gandhi's successes throughout his career depended upon a combination of deep religious conviction and astute political insight. He
was immovable when he was certain that one of his many moral
principles was involved. He was flexible whenever there was nego-
tiation within the limits of his principles. When his followers got
out of hand and practiced violence that he could not countenance,
he would punish himself by a fast. And as his devoted adherents
imagined him becoming daily more emaciated and risking death on
account of their misbehavior, they inevitably repented and, like
naughty children, promised not do to it again. His motive in all this
was religious, but the effect was to reveal his power upon the whole
movement that he had created. Who could venture to disobey a
revered and beloved leader who would inflict upon himself such
suffering, and perhaps death, in expiation of the sins of others? It
was a perfect technique, but it was perfect bcause in his own mind it
was not a technique, but obedience to the dictates of duty.

Gandhi's moral sense had various aspects that are strange to
most modern Europeans. Matters of diet had an importance to him
which is a little puzzling. In the midst of events of the most enormous importance, it would occur to him that he ought not to eat salt
or pulse, and he would feel about this with the same earnestness
that he felt about the fate of India. For example, he took a vow
against milk, but once, when he was very ill, the doctor said he
would die unless he took milk. His wife pointed out to him that the
word he had used in his vow applied only to the milk of the cow or
the buffalo, and did not include the milk of the goat. It was therefore
permissible for him to drink goat's milk. He was aware that his
death would be a loss to India, and on this ground he allowed
himself to accept his wife's argument, although it appeared to him
somewhat sophistical. His own account of the matter is as follows:

> The will to live proved stronger than the devotion to truth, and for
> once the votary of truth compromised his sacred ideals by his eager-
> ness to take up the *Satyagraha* fight. The memory of this occasion
> even now rankles in my breast, and fills me with remorse, and I am
> constantly thinking how to give up goat's milk. But I cannot yet free
> myself from that subject of my temptations, the desire to serve which
> still holds me.

Many modern Europeans will have difficulty in understanding his motives for the vow of complete chastity in marriage which he made at a time when he was trying to help the Zulus who were being persecuted for what the government chose to call a "rebellion." He felt, so he tells us, that he could not be wholehearted in his work, or have all the strength of endurance that it demanded, unless he gave up the joys of family life. This attitude was common in the early Church but now, to a European, feels somewhat strange. Probably for him the decision was a right one. He did and endured things which it is very difficult to do and endure. In spite of bad health, he continuously risked his life by fasts and other hardships. It may be that no less absolute devotion would have enabled him to achieve the great measure of success which he did finally achieve. As to this, no one except himself could be the judge. However that may be, it is impossible to understand him psychologicaly so long as we think of him in purely modern terms. To build him up psychologically from European ingredients we must make a combination of early Christian saints with medieval ecclesiastics, adding to both, however, something of the sweetness of St. Francis.

For India, which is not a modern country, his character and his religion were what was needed. A more modern-minded man, for example, could not have been nearly so successful in the campaign on behalf of the untouchables. But while his memory deserves to be revered, it would be a mistake to hope that India will continue to have the outlook that to him seemed best. India, like other nations, has to find her place in the modern world, not in the dreams of a bygone age. His work is done, and if India is to prosper, it must be along other roads than his.

21

The Theologian's Nightmare

The eminent theologian Dr. Thaddeus dreamt that he died and pursued his course toward heaven. His studies had prepared him and he had no difficulty in finding the way. He knocked at the door of heaven, and was met with a closer scrutiny than he expected. "I ask admission," he said, "because I was a good man and devoted my life to the glory of God." "Man?" said the janitor, "What is that? And how could such a funny creature as you do anything to promote the glory of God?" Dr. Thaddeus was astonished. "You surely cannot be ignorant of man. You must be aware that man is the supreme work of the Creator." "As to that," said the janitor, "I am sorry to hurt your feelings, but what you're saying is news to me. I doubt if anybody up here has ever heard of this thing you call 'man.' However, since you seem distressed, you shall have a chance of consulting our librarian."

The librarian, a globular being with a thousand eyes and one mouth, bent some of his eyes upon Dr. Thaddeus. "What is this?" he asked of the janitor. "This," replied the janitor, "says that it is a member of a species called 'man,' which lives in a place called 'Earth.' It has some odd notion that the Creator takes a special interest in this place and this species. I thought perhaps you could enlighten it." "Well," said the librarian kindly to the theologian, "perhaps you can tell me where this place is that you call 'Earth.'" "Oh," said the theologian, "it's part of the Solar System." "And what is the Solar System?" asked the librarian. "Oh," said the theologian, somewhat disconcerted, "my province was Sacred

From *Fact and Fiction* by Bertrand Russell. Copyright © 1961 by George and Allen Unwin. Reprinted by permission of the publisher.

Knowledge, but the question that you are asking belongs to profane knowledge. However, I have learnt enough from my astronomical friends to be able to tell you that the Solar System is part of the Milky Way." "And what is the Milky Way?" asked the librarian. "Oh, the Milky Way is one of the Galaxies, of which, I am told, there are some hundred million." "Well, well," said the librarian, "you could hardly expect me to remember one out of so many. But I do remember to have heard the word 'galaxy' before. In fact, I believe that one of our sub-librarians specializes in galaxies. Let us send for him and see whether he can help."

After no very long time, the galactic sub-librarian made his appearance. In shape, he was a dodecahedron. It was clear that at one time his surface had been bright, but the dust of the shelves had rendered him dim and opaque. The librarian explained to him that Dr. Thaddeus, in endeavoring to account for his origin, had mentioned galaxies, and it was hoped that information could be obtained from the galactic section of the library. "Well," said the sub-librarian, "I suppose it might become possible in time, but as there are a hundred million galaxies, and each has a volume to itself, it takes some time to find any particular volume. Which is it that this odd molecule desires?" "It is the one called 'The Milky Way,'" Dr. Thaddeus falteringly replied. "All right," said the sub-librarian, "I will find it if I can."

Some three weeks later, he returned, explaining that the extraordinarily efficient card index in the galactic section of the library had enabled them to locate the galaxy as number QX 321,762. "We have employed," he said, "all the five thousand clerks in the galactic section on this search. Perhaps you would like to see the clerk who is specially concerned with the galaxy in question?" The clerk was sent for and turned out to be an octohedron with an eye in each face and a mouth in one of them. He was surprised and dazed to find himself in such a glittering region, away from the shadowy limbo of his shelves. Pulling himself together, he asked, rather shyly, "What is it you wish to know about my galaxy?" Dr. Thaddeus spoke up: "What I want is to know about the Solar System, a collection of heavenly bodies revolving about one of the stars in your galaxy. The star about which they revolve is called 'the Sun.'" "Humph," said the librarian of the Milky Way, "it was hard enough to hit upon the right galaxy, but to hit upon the right star in the galaxy is far more difficult. I know that there are about three hundred billion stars in the galaxy, but I have no knowledge, myself, that would distinguish one of them from another. I believe, however, that at one time a list of the whole three hundred billion was demanded by the Administration and that it is still stored in the basement. If you think it worth while, I will engage special labor from the Other Place to search for this particular star."

It was agreed that, since the question had arisen and since Dr. Thaddeus was evidently suffering some distress, this might be the wisest course.

Several years later, a very weary and dispirited tetrahedorn presented himself before the galactic sub-librarian. "I have," he said, "at last discovered the particular star concerning which inquiries have been made, but I am quite at a loss to imagine why it has aroused any special interest. It closely resembles a great many other stars in the same galaxy. It is of average size and temperature, and is surrounded by very much smaller bodies called 'planets.' After minute investigation, I discovered that some, at least, of these planets have parasites, and I think that this thing which has been making inquiries must be one of them."

At this point, Dr. Thaddeus burst out in a passionate and indignant lament: "Why, oh why, did the Creator conceal from us poor inhabitants of Earth that it was not we who prompted Him to create the Heavens? Throughout my long life, I have served Him diligently, believing that He would notice my service and reward me with Eternal Bliss. And now, it seems that He was not even aware that I existed. You tell me that I am an infinitesimal animalcule on a tiny body revolving round an insignificant member of a collection of three hundred billion stars, which is only one of many millions of such collections. I cannot bear it, and can no longer adore my Creator." "Very well," said the janitor, "then you can go to the Other Place."

Here the theologian awoke. "The power of Satan over our sleeping imagination is terrifying," he muttered.

Bibliography

A Complete List of Bertrand Russell's Books

1896   *German Social Democracy*

1897   *An Essay on the Foundations of Geometry*

1900   *The Philosophy of Leibniz*

1903   *The Principles of Mathematics*

1910   *Philosophical Essays*

1912   *Problems of Philosophy*

1913   *Principia Mathematica* (with A. N. Whitehead)
        Volume I (1910)
        Volume II (1911)
        Volume III (1913)

1914   *Our Knowledge of the External World*

1916   *Justice in Wartime*
        Principles of Social Reconstruction

1917   *Political Ideals*

1918   *Mysticism and Logic*
        Roads to Freedom

1919   *Introduction to Mathematical Philosophy*

1920   *The Practice and Theory of Bolshevism*

1921   *The Analysis of Mind*

1922   *The Problem of China*

1923   *The ABC of Atoms*
        The Prospects of Industrial Civilization (with Dora Russell)

1924   *Icarus or the Future of Science*

1925   *The ABC of Relativity*
        What I Believe

1926   *On Education*

1927   *The Analysis of Matter*
        An Outline of Philosophy
        Selected Papers of Bertrand Russell

1928   *Skeptical Essays*

1929   *Marriage and Morals*

1930   *The Conquest of Happiness*

1931   *The Scientific Outlook*

1932   *Education and the Social Order*

1934   *Freedom and Organization 1814-1914*

1935   *In Praise of Idleness*
        Religion and Science

1936   *Which Way to Peace?*

1937   *The Amberley Papers* (with Patricia Russell)

1938   *Power*

1940   *An Inquiry into Meaning and Truth*

1945   *History of Western Philosophy*

1948   *Human Knowledge: Its Scope and Limits*

1949   *Authority and the Individual*

1950   *Unpopular Essays*

1951   *New Hopes for a Changing World*
        The Wit and Wisdom of Bertrand Russell
            (edited by L. Denonn)

1952   *Dictionary of Mind, Matter, and Morals*
            (edited by L. Denonn)
        The Impact of Science on Society

1953   *The Good Citizen's Alphabet*
        Satan in the Suburbs

1954   *Human Society in Ethics and Politics*
        Nightmares of Eminent Persons

1956   *Logic and Knowledge* (edited by R. C. Marsh)
        Portraits From Memory

1957   *Understanding History*
        Why I Am Not A Christian (edited by P. Edwards)

1958   *Bertrand Russell's Best* (edited by R. Egner)
        Vital Letters of Russell, Krushchev, and Dulles

1959   *Common Sense and Nuclear Warfare*
        My Philosophical Development
        Wisdom of the West (edited by P. Foulkes)

1960   *Bertrand Russell Speaks His Mind*

1961   *The Basic Writings of Bertrand Russell* (edited by
            R. Egner and L. Denonn)
        Fact and Fiction
        Has Man A Future?

1963   *Unarmed Victory*

1965   *On the Philosophy of Science* (edited by C. Fritz)

1967   *War Crimes in Vietnam*

1968   *The Art of Philosophizing*

1969   *Autobiography*
            Volume I (1967)
            Volume II (1968)
            Volume III (1969)
        Dear Bertrand Russell (edited by B. Feinberg and R. Kasrils)

1972   *The Collected Stories of Bertrand Russell* (edited by
            B. Feinberg)

Selected Books on Russell's Life and Views

Aiken, Lillian. *Bertrand Russell's Philosophy of Morals.* New York: Humanities Press, 1963.

Ayer, A. J. *Bertrand Russell.* New York: Viking Press, 1972.

Clark, Ronald. *Bertrand Russell and His World.* New York: Thames and Hudson, 1981.

———. *The Life of Bertrand Russell.* New York: Alfred Knopf, 1976.

Crawshay-Williams, Rupert. *Russell Remembered.* London: Oxford University Press, 1970.

Dewey, John (ed.). *The Bertrand Russell Case.* New York: Viking Press, 1941.

Feinberg, Barry and Ronald Kasrils (eds.). *Bertrand Russell's America. His Transatlantic Travels and Writings: 1896-1945.* London: George and allen Unwin, 1973.

———. *Bertrand Russell's America: 1945-1970.* Boston: South End Press, 1983.

Saur, K. G. *Bertrand Russell: A Bibliography of His Writings 1895-1976.* Connecticut: Linnet Books, 1981.

Schoenman, Ralph (ed.). *Bertrand Russell: Philosopher of the Century.* Boston: Atlantic Monthly, 1967.

Tait, Katherine. *My Father Bertrand Russell.* New York: Harcourt Brace Jovanovich, 1975.

Wood, Alan. *Bertrand Russell: The Passionate Skeptic.* New York: Simon and Schuster, 1958.

Index of Names

Adam, 219, 241, 243, 257, 274ff.
Amberley, Viscount John, 15, 39
Amberley, Viscountess Kate, 15, 39
Anaxagoras, 311
Anthony, Saint, 256
Aquinas, Saint Thomas, 57, 110, 211ff., 298
Archimedes, 285, 309
Aristarchus, 309
Aristotle, 145, 207, 208, 220, 228, 232, 241, 309ff.
Assisi, Saint Francis of, 110, 135, 143, 335
Augustine, Saint, 57, 213, 214, 241, 243, 244, 273, 274
Aurelius, Marcus, 235

Bacon, Francis, 241
Bergson, Henri, 190, 199, 200
Berkeley, Bishop George, 173, 178, 179
Black, Dora, 24, 26, 27
Bohr, Niels, 30
Born, Max, 32
Bradley, Francis H., 42, 43
Bruno, Giordano, 202, 245

Buddha, 67, 75
Butler, Samuel, 69, 214

Caesar, Julius, 218, 226, 285, 316
Cain, 221
Calvin, John, 243, 245
Christ, Jesus, 11, 65ff., 75, 76, 112, 220, 226, 251, 265, 301, 314

Dante, Alighieri, 110
Darwin, Charles, 62, 209, 253, 260, 311
Descartes, René, 54, 156, 170, 178, 241, 310
Dickinson, Sir John, 23

Eddington, Sir Arthur, 169, 172, 176ff., 185, 187
Einstein, Albert, 28, 30, 60, 169, 198
Eliot, T, S, 19, 127
Ellis, Havelock, 27
Empedocles, 273
Erasmus, Desiderius, 207

Franklin, Benjamin, 209

345

Subject Index

Acquiescence, 102ff.
Agnosticism, 24, 40, 73ff., 85, 123
Asceticism, 291, 292
Atheism, 11, 16, 73, 85

Bible, absurdities in, 74; atrocities in, 75, 215, 291; as behavorial grab bag, 74, 84, 215
Bigotry, 87, 220ff., 265ff., 285, 296ff.
Buddhism, 9, 81

Catholicism, 10, 109ff.
Censorship, 267
Christian, definition of, 57ff., 76ff.
Christianity, 9, 224, 244, 258, 274, 284; opposition to: (anesthetics) 219, 290; (artificial insemination) 84; (Association for the Prevention of Cruelty to Animals) 211; (birth control) 9, 10, 15, 84, 229ff., 245, 263; (cremation) 212; (dissection) 212; (divorce) 70, 84, 213; (euthanasia) 211, 263; (evolution) 253, 263, 311, 312; (free think-

ers) 240, 245, 263; (lightning rods) 209, 210; (progress) 69ff., 79; (science) 81ff., 167ff., 209; (sex) 213ff.; (sex education) 26; (witchcraft) 208, 215, 234, 241, 253; (equal rights for women) 230ff.
Christian love, 76
City College of New York, 27ff.
Communism, 9, 25, 81, 264ff., 292
Creator, see God

Deity, see God
Dogma, danger of, 9, 11, 69, 79, 86, 91, 251ff., 264

Emergent evolution, 184ff., 189ff. See also Evolutionary theology
Evolution, 179ff., 217, 253, 257, 260, 261, 311
Evolutionary theology, 179ff., 189ff.

Faith, 10, 11, 80, 81, 281ff., 286, 287
Fear, 15, 70ff., 234, 236, 254ff.

349

GREAT BOOKS IN PHILOSOPHY PAPERBACK SERIES

ESTHETICS

- ❏ Aristotle—*The Poetics*
- ❏ Aristotle—*Treatise on Rhetoric*

ETHICS

- ❏ Aristotle—*The Nicomachean Ethics*
- ❏ Marcus Aurelius—*Meditations*
- ❏ Jeremy Bentham—*The Principles of Morals and Legislation*
- ❏ John Dewey—*Human Nature and Conduct*
- ❏ John Dewey—*The Moral Writings of John Dewey, Revised Edition*
  (edited by James Gouinlock)
- ❏ Epictetus—*Enchiridion*
- ❏ Immanuel Kant—*Fundamental Principles of the Metaphysic of Morals*
- ❏ John Stuart Mill—*Utilitarianism*
- ❏ George Edward Moore—*Principia Ethica*
- ❏ Friedrich Nietzsche—*Beyond Good and Evil*
- ❏ Plato—*Protagoras, Philebus,* and *Gorgias*
- ❏ Bertrand Russell—*Bertrand Russell On Ethics, Sex, and Marriage*
  (edited by Al Seckel)
- ❏ Arthur Schopenhauer—*The Wisdom of Life* and *Counsels and Maxims*
- ❏ Adam Smith—*The Theory of Moral Sentiments*
- ❏ Benedict de Spinoza—*Ethics* and *The Improvement of the Understanding*

METAPHYSICS/EPISTEMOLOGY

- ❏ Aristotle—*De Anima*
- ❏ Aristotle—*The Metaphysics*
- ❏ Francis Bacon—*Essays*
- ❏ George Berkeley—*Three Dialogues Between Hylas and Philonous*
- ❏ W. K. Clifford—*The Ethics of Belief and Other Essays*
  (introduction by Timothy J. Madigan)
- ❏ René Descartes—*Discourse on Method* and *The Meditations*
- ❏ John Dewey—*How We Think*
- ❏ John Dewey—*The Influence of Darwin on Philosophy and Other Essays*
- ❏ Epicurus—*The Essential Epicurus: Letters, Principal Doctrines, Vatican Sayings, and Fragments*
  (translated, and with an introduction, by Eugene O'Connor)
- ❏ Sidney Hook—*The Quest for Being*
- ❏ David Hume—*An Enquiry Concerning Human Understanding*
- ❏ David Hume—*Treatise of Human Nature*

- ❑ William James—*The Meaning of Truth*
- ❑ William James—*Pragmatism*
- ❑ Immanuel Kant—*The Critique of Judgment*
- ❑ Immanuel Kant—*Critique of Practical Reason*
- ❑ Immanuel Kant—*Critique of Pure Reason*
- ❑ Gottfried Wilhelm Leibniz—*Discourse on Metaphysics* and the *Monadology*
- ❑ John Locke—*An Essay Concerning Human Understanding*
- ❑ George Herbert Mead—*The Philosophy of the Present*
- ❑ Charles S. Peirce—*The Essential Writings*
  (edited by Edward C. Moore, preface by Richard Robin)
- ❑ Plato—*The Euthyphro, Apology, Crito,* and *Phaedo*
- ❑ Plato—*Lysis, Phaedrus,* and *Symposium*
- ❑ Bertrand Russell—*The Problems of Philosophy*
- ❑ George Santayana—*The Life of Reason*
- ❑ Sextus Empiricus—*Outlines of Pyrrhonism*
- ❑ Ludwig Wittgenstein—*Wittgenstein's Lectures:*
  Cambridge, 1932–1935 (edited by Alice Ambrose)

PHILOSOPHY OF RELIGION

- ❑ Jeremy Bentham—*The Influence of Natural Religion*
  on the Temporal Happiness of Mankind
- ❑ Marcus Tullius Cicero—*The Nature of the Gods* and *On Divination*
- ❑ Ludwig Feuerbach—*The Essence of Christianity*
- ❑ David Hume—*Dialogues Concerning Natural Religion*
- ❑ William James—*The Varieties of Religious Experience*
- ❑ John Locke—*A Letter Concerning Toleration*
- ❑ Lucretius—*On the Nature of Things*
- ❑ John Stuart Mill—*Three Essays on Religion*
- ❑ Friedrich Nietzsche—*The Antichrist*
- ❑ Thomas Paine—*The Age of Reason*
- ❑ Bertrand Russell—*Bertrand Russell On God and Religion*
  (edited by Al Seckel)

SOCIAL AND POLITICAL PHILOSOPHY

- ❑ Aristotle—*The Politics*
- ❑ Mikhail Bakunin—*The Basic Bakunin: Writings, 1869–1871*
  (translated and edited by Robert M. Cutler)
- ❑ Edmund Burke—*Reflections on the Revolution in France*
- ❑ John Dewey—*Freedom and Culture*
- ❑ John Dewey—*Individualism Old and New*
- ❑ John Dewey—*Liberalism and Social Action*

- ❏ G. W. F. Hegel—*The Philosophy of History*
- ❏ G. W. F. Hegel—*Philosophy of Right*
- ❏ Thomas Hobbes—*The Leviathan*
- ❏ Sidney Hook—*Paradoxes of Freedom*
- ❏ Sidney Hook—*Reason, Social Myths, and Democracy*
- ❏ John Locke—*Second Treatise on Civil Government*
- ❏ Niccolo Machiavelli—*The Prince*
- ❏ Karl Marx (with Friedrich Engels)—*The German Ideology*, including *Theses on Feuerbach and Introduction to the Critique of Political Economy*
- ❏ Karl Marx—*The Poverty of Philosophy*
- ❏ Karl Marx/Friedrich Engels—*The Economic and Philosophic Manuscripts of 1844* and *The Communist Manifesto*
- ❏ John Stuart Mill—*Considerations on Representative Government*
- ❏ John Stuart Mill—*On Liberty*
- ❏ John Stuart Mill—*On Socialism*
- ❏ John Stuart Mill—*The Subjection of Women*
- ❏ Montesquieu, Charles de Secondat—*The Spirit of Laws*
- ❏ Friedrich Nietzsche—*Thus Spake Zarathustra*
- ❏ Thomas Paine—*Common Sense*
- ❏ Thomas Paine—*Rights of Man*
- ❏ Plato—*Laws*
- ❏ Plato—*The Republic*
- ❏ Jean-Jacques Rousseau—*The Social Contract*
- ❏ Mary Wollstonecraft—*A Vindication of the Rights of Men*
- ❏ Mary Wollstonecraft—*A Vindication of the Rights of Women*

GREAT MINDS PAPERBACK SERIES

ART

☐ Leonardo da Vinci—*A Treatise on Painting*

CRITICAL ESSAYS

☐ Desiderius Erasmus—*The Praise of Folly*
☐ Jonathan Swift—*A Modest Proposal and Other Satires*
    (with an introduction by George R. Levine)
☐ H. G. Wells—*The Conquest of Time*
    (with an introduction by Martin Gardner)

ECONOMICS

☐ Charlotte Perkins Gilman—*Women and Economics:*
    A Study of the Economic Relation between Women and Men
☐ John Maynard Keynes—*The General Theory of Employment,*
    Interest, and Money
☐ John Maynard Keynes—*A Tract on Monetary Reform*
☐ Thomas R. Malthus—*An Essay on the Principle of Population*
☐ Alfred Marshall—*Money, Credit, and Commerce*
☐ Alfred Marshall—*Principles of Economics*
☐ Karl Marx—*Theories of Surplus Value*
☐ David Ricardo—*Principles of Political Economy and Taxation*
☐ Adam Smith—*Wealth of Nations*
☐ Thorstein Veblen—*Theory of the Leisure Class*

HISTORY

☐ Edward Gibbon—*On Christianity*
☐ Alexander Hamilton, John Jay, and James Madison—*The Federalist*
☐ Herodotus—*The History*
☐ Thucydides—*History of the Peloponnesian War*
☐ Andrew D. White—*A History of the Warfare of Science*
    with Theology in Christendom

LAW

☐ John Austin—*The Province of Jurisprudence Determined*

PSYCHOLOGY

☐ Sigmund Freud—*Totem and Taboo*

RELIGION

- ☐ Thomas Henry Huxley—*Agnosticism and Christianity and Other Essays*
- ☐ Ernest Renan—*The Life of Jesus*
- ☐ Upton Sinclair—*The Profits of Religion*
- ☐ Elizabeth Cady Stanton—*The Woman's Bible*
- ☐ Voltaire—*A Treatise on Toleration and Other Essays*

SCIENCE

- ☐ Jacob Bronowski—*The Identity of Man*
- ☐ Nicolaus Copernicus—*On the Revolutions of Heavenly Spheres*
- ☐ Marie Curie—*Radioactive Substances*
- ☐ Charles Darwin—*The Autobiography of Charles Darwin*
- ☐ Charles Darwin—*The Descent of Man*
- ☐ Charles Darwin—*The Origin of Species*
- ☐ Charles Darwin—*The Voyage of the* Beagle
- ☐ Albert Einstein—*Relativity*
- ☐ Michael Faraday—*The Forces of Matter*
- ☐ Galileo Galilei—*Dialogues Concerning Two New Sciences*
- ☐ Ernst Haeckel—*The Riddle of the Universe*
- ☐ William Harvey—*On the Motion of the Heart and Blood in Animals*
- ☐ Werner Heisenberg—*Physics and Philosophy:
  The Revolution in Modern Science* (introduction by F. S. C. Northrop)
- ☐ Julian Huxley—*Evolutionary Humanism*
- ☐ Edward Jenner—*Vaccination against Smallpox*
- ☐ Johannes Kepler—*Epitome of Copernican Astronomy
  and Harmonies of the World*
- ☐ Charles Mackay—*Extraordinary Popular Delusions
  and the Madness of Crowds*
- ☐ James Clerk Maxwell—*Matter and Motion*
- ☐ Isaac Newton—*The Principia*
- ☐ Louis Pasteur and Joseph Lister—*Germ Theory and Its Application
  to Medicine and On the Antiseptic Principle of the Practice of Surgery*
- ☐ William Thomson (Lord Kelvin) and Peter Guthrie Tait—
  The Elements of Natural Philosophy
- ☐ Alfred Russel Wallace—*Island Life*

SOCIOLOGY

- ☐ Emile Durkheim—*Ethics and the Sociology of Morals*
  (translated with an introduction by Robert T. Hall)